Praise for Call Me Legachi

Adesuwa O'Man Nwokedi never disappoints, never!

—Temitope Adeniran, Goodreads Reviewer

Legachi's journey to London and all she experienced there was so well written. Took me way back to my first experience in London. (The encouraging Nigerians and the yeye ones that would try to discourage you.)… This book is awesome! Can't wait for everyone to read it.

—Amaka Azie, Author of The Governor's Daughter

I love how Adesuwa always presents strong themes subtly in her books. Like marital tension and how it ends up affecting the children one way or the other. Like how immigrants "borrow" other people's identity to get jobs to survive. Like how so many Nigerians would rather leave their white-collar jobs in Nigeria to take up menial jobs abroad, all in the name of greener pastures. It makes her stories real and not just fiction in a vacuum, because fiction, to me, must have an element of fact.

—Iyanuoluwa Olorode, Goodreads Reviewer

Legachi's story was relatable and eye-opening on many levels. The people she met on the journey to finding herself serves as a reminder that different people will come into one's life to make things happen or otherwise. Highly recommend this book to lovers of secrets & lies, single dads and nanny romance tropes.

Margaret Adetimehin, Author of Escape, A Twin Bliss Resort Novel

Cover Design: Margaret Adetimehin
Formatting & Interior: Margaret Adetimehin
For more information, kindly visit https://thefertilechick.ng/

Printed and bound in the United States of America
First Edition: August 2022
10 9 8 7 6 5 4 3 2 1

Dedicated to the memory of my dear friend
Legachi Peggy Madu-Uzuokwu
(1975-2020)

One

Write Off

Legachi

I sit on the toilet seat, scrolling through my phone as I wait for Mezie's call, away from the blare of the all-night prayer session from my flat mate's phone. For a device that small, its audio quality rivals the output from many heavy-duty speakers.

As I mindlessly skim the images on my Instagram feed, I pause when I see a picture of a former colleague, Doris. I feel the familiar jaws of envy clench my chest as I look at her smiling back at the camera, her killer body in full-on assasin mode in a tiny red bikini, the backdrop of a brilliant blue ocean and clear blue skies the give away that she's holidaying in yet another exotic location. I roll my eyes at the #WorkHardPlayHarder caption of the picture and let out a long hiss as I scroll past it.

The privacy of my toilet is the only place I can express this unjustified jealousy, unjustified because not only is she one of the nicest people I have ever met, she's also one of the most brilliant and hard working. Two years after we were both hired by First Guaranty Bank, FGB, she got a scholarship to an American Ivy League University and was promptly hired by an investment bank on Wall Street subsequently after. Now, five years later, she is a Senior Vice President and living the high life... while I have only been able to move one step higher in my bank's Pecking Order.

I scroll back to her picture to scrutinize it, squinting to see if her tiny waist and rounded hips are the result of hard work... or hard cash. But what I see instead is a new comment from the very person whose call I'm waiting for. Mezie.

Looking smoking hot is his comment, accompanied by five exploding bomb emojis. I know, because I count them all. Here I am, waiting for his call, while he's busy commenting on social media. Letting out yet another hiss, I dial his number instead, ignoring the fact that it will cost me a fortune. The sketchy Internet service in my area is only tolerable for a few eppileptic moments online, so video or voice calls on WhatsApp are almost an impossibility, something Mezie and I had to find out the hard way.

"I see you've been busy on Instagram," I retort, when the line connects. "Didn't you say you were going to call me at 11?"

"Madam, I've had a long day. This nagging is the very last thing I need now," is his equally terse answer. "It's only ten minutes past. Besides, now that you've called me, have you died?"

"You know this call is very expensive for me."

"And I'm the one it's not expensive for, *abi*?"

"I thought you said international calls are cheaper with your new line," I counter. There is silence and I wonder if the line has disconnected. "Hello?"

"That echo. Legachi, are you calling me from the toilet again?" he asks, his voice elevated in what I can now tell is the beginning of an explosive fit. "How many times have I told you not to call me while you're taking a shit?"

2

"I'm not taking a shit, Mezie," I protest. "I came here because the noise from Chineme's prayer session was loud."

"Talking to your boyfriend from the toilet is just downright disrespectful. Later, *abeg*!"

And the line disconnects.

I stare at my phone for several minutes, a thick lump forming in my throat. In the year it has been since he left for London, our relationship has deteriorated a little more every day. We have been together since meeting at FGB seven years ago. I was assigned to his team and he took an instant liking to me. Only a rank higher than I was as an Executive Trainee, he still fancied himself my mentor, even though I soon became more knowledgeable of the job than he was. Muscled and standing over six feet tall, he was neither conventionally handsome nor the smartest pea in the pod, but it didn't take long for me to lose my head to him.

We soon became inseparable. Last year, the opportunity arose for a scholarship abroad. Going away wasn't on my radar and when he insisted on taking the exam, I hadn't been too worried because, I'm now sorry to admit, I thought there was no way he would pass the exam. And I was right. He hadn't passed, but rather than shrug it off and move on with his life, it just made him even more determined to leave the country somehow. So, he'd gotten himself a tourist visa, sold his belongings, quit his job, and left for London, where he has been trying to get himself reasonable employment ever since.

Rising from my sitting position, I tell myself he is only taking out the frustration of his predicament on me. I need to be more patient with him. I shouldn't have called him from the toilet, knowing fully well it irritates him when I do.

I open the door and see Chineme now on her feet, *kabashing* with her online companions. Our eyes meet and I can see the disapproval in hers, not only because I'm not praying along with her but that I have been talking on the phone with my 'partner in sin', as she has labelled Mezie since walking in on us having sex several years ago.

3

Well, to each their own, I guess. I avert my eyes and walk quickly across the room, letting myself out and shutting the door behind me.

A distant relative, she'd been the only one I could think of when I found the self-contained room in Victoria Island. I couldn't afford the rent on my own and, as she too had just started working on the island, I had asked her. Big mistake. I'm not sure if the proximity to work is enough to justify the constant verbal and non-verbal harrassment I get from her, not to mention that she is, without a doubt, the sloppiest person I have ever met in my life. It has been seven years, but I am yet to get accustomed to her habit of soaking her underwear in buckets for weeks on end, the unwashed plates and cutlery stacked under her bed, or the perenial odour that follows her even after just having a shower. But hopefully, I won't have to deal with any of that for much longer.

Leaning on a neighbour's car, I dial Mezie's number again.

"Babe, I'm sorry about calling you from the toilet," I apologise. "I'm outside now."

"At this time of night?" he grunts.

"I told you Chineme and her people are at it again. Coming outside was the next best thing."

"This long distance thing is beginning to get old, Legachi," he sighs. "Like, really old. I don't know how much longer I can go on like this. It's bad enough I can't see you, but even talking to you is now an issue. This is starting to feel like a write off."

Ah! Write off *ke*?

I feel the all-too familiar panic engulf me. It is not the first time he has made this complaint and the thought of losing him makes me feel physiclly ill. It is one of the reasons I recently sat for the same *Skyline* exam he took last year, hoping I will be more successful than he was and be awarded a scholarship, so I can join him there in England.

"Babe, don't talk like that," I plead. "Let's pray that I pass the scholarship exam. If I do, I'll be with you in a matter of months."

"Scholarship exam my foot! That *Skyline* program is a waste of time. Only people that have connections get their scholarships, so you better not waste any time banking on it. Or have you forgotten what happened to me?"

It is on the tip of my tongue to tell him he didn't pass because he neither had the aptitude nor prepared enough for it, but I know this will worsen an already bad situation.

"I'll talk to you tomorrow," he says, sounding just as weary as I feel. "Later."

My heart is heavy as the line disconnects for the second time that night. I can't afford to lose him. At the age of 31, starting over is not an option for me. Mezie is insanely attractive and can get any woman he wants. As for me, I'm not exactly a head turner. The odds of finding another guy like him are slim to none.

I cast a furtive glace up to the heavens, tempted to run back into the house to join Chineme's prayers, to beg God to grant me this one thing, this one thing I desire with every inch of my heart.

Roman

I am out of the northbound Jubilee line train as soon as the doors slide open, shoving my way past the unruly commuters who don't have enough travel decorum to wait for people to alight before they board. I run all the way up the escalators and make a mad dash out of the station on to Avenue Road.

At 8pm, I am two clear hours later than when I should have picked Luna up from her day care centre. Three, if you discount the grace hour. As much as I have tried to limit my hours at the hospital to a maximum of five, there are days like this when it is out of my control. Thankfully, the owner of the childcare facility, Cheryl, lives on the premises, which is the main reason I chose it over other less expensive and easier accessible options. But as I half walk and half run down the street, the hefty penalty I will have to pay booms in my head like a trombone.

The frown on Cheryl's face when she opens the door does very little to conceal her disapproval.

"I'm so sorry about this," I say, as she hands over my sleeping daughter. "It got crazy at the hospital."

Her deadpan face shows her disinterest in my worn excuse. She hands me a slip and the amount I see is jarring. But at £2 for every minute after 6pm, it is expected.

"Do us a favour and let it slide this time?" I ask, giving her what I hope is my most charming smile. "It's not like I'm late every day. And I was saving lives and all."

"Nice try," she chuckles, shaking her head. "Luna had some sniffles this evening, so you might want to keep an eye on her this weekend."

I nod in acknowledgment, disappointed my attempt to charm myself out of the penalty has failed... again. It'll be yet another expensive month.

"Thanks, Cheryl," I force a smile as I accept my daughter's bag with my free arm. "Have a good weekend."

"You too, Roman," she says, shutting her door.

It's a short bus ride home and, once there, Luna remains asleep as I get her out of her clothes and into her nightwear. My phone vibrates as I tuck her in, and I pad silently out of the room to answer it.

"Chudi and I are heading out now," comes my friend, Sean's voice. "Are you already on your way? Remember, it's *Thirst Bar* not *Barrio*."

I grimace as I remember I was supposed to find a babysitter for the evening for a long-delayed hangout with my friends.

"What the hell is that sound? Don't tell me you didn't get a sitter?" comes Sean's elevated voice.

"I didn't get a sitter, mate," I say, opening my bedroom door, feeling just as regretful as my friend is disappointed. It's a mutual friend's 35th birthday, and I'd looked forward to a chance to hang out with them after such a long time.

"How long is this going to go on, Roman?" Sean sighs in his exasperation. "You're not the only single dad in the world. You don't have to turn yourself into a hermit. You're writing yourself off socially."

A sardonic smile forms on my face as I think of the many other ways I am 'writing myself off'. With my drastically reduced hours, the fortune I pay in penalties to Luna's day care, not to mention that I have had to temporarily drop out of my hospital's advanced specialization training in endocrinology because of its demanding hours, I might just be doing the same financially and professionally.

But it is what it is.

As I unbutton my shirt, my phone vibrates with a text message. I'm smiling as I open it, thinking it's from yet another disappointed friend, but the smile is replaced by a frown when I read the message. It is not a friendly one... not in the least. Deleting it, I block the unfamiliar number, making that the fifth such one I have had to block in a month. But I'm ready to block as many more as I need to, to make sure messages like this become a thing of my past.

Two

Staking Claim

Roman

I jolt myself awake just in time not to miss my stop at Westminster Station on Monday morning. I buy myself a cup of coffee as I make the walk to the hospital, needing every ounce of caffeine I can get. Luna's sniffles manifested into a full-on cold this past weekend, so neither of us got much rest. But after dropping all my weekend shifts, dropping another one today isn't even an option.

"You look totally washed!" my friend, Yash, exclaims when I walk out of the elevator on to the outpatient floor where I have consultations that morning. "Let me guess; another tough weekend?"

"You called it," I answer with a shrug.

"Why don't you just get a live-in Au Pair? After Brexit, the European ones are even cheaper than they were before. Kavya keeps threatening to get one and send her mother back to India."

"Weren't Kavya's parents born here in England?"

8

He chuckles. "Yeah, but it still feels good seeing the look on my mother-in-law's face when she hears it."

I shake my head and smile as I walk down the hall. "You should count yourself lucky her mother is around to help you guys out. Mine lives over an hour away and would rather slit her throat than move to London. Left to her, Luna would live with her in Chelmsford."

"And would that be such a bad idea?" Yash asks, walking fast to keep in step with me. "You'd get your life back and be able to do the things you haven't been able to."

We both know he's talking about the specialization program I have suspended. Even though we wrote our MRCP exams at the same time, he has since been able to qualify as a Specialist Oncologist, a feat I'm at least two years away from.

"Moving Luna to my mom's isn't an option, Yash. And I'm not interested in getting an Au Pair, either," I say, walking into the consulting room. "Have you forgotten what happened with the last one?"

Just before Christmas, I hired Astrid, a Swedish Au-Pair. Pleasant and well spoken, I was relieved to have finally found decent childcare. That was until schedules at the hospital were rearranged and I left for home several hours earlier than I normally did… and found that she had been harbouring her boyfriend in her bedroom for Lord knows how long. Walking into my house and seeing the half-naked man with the body of a wrestler, remains one of the most surreal events of my life. I can only imagine how men who catch their wives cheating feel. Even though Astrid pleaded, saying she'd only taken him in because he had nowhere else to go, the fact that she'd put my daughter's life at risk with a strange man in the house was enough reason for me to let her go. And I have been too scared to go down that route again.

"Besides, they're too expensive," I say, setting down my cup of coffee. "And with my reduced hours, I might not be able to afford one."

He doesn't laugh at my joke and instead scoffs. "Carry on the way you are, and soon you really won't. Get your shit together and get childcare, Roman."

The smile fades from my face and I nod in agreement. He's right. I do need to get my shit together.

"Anyway, Kavya said to invite you and Luna for dinner anytime you're free this week," he wiggles his bushy brows and winks, my cue that I won't like the next thing he says. And I'm right. "There's someone she wants you to meet."

I glare at him and sit, not even bothering to respond to what has to be the most annoying collection of words ever; 'someone I/we/she/he want(s) you to meet'.

"Seriously, I've met her," Yash says, sitting on the patients' chair opposite me. "Her name is Jessica, and she's really fit… "

"Again, you forget what happened the last time someone tried to play matchmaker with me," I find the need to remind him.

"Come on, man. That was so long ago!" After a long pause, he adds, "Sekani would want you to move on, and you know it."

Hearing my late wife's name is enough to make me still. I glance up at him from the computer I'm powering on, and even he knows he's overstepped.

"Just think about it," he says, rising to his feet. "She's a real stunner. Tall and slim like you like them."

"Bye, Yash."

Alone in the room, my mind wanders to the woman who still holds my heart, years after her passing. I smile at the mental image that forms in my mind, one of her the way she was before the aggressive cancer ravaged her body. Tall, willowy and with glossy mahogany coloured skin, we'd met as medical students at Queen Mary University. Away from her family in Malawi for the first time, I'd been more than glad to ease her homesickness and help her settle in. We were inseparable all through medical school and as we wrote our qualifying exams, finally marrying the year we both passed the final MRCP exam. We had a beautiful, blissful marriage... until cervical cancer cut our love story short.

Flipping open my wallet, I smile at her glowering passport picture tucked there, right beside one of a grinning Luna. It is one of the very few pictures where her brilliant white teeth are not on full display in what was her signature grin. But frowning or not, she is still staking claim, not only in my wallet but from almost every room in my house where her pictures hang beautiful and graceful, just like her.

"What should I do, babes?" I ask her. "Should I bite the bullet and get another Au-Pair?"

I look at the picture as if expecting a response. Several minutes pass and it is the ringing of the telephone on my desk that brings me back to reality. I sigh as I realise the decision is mine to make, not someone long gone.

Later that morning, in between consultations, I pick up my phone, dial the agency's number, and ask them to send an Au Pair for me to interview. Surely, I can't have a stroke of bad luck two times in a row, can I?

Legachi

I refresh the *Skyline* website for what might just be the hundredth time that day. Scratch that. Thousandth. It is Monday, the day the results of the scholarship exam are to be published. I click my tongue in my rising impatience. It is already 2pm. Would publishing the results earlier in the day have been so hard? Because their process involves not just scoring candidates on their exam but also running paperwork with their partner universities, we have already had a two-month wait to get to this point.

"Babe, how far?" Franca, a friend who also wrote the exam, calls me on the phone yet again. "*You don see am?*"

"Is it not the same website you're also checking?" I retort. "Why are you asking as if mine will show me something different?"

"Didn't these people say the results would be out on the 14th?" Franca wails. "*Which kin' tension be dis na?*"

I sigh as I refresh the page yet again. Nothing. It starts to dawn on me that this might just be a precursor to the real bad news. What if neither of us is successful?

"Babe, keep checking *abeg!*" Franca pleads. "I'll be doing the same here. If you see something first, call me. I'll also call if I do."

She is off the phone before I can even answer, probably to harass someone else who wrote the exam. Realising I might be setting myself up for the biggest disappointment of my life, I close the page. I've already wasted enough of the day on it.

Rising to my feet, I decide to go to the cafeteria for lunch. There's no need starving myself. If I'm going to get my heart broken, it might as well be on a full stomach.

Walking into the bustling lunchroom, I buy a plate of white rice, stew, beef and a sprinkling of plantain fried so tiny, they look like specks of dust on my plate. I walk over to a table where three of my colleagues already sit; Ukpono, Chioma and Josephine. If the word *frenemy* were a person, it would be each one of them. Even though we are cordial, I know there is no love lost and that they talk about me behind my back. And truth be told, I do the same. But I'd rather not eat alone, so I place my tray on their table, with an overenthusiastic "Hello!"

"How now?" Ukpono answers, not looking up from the phone they are all huddled over. "This Doris girl, are you sure she hasn't had surgery. Was her waist always this small?"

"When you have the kind of money she does, is that even the issue?" a wistful Josephine says, her eyes so wide I know she wishes she could hop right into phone to join Doris in her exotic holiday location. "*Na wa o!* See how she's balling while I'm here eating *moin moin* and fish."

"Wasn't she an ABO when she was here? Now she's a Goldman Sachs Senior Vice President! This life isn't fair at all *sha!*" Ukpono whinges.

I am consoled I am not the only one eaten up with envy over our former colleague's success.

"Mezie even left a comment on the post," Chioma laughs.

"That one still *dey?*" Josephine scoffs. "What is he even up to in that London *sef?*"

Ukpono finally spares me a look, her smile mocking. "See his babe *na.* Ask her."

All three pairs of eyes turn to me, and I can't tell if they are really curious or just want to make fun of me. For all the time Mezie and I were together before he left, they weren't the only ones who constantly teased our unlikely pairing; him, tall, strapping and charming, and me, well, none of the above.

But I'll be damned if they make me cower like I used to.

"He's fine," I answer, forcing a bright smile. "He's doing very well."

Ukpono raises a brow, her gaze disbelieving. "Doing very well with what? That's not what I heard."

"He just got a good job with a building firm just outside London," I hear myself saying, referring to the interview he told me has today and praying with all my heart he gets the job. "He's doing great."

"That's good to know," Chioma says, shrugging. "After he threw his job here away, I was afraid he would end up working as a bus driver there or something."

"Or at McDonalds!" Ukpono guffaws, and the other girls laugh along with her. I have to fight off the temptation to claw out their eyes, all six of them.

"And you're here waiting for him?" Josephine taunts. "You think he hasn't found himself one hot London babe by now?"

This hits the very mark she intended, but I will not give them the satisfaction of seeing how affected I am hearing that. Instead, I'm determined to stake my claim.

"Of course, we're still together," I laugh. "As a matter of fact, I'll be joining him there soon."

Thankfully, they are distracted by something else on Josephine's Instagram feed, and I return my attention to my plate. But my appetite has since fled, not just the room but the entire building.

Back at my desk, I let out a deep sigh. A part of me wants to return to the *Skyline* website but another part of me wants to manage my expectations. The way it's looking, I might just have to toe Mezie's line and join him in London on a tourist visa.

I am about to continue working on a report my boss has asked for, when the notification of an email to my private account flashes at the top of my screen. My breath catches in my breath when I see it is from *Skyline*, and my heart starts to race as I wonder if it is a rejection letter. I look around to be sure nobody is standing around; the fewer people to witness my shame, the better.

But when I click open the email, a rejection letter it is not.

Dear Legachi Elizabeth Onyema,

Congratulations. You have been selected for our prestigious Skyline Scholarship Program. In partnership with Middlesex University, London, you have been offered admission for an **M.Sc. in Global Supply Chain Management**, *starting in September 2018. This scholarship covers tuition and living expenses, and also…*

I don't even finish reading it as I let out a loud yelp, goose bumps forming all over my body. I shoot to my feet and squeal, not caring about the several curious glances thrown my way in the open plan office. God has answered my prayers.

I am finally on my way to my Mezie.

Three

New Beginnings

Legachi

Y ou got it?!"

I smile, smug from the good news I have just given him. I am pleased not only to have proved his theory about *Skyline* wrong, but that he can admit how much he underestimated my ability to pass the exam.

"I sure did! I told you the thing isn't a scam."

"And they're paying your full tuition?"

"Full tuition and living expenses for the entire year! The same thing on offer last year."

"This is unbelievable. Send me the letter so I can see for myself."

I frown, his doubt making my excitement ebb. Does he think I'm lying or what? Deciding I lose nothing by sending him the letter, especially as he'll see it eventually anyway, I do just that.

"Unbelievable!" he exclaims, when he reads it. "The full £16,000 tuition and another £8,000 for living expenses? Unbelievable!"

"Believe o!" I chuckle. "It takes into account the ten months of the academic year, from September this year to June next year."

"Are they going to give you the cash?"

I frown. "Not the tuition, I don't think. And I'd much rather they sort out my campus accommodation on my behalf and give me whatever's left."

"Campus accommodation? Why? When I'm here?"

Oh. Okay. I hadn't quite thought of that. "You want me to stay with you?"

"Baby, that's what makes the most sense. Why would you blow all that money on accommodation when your man is here? Tell them you'd rather have the cash for living expenses."

I am slightly disappointed. I've been looking forward to the experience of school accommodation abroad, an experience I know will be worlds apart from my experience at ABSU. But Mezie does have a point though. Besides, what better way to make up for lost time than us living together?

"They sent an acceptance form which I'm supposed to fill," I say. "There's also a contact number, so I'll call tomorrow to ask."

"Fantastic!" he exclaims, his voice finally conveying the excitement I've been expecting. "I'm so happy you're finally coming! I've missed you too much."

I beam, also ecstatic. "Me too. This past year has been awful without you."

"So, when you ask them about the cash, you'll transfer it to me, right? I'll keep it safe till you get here," he pauses before he asks. "Maybe I could pay for my PMP certification from the money? You know that's what's stopping me from getting a good job here. It's £3,000, and I haven't been able to raise that kind of money."

I shrug. If I won't be paying rent, surely I can spare that, especially as it's for a good cause.

"Sure, we can do that," I answer, loving how we're now planning as a unit.

"You're the best!" he exclaims. "I love you. I can't wait for you to get here. Things are going to be so wonderful. By the time I get my PMP certification and get a great job, we'll move to a nicer apartment in a nice neighbourhood. With your Masters, you'll also get a nice job. We'll be a power couple."

I hesitate before asking what I have been dying to since the thought of joining him in the UK took root in my mind. "Are we going to get married as soon as I get there? Something small to formalise things?"

"Why will we elope when we have families back home?" he retorts. "Babe, that's the thing about you. You're always jumping the gun. After your program, we'll come back home for our traditional marriage before any other formalisation can happen. You know I'm a traditional man."

It is on the tip of my tongue to retort that he's a 'traditional man' but has no issues with us living together before we are wed. But I decide against it, not wanting to upset him. I chid myself for getting too carried away and decide to focus on this win.

When I get to London, we'll figure out the rest.

Roman

I look at the brunette sitting in front of me, the Au Pair the agency has sent, Greta, is a young Danish girl who has been in London less than a year. Her English isn't great, and it is an initial worry for me, especially with Luna just becoming conversational. But demure and diminutive, she is nothing like the buxom Astrid, which could be a good thing as there's a lower chance of me stumbling on any strange men in my house.

Or is there?

Last minute, I decide that is a risk I can't take.

"It's not a live-in position," I tell her. "Will that be a problem?"

"I live Belsize Park," she beams as she raises a finger. "Only one bus."

Perfect.

We finalise plans for her to come in the mornings, early enough to prepare and take Luna to day care, and leave when I get back from the hospital at 9pm. On nights I have social events, she'll sleep in, but only on those. Everything is sorted.

She starts work the next day, arriving nice and early at 7:30am. She is effective enough, except her culinary skills are abysmal. I end up having to trash the soggy oatmeal she made for Luna's breakfast and make a quick sandwich for her lunch box instead. But as she giggles with Luna, I decide it is a flaw I'm happy to ignore. All I need is for her to take care of my child. Any other thing is a plus.

—

That Friday night, I am comfortable enough to ask her to watch Luna while I meet up with my friends for drinks. Journeying to the West End bar with Yash is surreal, and I can't believe how long it has been since I've been out and about.

"Ah, there he is! Mr. Mom himself!" Sean teases, as we walk up to where he and Chudi are seated at the bar. "I was actually getting ready to hear you call to complain about not having a sitter."

"He not only has a sitter now, but an Au Pair!" Yash declares, proud of himself for whatever way he might have influenced that decision.

Chudi raises a bemused brow. "Another Au Pair? You didn't learn your lesson the last time?"

"Not all Au Pairs are like that," Yash answers for me. "He was just unlucky."

"*Nyansh*, let the man talk for himself. *Abi* you're his mouthpiece?" Sean cuts in, chuckling at the nickname he and Sean have called Yash for as long as they have known him. It has been almost ten years, but they can't seem to get over how much his name sounds like the Nigerian term for a woman's backside.

"No mind *Nyansh*," Chudi laughs, also amused. I guess Yash will have to accept it's a joke that will never get old.

"She's not living in the house, so won't be able to harbour any strange men," I say in my defence.

"It's not even wise, considering the way women accuse guys of all sorts these days," Chudi says. "You don't need that, man."

"Exactly why this arrangement works for us. Besides, she's great with Luna."

"*Besides*, it's about time you had a life, man!" Sean cuts in, throwing his arm around my neck. "It's been too long, bruv!"

That it sure has.

We are soon drinking shots and talking and laughing a little too loud. But then again, so is everyone else in the bar. Loosened by alcohol for the first time in forever, everything my friends say sounds funny and everything around me looks that much better. A woman walks in, and Sean beckons her over. I realise her being there is probably no accident, but I'm too merry to care.

"This is Lara's friend, Itunu," Sean says as loudly as he can over the loud house music now playing. Lara is his wife. "Itunu, this is Roman."

I smile at the beautiful, willowy woman who has a striking resemblance with Sekani. Like Sekani, she stands a few inches taller than me, and I peg her at about 5 feet 11 inches or even 6 feet. This is a turn on for me as, at 5 feet 9 inches, I have always liked my women taller. She has the same large eyes, angular cheekbones, and small lips as Sekani, but her honey-coloured skin is a few shades lighter than Sekani's rich dark colouring. On another day, I would have balked at any kind of set up, lest of all with my dead wife's doppelgänger. But as a slow, dimpled smile forms on her face, I decide a short chat won't be that bad.

"Hi, Itunu," I say, shaking her supple soft hand. "It's good to meet you."

"He's a doctor!" Sean declares, before winking at me and shuffling away.

I smile and shake my head. He's lucky I'm too inebriated to take offense.

"Sean is such a funny guy," she giggles.

"He's a muppet, that's what he is," I chuckle along with her.

"He's my friend's husband, so watch it," she says, a mischievous glint in her eye.

"And he's my friend of almost twenty years," I counter, enjoying the verbal exchange.

"Oh, wow. That's a long time. You don't look old enough to have had a friendship that long."

I laugh and cock my head to the side. "Oh yeah? I'm a lot older than you think."

"Well, I look forward to learning a whole lot more about you," she says, holding my gaze.

I might have been out of the game for a long time, but not long enough not to know when a woman is interested... and she's definitely interested. I smile at her, not breaking our gaze. There just might be something here.

"So, what do you do?" I ask.

"I'm a Visual Merchandiser," she answers, the mischievous glint still in her eyes.

I stare back, not having the slightest clue what that is, and she laughs, a nice sound that sounds like dainty bells ringing.

"I conceptualize and design store displays," she answers, still smiling. "Basically, it's my job to ensure store displays are aesthetically appealing enough to entice customers to check out and ultimately buy the store's products."

I nod, surprised there's a whole ass job for that. "Just any store or any one in particular?"

"I've worked with several brands, but I've been with *Gucci* for the last four." Then leaning in, her smile turns coy. "I was a model in my early twenties though."

"No shit!" I answer in feigned surprise. Of course, that doesn't surprise me. With her looks, I'm surprised she isn't still one.

"I still do model on occasion though," she answers, as if reading my mind. "Just no longer as often."

"How long have you lived in London?" I ask as, though almost imperceptible, I can hear a faint Nigerian accent.

"About four years. I moved here when I got the job at *Gucci*. I was in Manchester before that."

When I frown in my confusion, she shrugs. "I moved here from Lagos thirteen years ago as a teenager." She giggles and covers her face with well-manicured hands. "Oh dear, I've disclosed my age!"

"Not really," I chuckle back. "You've only given me the assurance that you're old enough for this discussion."

"What about you?" she asks, leaning closer. "From your accent, you were probably born here. Or came here as a young child?"

"Born here," I answer. "My father moved here in the late '70s."

"Have you been to Nigeria before?"

The smile on my face wanes. "A few times."

"Well, we have to do something about that," is her coy response. "I might need to take you back to my apartment to school you a little more about the homeland."

I'm about to respond that I'll be too happy to be schooled, when I make eye contact with a woman sitting at the other end of the bar. I look away but turn to look again when I realise she, and another woman sitting next to her, are not only still staring at me, but glaring.

Suddenly, recognition sets in... and I know I need to be as far away from that bar as I can get.

"It was great meeting you, Itunu," I say, dropping my glass on the counter and motioning to Sean that I'll reimburse him later. "I'm sorry, but I have to go."

Her mouth parts in her surprise, but I don't even tarry long enough to offer any further explanation. I turn around and struggle through the teeming crowd, which seems to have multiplied in the couple of hours I've been there.

As I walk briskly towards my car, I am reminded why I no longer do things like this. Being out on the town has resurrected things I need long dead.

Four

Skyline

SEPTEMBER 2018

Legachi

I curse as the *No Service* message flashes on the screen of my dodgy Wi-Fi modem. Sitting in front of my personal laptop with my earphones plugged in, with less than a minute before the commencement of the Skyline Zoom call, this is the worst possible time for me not to have Internet access. I cast a desperate look at my office computer and consider using it, and the more stable official Internet connection, for the meeting. But as the port for external headphones has never worked in all the time I have used the device, and with how packed and noisy my floor is, using my official computer will not be the wisest of ideas.

At 4pm, it is peak time at the bank and, even though I have only one more week left there, the last thing I need is an audience for this call with the executives of the organization giving me the scholarship and, indeed, the chance of a lifetime. Making the last minute decision to hotspot from my phone, I grab my personal laptop and dash into the small meeting room adjacent to my desk, locking the door behind me for good measure. By the time I log in using the earlier shared credentials, it is already two minutes past 4pm.

My heart races as I stare at the boxes of each of the 28 attendees, many of whom have their cameras switched off and microphones muted. Five of the boxes with their cameras switched on show pleasant-faced people who, if the Skyline logo used as their respective backgrounds is anything to go by, are executives of the scholarship organization. A Caucasian woman, who looks to be about the same age as me, is talking animatedly and I have to keep myself from continuing to stare at the names on the boxes of the other attendees so I can pay attention to what she is saying.

"Before I go on, I think it'll be a nice idea for us to turn on our cameras, so that we can get to know each other better," the woman suggests, a bright smile on her face. "With all of you headed to schools all across the world, this might be the only time our class of 2018 will be on the same call, so it'll be nice to place some faces behind the names we've been corresponding with all these months."

My heart skips a beat at the prospect of turning on my camera. Patting my curly wig, I run my tongue across my teeth to make sure there is no recalcitrant residue from the meal of rice and *efo-riro* I've just had for lunch. I linger for a few seconds, waiting to see if the other people on the call will also not be eager to turn on their cameras, but as their images start to appear one by one, I have no choice but to turn mine on as well.

"Fantastic!" the Caucasian woman says. "It's so great to see all your faces. Later in this call, we'll all get the chance to introduce ourselves. For those who missed my introduction earlier, my name is Melanie. Also, if you have any questions, you can send them through the chat box or wait till I'm done with my presentation."

I stare back at the screen, not quite sure what to do with my face. The fact I am visible to all these strangers is making my heart race a mile a minute. If there is one thing I don't like, it's being in the spotlight.

I listen as Melanie talks about the Skyline scholarship and it being an opportunity to broaden our respective horizons, with unlimited opportunities at our fingertips. As she reiterates how their focus is on the wellbeing of future leaders being well equipped, evidenced by their various student loans and different tiers of scholarships, I start to relax, delighted that I am the beneficiary of one of their most robust scholarships; full tuition and board.

She continues to talk for another fifteen minutes before she calls on three panellists, all of whom have benefitted from the Skyline scholarships, and I listen with rapt attention as they each talk about their experience and how the scholarship changed their lives. I am particularly interested in the only woman among the three, the one who schooled in the United Kingdom, curious about how easy it was for her to remain there when her program was over. But curious though I might be, I am not brave enough to type my question in the chat box, worried the other people on the call would think it stupid. And that is the last thing I want to be labelled, not especially when I am doing more than enough self-deprecation already.

"Join me," Melanie says, when the spotlight returns to her, "as I welcome the Fall intake of 2018. After the introduction by the Fall intake students, three beneficiaries who have spent more than a year in their respective schools will share brief tips on making the best of this amazing Skyline opportunity." She smiles. "It's a tradition and I hope you learn a thing or two, or even make new friends."

She squints and I wipe sweaty palms on my skirt, willing her not to call me first. My inner voice is screaming at me to look away from my screen, but with my heightened nerves, I remain rooted to the spot, wide eyes staring back at my screen.

"Can we start with you, urm… " she leans forward to squint as if trying to read the name in focus better. "Legachi?"

Drat!

Swallowing hard, I force a smile and wave. "Hi, I'm Legachi." I swallow again in a desperate bid to banish the quiver from my voice. Why on earth am I so nervous when most of the faces I see look way younger than me? Taking a deep breath, I go on. "I... I've been accepted as an M.Sc. student at Middlesex University, studying Global Supply Chain Management. It's an honour to be one of the selected few for the class of 2018."

I exhale as I mute my microphone, glad to have gotten it over and done with. But even though my microphone is now muted, my heart is still beating so fast, I am certain the throb at the centre of my neck is visible to all.

"Hi, I'm Berwa from Kenya, studying at Savannah University," comes the voice of a pretty girl with glossy dark skin. "My course of study is… "

"Sorry to cut you short," Melanie says, the spotlight returning to her. "Can we circle back to urm… Legachi?"

My eyes widen as my anxiety skyrockets again. Goodness, isn't she done with me?

"What country are you from?" she asks, smiling at her screen.

I manage a weak smile back. "I'm from Nigeria. Lagos, Nigeria," I add for emphasis.

"Thank you," she says, nodding. "Please proceed, Berwa."

The Kenyan girl finishes her introduction and is quickly followed by another Nigerian girl.

"Hi. I am Enitan Adebayo, from Nigeria. I'm in for a Masters in Film at The Empire Film School, London.". The Nigeria movie industry is growing, and I want to be a driving force."

My concentration starts to wane as the introductions continue. The call is already taking longer than I'd expected and I know it is only a matter of time before my Manager starts to look for me. With all the work he has been heaping on me since I tendered my notice, it's like he is trying to extract from me every morsel of productivity he possibly can.

My ears perk up when I hear someone mention she'll be schooling in East London. Her name is Aretta George and she says she'll be studying for an MA in French at the University of East London. I am tempted to send her a private message, to ask if we can meet up when I get to London.

"I am from Nigeria," Aretta continues, her voice steady and her gaze self-assured. "Born and bred in Lagos State. It's nice to meet you all."

I immediately cower, no longer confident enough to reach out to her. She looks like a posh girl, the kind I have felt inferior to pretty much my whole life. The last thing I need is to be shunned before I even leave the shores of Nigeria. Nah, it's best to let her, and indeed any of the other London-bound students, be. Thank God I have Mezie over there. I'll be okay.

With all the introductions done, Melanie introduces three students from the class of 2017, who have already spent a year in their different schools on the Skyline program, asking them to each share some advice for the new intakes.

I hardly listen to the first two, Tokun and Grace, as they drone on about how wonderful the program is. At the risk of sounding ungrateful, I've heard more than enough about how amazing and fantastic the *Skyline* scholarship is. Glancing at my watch, I am tempted to sneak out of the call. With only 24 people now on it, I see a few people have already done just that. But when the third student, Jamila, starts to speak, something in her sonorous, refined tone piques my interest.

"Hello, I'm Jemila Abeo, MA International Economics, American University. You'll experience a lot on this journey, but, no matter what, it's good to know there's a village cheering you on. On the serious side though, it's never too late to apply for internships or jobs."

Finally, someone with *real* talk and not sugar coated rambling. I look at her and even though she isn't smiling, her eyes are dancing like they hold some kind of secret. I desperately want to hear everything she has experienced in her one year but, again, I am too scared to type anything in the chat box. I make a mental note to look her up on Google, just to see what I'll find.

"Feel free to reach out to me if you have any issues," the guy, Tokun, says, grinning. "I always know someone that knows someone."

I have to keep myself from rolling my eyes. Indeed!

Thankfully, the call soon ends and I rush back to my desk, hopeful I haven't been missed. But as I try to return my attention to the work I have left on my table, I am tingling from the crown of my head to my toenails. Even with my fees paid, my living expenses transferred, and my one-way ticket already purchased, the whole thing has still seemed surreal, almost like it is one long dream I will soon awake from. But this call, this call where I have seen the faces and heard the voices of not only the people who have made this happen, but other beneficiaries like me, has made it so very real.

And I am beside myself with excitement!

Five

London

Legachi

I shiver as I walk along the jetway connecting the British Airways plane that has brought me from Lagos to Heathrow's Terminal 5, my thick denim jacket feeling no better than if it were a flimsy scarf. I marvel as two young girls walk past me, neither of them wearing any type of jacket, and one of them even in mid-calf cargo pants.

As the other passengers overtake me, I see that very few of them indeed have on any kind of outerwear. Another sharp gust of wind slaps me in the face, and I marvel anew, but as I get on the horizontal escalator, as larger than life adverts welcome me to London as I glide on the moving walkway, I forget the cold and take in my new reality. I have left Nigeria. I'm in London. I will soon be reunited with Mezie. And that is enough to make me excited all over again.

Going through immigration is a breeze. I stick to my scholarship story and, as Mezie advised, I make no mention of him at all. As I move on to get my luggage, I can't help but be amazed over how seamless the whole thing has been. I go through more stress flying from Lagos to Port Harcourt airport every Christmas. As I wheel the trolley bearing my suitcases, I am even angry with myself for all the time I wasted being nervous about this whole thing. It's been a walk in the park.

Stepping into the Arrivals terminal, I look around anxiously for Mezie. It is a little past 7am and I am surprised by how bright it already is. I stand in the middle of the hall, marvelling at the cocoon of steel the airport is, with its elegantly curved walls. I watch as nearby stalls are opened for the day and smile again as I hear people chatter as they walk past me, their accent another reminder that my situation has changed. London is no longer a dream, but now a reality.

"Legachi!"

I turn around when I hear Mezie's voice and squeal as I push past my trolley and run into his arms. He lifts me off the ground as we embrace, and I savour the feel and smell of his body again. Even though he feels bulkier and has on aftershave I don't recognise, he is still the man my heart has been pining for in the fifteen months he has been away.

"Wow! You're really here!" he says, pulling away to take a good look at me. "Was the flight stressful? You look tired."

I am crushed that my last-minute reapplication of mascara and lip gloss when the plane landed haven't quite achieved their aim.

"But you still look beautiful," he says, bending to kiss me on the tip of my nose. "I love your hair."

Of course, he loves my hair! Even though I'm not a fan of the hair colour, I have braided my hair in the honey blonde hue he likes. The braids are tiny enough to last me till Christmas, so I can only hope they age well.

"But it's cold *sha*!" I say, shivering as another gust of wind blows past. "I thought you told me it would still be warm and not to bother getting a winter jacket."

Before I left Nigeria, I'd asked how the weather was and he'd assured me that, at that time of year, it was still very much like Lagos.

"Just imagine Lagos in the evening, after it has rained," he'd said to me.

"So, I don't need to get a jacket or anything?"

"Which jacket? Is it those second-hand contraptions at *Tejuosho* you're calling jacket?" he'd guffawed. "Just wear your denim jacket and you'll be fine."

Except, I am not quite fine.

"Are you being serious?" he scoffs. "Is this what you call cold?"

That is when I realise he is only wearing a polo shirt over a pair of jeans.

"Babe, you better brace up. It's over twenty degrees now. In a few weeks, it's going to get much, much cooler," he says, reaching for my trolley and pushing it.

I fall into step with him, making a mental note to get ready for even worse weather soon. I interlink my arm with his as we walk, my eyes scanning the signs. As we walk past the exit sign for taxis and the car park, I look at him.

"Aren't we supposed to go through there?"

"No, we're taking the train. It's much cheaper," he answers. "You're lucky you arrived on a Saturday. If it were a weekday morning, we'd have had to wait till 9:30. Peak fares before then are crazy expensive."

"I have some money on me," I say, referring to the £1,000 I managed to convert from what was left of my salary after buying the foodstuff Mezie asked for, having transferred the agreed £8,000 to him as far back as July. After deducting the loan I'd taken from the bank to add to his travel fund the previous year, I was left with a fraction of my salary and a handshake as I bade my company farewell.

He stops abruptly and glares at me. "You better get rid of that wasteful mindset, Legachi. Do you have any idea what a taxi from here to Hackney will cost?"

My brows form a knot as I take in this piece of information, wondering if that cost is really worth the stress of us manoeuvring my two heavy boxes and large travel bag on a train. I immediately quash my concerns, confident he knows best.

But my every fear is justified as we huff and puff my luggage onto a packed train from the terminal to Gloucester Road Station, heaving the boxes up, down and up the escalators as we switch platforms, before boarding a Circle line train to Monument Station. As we stand in the packed carriage, I lose my footing several times, even as I hold on to the overheard safety straps as if my life depends on it. Mezie puts his arm around my torso to steady me, but I am already feeling weary from the tedious journey. So weary that I barely register this new commute experience, or even the people around me. I'm already over it.

"Are we almost there?" I ask, sleep colliding with muscle fatigue, eager to arrive where I will now call home.

"Almost," he answers, smiling at me. "You too, why did you pack such heavy bags? Did you move all your life's belongings? And don't say it's the noodles and plantain chips I asked you to buy that have made your boxes heavy."

I look away so as not to glare at him, thinking how convenient it is for him to forget that I had to empty two cartons of noodles and almost as many plantain chips, not to mention the foodstuff for soups he said he was craving, into said boxes. I had been too happy to dispose of my own personal effects, so only packed a handful of clothes. But today isn't the day for arguments.

We get to the station and board a bus this time. At this point, I'm sore in places I didn't even know exist.

"Almost home, babe," he winks at me, from where we stand.

I can only sigh in response. With my leg muscles beginning to buckle, I am desperate to rest them, even if only for a second.

"That's our stop," he says, as the bus pulls up where the destination sign indicates as Shore Road. "Don't worry, it's just a short walk to the house."

A 'short' walk ends up being nine minutes. Soon, we get to a block of flats, and it is another huffing and puffing up stairs this time, until we walk up to a door on the second floor of the building. As he makes to open it, I hear the blare of a TV from inside.

"You left your TV on?" I ask, surprised.

"Nah, must be Eche or Diran."

"Who are Eche and Diran?" I ask, just as the door opens.

I soon get my answer.

"Hey, man. *You don come?*" comes a voice from the short corridor we are now standing in.

I turn to see a large man emerge from a nearby room, a wide smile on his face.

"Yes *o*. My woman is here," Mezie declares. "Babe, this is my flatmate, Diran."

I am very confused as I shake his hand. Mezie never said anything about a flatmate.

"Welcome, our wife," Diran's grin is even broader. "Mezie has been so excited."

"*She don come?*" comes another voice from the living room the corridor leads into.

My heart catches in my throat at the sight before me. Seated in the living room, playing video games, are three guys. Empty pizza boxes and soda cans litter the floor, and the air is thick with smoke… from cigarettes and possibly something more potent. A woman dressed in a flimsy nightgown lies asleep on the other couch. It is an unpleasant throwback to my undergraduate years and the overcrowded quarters some of my male friends and classmates opted for. I shut my eyes, wanting the sight before me to be something my tired mind has conjured, but opening them again, I realise, with dismay, that this is no bad dream.

And it gets worse.

"Babe, meet my other roommates Eche, Nedu and Alex," Mezie beams. "Guys, *na my madam be dis o!*"

I force a smile through introductions and listening to the guys rave about how much Mezie has looked forward to my arrival. It is like I am having an out-of-body experience, like I am watching the situation from afar. No, this has got to be a joke. There has to be a punch line soon.

But there is no punch line. Instead, he leads me to a small bedroom which, after we've pushed in my suitcases and bags, has no standing space left. I feel myself getting lightheaded, so I sit on the bed. No, there must be some sort of mistake.

"I don't understand. What's this about flatmates, Mezie?" I ask, casting him a plaintive look, begging him with my eyes to put me out of my misery by telling me this is all a prank.

But instead, he frowns. "What do you mean 'what's this about flatmates'? Did I tell you I live alone? Do you know how expensive rent is here?"

My mouth opens but no words come out. I am rendered speechless.

"You're very funny o, Legs," he chuckles, pushing my suitcases under the bed. "Even with all my lamentation, you were expecting me to live in a flat alone? With which money *na*?"

"So, why did you ask me to come stay with you if you don't have a place to yourself?" I finally find my voice.

He looks at me. "I have a bed, Legachi. Or isn't that enough? Must you occupy every square inch of this flat before you're satisfied?"

A bed. My eyes widen when the import of what he has said hits me.

"Do you share this room with anyone?"

The shift of his eyes is my answer and I cover my face with my hands.

"Don't be melodramatic, Legachi. Nedu sleeps on that thing over there," he says, pointing at a sleeping bag tucked in the small crevice between the closet and the wall. "We have the bed to ourselves."

And the tears I have been keeping at bay pool in my eyes. Is this what I left my life back in Lagos for?

As if on cue, the one introduced to me as Nedu walks into the room. "Knock, knock," he says redundantly, a lopsided grin on his face. He doesn't make eye contact with me, and I can tell he is embarrassed for me… for all of us. "I came to get my charger."

Neither Mezie nor I say anything, sitting in silence as Nedu disconnects the charger from the wall socket and leaves the room, his gaze averted.

"Stop acting like this is new to you," Mezie mutters when we are alone. "You shared a room with Chineme."

"A room probably four times the size of this!" I exclaim, wiping tears from my face. "Mezie, this can't work. I can't live like this. You'll have to give me back that money so I can make accommodation arrangements with my school. Hopefully, it isn't too late."

A frown shadows his face. "What are you talking about? Didn't we agree I'd use from the money for my PMP exam?"

"Yes, but I should still have £5,000 left. I'm sure that can get me something, no matter how small."

"It's not up to £5,000. After paying for my exam, I had to sort out one or two things," he answers with a shrug. "There's very little left."

I look at him, and it feels like all the air has been sucked out of the room. I take one deep breath and then another, but it feels like my airway is restricted, unable to take in enough oxygen to power my lungs.

"Are you okay?" he asks in concern.

I say nothing as I rest my head on the pillow, the room spinning around me. Just when I thought things couldn't get any worse, they have gone straight to hell.

He rises from the bed and crouches before me. "Babe, it's not that bad. The guys are awesome. You'll like them." He wipes a tear as it rolls down my face. "It's only for a little while. In a matter of months, we'll be able to move somewhere better. Please don't cry." His face brightens. "I got a job last week."

This catches my attention. "Last week? And you didn't tell me?"

"I wanted to wait for you to get here."

"What kind of job is it?"

"It's just temporary, so don't shout," he warns, and I know I won't like what I hear. And I don't. "It's a Door Supervisor role at a lounge."

I might be simple minded, but not that simple minded not to know what the real interpretation is. "You mean a bouncer? A nightclub bouncer?"

He shrugs and rises. "Call it what you like, but it's a cool £14 an hour. It's only temporary, and once I've saved enough and passed my exam, I'll be able to get a much better job."

I sit up, no longer wanting to hear another word. "Where is the toilet?"

"The door right after this one."

The smell of stale urine hits me when I walk into the restroom, which clearly hasn't enjoyed a good clean in weeks, months maybe. From the plethora of towels hanging on the shower curtain rod, and the mishmash of both male and female bath products, I realise this is all we've got; Mezie, his flat mates, their very many female guests… and me.

Sitting on the ledge of the bath, I burst into tears. I haven't even been in the country six hours, but all my fantasies have already come crashing down. I remember how excited I'd been to move out of my flat in Lagos, ecstatic that my cohabitation with Chineme had finally ended. But sitting in the smelly cubicle, I would do anything, absolutely anything, to open my eyes and find myself back in my old flat.

I sit there for several minutes, weeping. When I'm spent, I rise and walk to the sink to wash my face. Standing before the toothpaste-stained mirror, it is so dirty I can barely see my reflection. But from what I can make out, I behold the puffy eyes of the woman staring back at me and remind her of the reasons she is here; to go to school and, more importantly, be reunited with the love of her life. As disappointing and soul crushing as this living arrangement is, neither of those has been compromised.

I walk out of the toilet and hear Mezie's voice in the living room. I decide to start trying to blend in with my new gang and walk there to join them.

"Babe, do you think you can organize me a couple packs of the noodles you brought?" Mezie asks, not looking up from the PS4 console in his hands.

I turn to look at him. Surely, he can't expect me to cook him a meal, when I haven't even as much as had a shower, or even slept!

"She brought noodles?" Eche exclaims. "*Abeg, no forget your homeboy o!*"

And that is how I am roped into cooking a large pot of garnished noodles for not just the guys, but the woman who is still lying on the couch with no plans of vacating it anytime soon. As the noodles cook, I am told where to find a frozen pack of chicken in their freezer and end up having to cook that as well. By the time I dish the garnished noodles, boiled eggs and fried chicken, I'm falling asleep on my feet.

"Mezie, *you dey enjoy o!*" Alex raves, as he devours his food. "Good food and good pussy! You're a lucky man."

I am appalled by the crudeness of the statement, but Mezie clearly isn't. Instead, he laughs heartily along with the others.

"Aren't you eating?" Nedu asks, as I make to leave the room.

I force a smile and shake my head. "Maybe later. I'm quite tired."

Turning around, I return to the bedroom, take off the sneakers that have been on my feet for almost twenty-four hours, lie on the bed and I am asleep before my head even hits the pillow.

The smell of aerosol rouses me, and I open my eyes to see Mezie dousing himself with body spray before he slips on a crisp white shirt. Our eyes meet and he smiles.

"You're finally awake," he remarks. "I thought you were going to sleep till tomorrow."

"Are you going out?"

He rolls his eyes, returning his attention to buttoning his shirt. "It's Saturday night, babes. I'm working tonight."

I sit up and watch as he wears a pair of black trousers, before pulling on a smart black blazer. It's a very different look from the tight jeans and muscle tops bouncers in Nigerian nightclubs wear, so maybe it's not so bad a gig after all.

"Is it far from here? The club."

"Just about twenty minutes," he answers, pinning on a nametag.

"Harry?" I ask when I read the name inscribed on it.

He sighs, and I see he is already getting impatient with my questions. "I can't work here legally, Legachi. You know quite well that my visiting visa has long expired. I had to pay good money to use someone's N.I. number to get this job."

"And his name as well?"

He shrugs. "It is what it is." He combs his hair, sprays a heady perfume and turns to me. "You'll need to make more noodles if you want to eat. The guys cleared everything in the pot."

My stomach growls in response, the hunger I have been keeping at bay rearing its head with a vengeance.

"Don't wait up," he says, planting a kiss on my forehead before walking out of the room.

When he leaves, I make sure the door is locked before getting out of my clothes. I reach for his discarded towel, pushing to the back of my mind my disdain for wet towels, wrap it around my body and open the door tentatively, rushing into the bathroom before any of the guys can see me. Once in there, I select the bath gel that looks the most like what a woman would use and make a mental note to buy my own toiletries as soon as I possibly can. Back in the room, I wear a pair of tracksuit bottoms and a long-sleeved t-shirt I had the good sense to pack, lie on the bed, nibble on a pack of plantain chips, and drift off to sleep.

I hear the grunting and groaning in my sub-consciousness. It sounds like it's coming from far away, like maybe someone nearby is watching porn. But as I drift back to consciousness and my eyes open, I am horrified to see that it is neither coming from far away nor from anyone's screen. Right there on his sleeping mat, limbs are intertwined as Nedu and a light skinned woman, who is moaning uninhibited, are having sex. I am too stunned to close my eyes or even look away, but throw the duvet over my head when they switch positions. How long are they going to go at it? Don't they know someone else is in the room?

From underneath the covers, I do everything to distract myself from what I am unwillingly witnessing; count to ten thousand, recite the Periodic Table... but none of it works and I have to listen until they both moan as they reach their release. Afterwards, they laugh and chat for a while, until the silence lets me know the coast is clear and they have fallen asleep. I sigh deeply as I emerge from beneath the sheets. No, we can't live like this. We simply can't. I am suddenly remorseful about the one time Chineme caught Mezie and I having sex, now understanding how traumatising the sight must have been for her.

I drift off to sleep but I am awakened a few hours later as Mezie slips into the bed next to me.

"Welcome back," I say, happy to have him home. "How was work?"

"It was good," he says, slipping his hand beneath my t-shirt.

My eyes widen with terror. "Mezie, what are you doing?" I whisper hoarsely as his hand cups my breast.

"I've missed you," is his raspy response. "I've longed for you for over a year."

"But not here!" I whisper back, not wanting to give Nedu and his female companion the same spectacle they subjected me to.

But Mezie is too far-gone. He pulls me closer, so close I can feel his erection, just as his hand slides beneath the band of my trousers.

"Mezie!" I snap, pushing his hand away. "There are people here!"

"So what? It's his room too. We're all adults."

"I didn't come here to act porn for your friends," I whisper, turning to glare at him.

"Is this what I get for being faithful to you?" he whispers back, the anger in his eyes matching mine. "I've waited for you all this time and you want to deny me now that you're finally here?"

His words make me feel guilty. I also desperately want to be sexually reunited with him, but just not in the full glare of other people.

"They're sleeping, babe," Mezie says, seeing a crack in my armour. "And we'll be quiet. I promise."

Reluctantly, I give in, but as he thrusts on top of me, I am unable to even enjoy it, my eyes on Nedu and his babe the whole time, sick to my stomach that they know what Mezie and I are doing. Thankfully, it is soon over, and as he rolls over to sleep, I lie awake in the darkness, with tears in my eyes.

Six

Sex Life

SEPTEMBER 2018

Roman

My phone rings as I step out of the train station and I immediately reach for it in my pocket, thinking it might be Greta calling about Luna. It's a Saturday morning and I have started taking on the extra workload I need to fast track my specialization. It has been four months and things are going great with Greta. She and Luna get along, and I can put in more hours at work. It's been a win-win situation.

Except it isn't Greta calling. I shut my eyes and grimace as Itunu's name flashes on the display of my phone, tempted to ignore the call as I have been doing for the last few weeks. After running out on her when we met months ago, she'd gotten my number from Sean and called. I'd been happy to hear from her and we met up for dinner that night. But unlike the last time when our conversation had flowed seamlessly, without the support of alcohol, I found her incredibly boring. My mind wandered as she'd droned on about topics I had no interest in. It was a big disappointment and I found myself counting the minutes till it was over. But when she invited me to her flat afterwards, I'd reconsidered, especially as it had been a while since I'd had sex and I could have done a whole lot worse than the gorgeous, sexy woman who was offering. Alas, even that proved to be as uneventful as our stilted conversation. It wasn't bad, but it wasn't great either. Wanting to give it more of a chance, we met up a few more times, but rather than get better, it only got worse. So, I decided it wasn't worth the trouble and ended things the way I knew best; ghosting her. But she has proven relentless and has hounded me ever since.

Looking at the ringing phone, I decide it's childish to continue ignoring her, and answer the call.

"Hey, stranger," comes her sultry voice as the line connects.

"Hi, Itunu. How are you doing?"

"Not great. You haven't been returning my calls."

"Yeah, I'm sorry about that," I say, feeling anything but. "I've taken on more work at the hospital, so it's been really busy." At least, that much is true.

"Are you there right now?"

"Just walking in," I answer, smiling in greeting as I walk past familiar faces in the hospital lobby.

"It's 10am, so you'll probably be off work by evening, right?"

"Not necessarily," I stutter, even though she is right and I am scheduled to have an eight-hour shift. "Some calls can run for as long as twenty-four hours."

"But I know you won't leave your kid with her nanny for twenty-four hours," she chuckles. "Meaning you'll be free this evening. Unless you have other plans?"

I pause in front of the elevator, wanting to tell her she is wrong and I'm indeed working that evening, or that I do have other plans. But I feel a stir in my groin and wonder how bad it would be to accept whatever she's offering that night. Maybe all it will take will be for me to spice things up a bit. Maybe I can put in more effort to make things with her more exciting.

"Actually, I don't," I answer, smiling. "What do you have in mind?"

"How about we meet up at *Le Gavroche* and take it from there?"

I wince at the mention of the upscale restaurant, a reminder of her penchant for expensive dining.

"Sure. See you there."

"9 o'clock?"

"Let's make it 8," I say, thinking how both the meal and sex afterwards need to be over for me to be home before midnight.

Mistaking my request for an earlier time for eagerness, she giggles. "8 it is."

The line disconnects just as the elevator door opens. Walking in, I decide that even if things are still uninteresting with Itunu that night, I will make more of an effort to put myself out there. Dating after Sekani has been a disaster, yes, but I need to at least try if I don't want to end up alone for the rest of my life.

—

"You're sure it's okay? I know you didn't plan to stay overnight," I say to Greta, who agrees to the extra hours with little or no coercion. Since I started taking on-call shifts at work, she has had cause to spend quite a few nights, a far cry from our initial agreement.

"Yes, I'm sure," she grins, nodding. "I'll go home tomorrow."

I smile back before making my way upstairs. She is always so eager and enthusiastic, and that has made the fact I still have to make Luna's meals not too bad to bear. Nobody is perfect.

Once in my bedroom, I strip off my clothes, instruct my virtual assistant to play Jay Z's *The Blueprint* album, and walk into the bathroom. As I shower, I rap along to *Bonnie & Clyde*, pumping myself for the evening. Maybe what I really need in this life of sin is 'me and my girlfriend'. I am still rapping and singing as I walk into the room nude, my towel flung over my shoulders. But the sight that meets me makes me stop dead in my tracks, the song evaporating from my lips, even as Beyoncé continues to belt the bridge. Greta is on my bed completely naked.

"What the!" I exclaim, tying the towel around my waist. "What the hell is this?"

She smiles, as if my surprise is part of the game, and parts her legs wider, to reveal fleshy labia beneath well-trimmed pubic hair the same shade of brown as her hair. But rather than excite me, I am repulsed.

"Luna is sleeping," she says, as if that is supposed to make a difference. She runs her tongue across her lip in some kind of medieval invitation, and that for me is the last straw.

"Get the fuck off my bed and put some clothes on!" I yell, as I retreat into the bathroom. "You better not be here when I come back."

I slam the door shut. Fuck! This girl could not have chosen a worse time to pull a stunt like this. I panic as I think about all the ways she can spin this, thinking how everyone would believe any tale of a traumatized Au Pair sexually harassed by her employer, and I hate myself for putting myself in this kind of situation.

I wait a few more minutes, before cautiously opening the door. Thankfully, she's gone. I ignore the white poplin Tom Ford shirt and Roberto Cavalli jeans I'd planned to wear that evening, and instead throw on an old t-shirt over tracksuit bottoms. There will be no outing for me tonight.

The fully dressed Greta I meet downstairs is the same demure and shy person I employed, and not her seductress alter ego. Her face is pale, and she is wringing her fingers in her nervousness. I am relieved to see that she is just as disturbed by what has just happened.

"I so sorry," she says, in her broken English. "I didn't understand. I thought is why you ask me to stay."

My eyes widen in my panic. "You've stayed overnight several times. Have I ever done or said anything for you to even think there's anything more to it? I asked you stay tonight because I have a date. *Had* a date."

"I so sorry," she repeats, her eyes tearing. "It was mistake. It will never happen again."

"You bet it won't," I answer firmly. Hell no, am I going to allow this European Jezebel destroy my life. People have lost their medical licenses for less serious offenses than what I could be accused of. God knows I have more than enough troubles to deal with already. "I'm afraid I have to let you go, Greta. I'll pay you for an additional week in lieu of notice, but that's just me being nice."

She nods, accepting that I am indeed being gracious. I wait as she goes to retrieve her handbag and other personal effects, and as she walks out of the house, her head bowed. All I can do is pray she doesn't try to stir up some kind of trouble for me.

It isn't until my phone rings that I remember the date I'm supposed to be headed for. At 8:15pm, I'm already late.

"I'm so sorry, Itunu, but I can't make it," I say, happy it's not an excuse I'm making up. "I just had some major drama with my Au Pair."

"What kind of drama?"

I find myself telling her the story and we are soon laughing hysterically over the failed seduction.

"That girl sure is ambitious! Aiming for a whole doctor!"

"Is that even the case or how she could have pulled a hashtag *MeToo* stunt on me?"

"I don't think that's what she wanted to do. She's probably been crushing on you since the day you hired her. Girl was just shooting her shot."

Somehow, the thought of that unsettles me even more.

"So, I'm afraid I can't come out," I repeat my earlier pronouncement. "There's nobody to watch Luna."

"If you can't come out, I could come to you," she says. "I could get some takeaway and be at your place in about an hour?"

It is on the tip of my tongue to tell her no. I have never brought a woman home, as the last thing I want is to confuse Luna. But as my stomach growls and with nothing interesting in my fridge, I think it might not be such a bad idea, especially with Luna already asleep. And I could do with some company after tonight's episode.

"Sounds good," I answer. "I'll text my address."

I go back upstairs, spritz on some body spray and change the sheets, more to get rid of the image of Greta's naked body on them than to make a good impression on Itunu. Back downstairs, I put on some rap music to loosen myself up and by the time Itunu knocks on the door an hour later, I'm ready for her.

"Hi, beautiful," I say, taking in the drop dead gorgeous, tall supermodel in front of me. Wearing a black leather jacket over a short dress with a neckline that runs all the way down to her waist, baring her modest cleavage, I wonder why I could possibly be running away from a beauty like this.

"Hey, sexy," she purrs, walking past me into the house. "Wow! Your place is beautiful."

I smile, proud again of the money, time and energy that went into decorating the terrace house I bought a little over a year ago. As I don't have people over often, it feels good to see the awe on the face of anyone seeing it for the first time. With a very minimalist, monochromatic scheme of white, grey and black, wood accents and LED recessed and pendant lights, it is a play of modern and traditional with the velvet-upholstered furnishing I chose to make the place Luna-friendly.

"Very, very nice. I'm impressed," Itunu says, a smile on her face as she continues to look around. Her eyes fall on the large portrait of Sekani and I on our wedding day and she gasps. "Is that her? Your late wife?"

I nod and walk to where she stands before the picture, remembering the very moment Sekani and I posed for this picture. It was after the wedding reception and as we were leaving the hall, Sekani had spotted a lake.

"We have to take a picture there, Roman!" she'd squealed, grabbing my hand and pulling me in the lake's direction.

"But honey, the photographer... "

"Forget the photographer!" she'd laughed, raising her hands and twirling in her excitement. "Janine can take the picture with her phone. It doesn't have to be perfect, and we don't even have to do anything with it. We just can't pass up this chance."

I'd been heart warmed by her exhilaration and joy, which matched mine. After so many years together, we'd finally made it official, and I couldn't wait to spend the rest of my life with her.

"It'll be perfect," I'd said, taking her hand. "It'll be perfect because you're in it."

"Oh, Roman," she'd said, her voice but a whisper as she looked at me, peace and contentment in her eyes. "I love you so much."

That had been the moment her best friend, Janine, captured, and which now hangs on my wall.

"She was very beautiful," Itunu says, a sympathetic smile on her face. "You both looked so in love."

I nod, looking at the picture as if seeing it for the first time. "We were."

"You also have a type," she adds with a wink.

I smile and shrug. Even a blind man would be able to see their physical similarities. But unfortunately, that is where their similarities end. With Sekani's broad knowledge of pretty much everything under the sun, from current affairs, to sports, to pop culture, to even the sole topic that interests Itunu, fashion, she was able to keep anyone she conversed with not only engaged but intrigued.

"I got us Italian food," Itunu says, raising the bag in her hand. "I stopped at *Canto Corvino* on my way here. That's what held me up."

My stomach churns. I'm not a fan of Italian food. All the cheese and tomatoes do not do much for me. But I force a smile. "Great!"

I lead her to the kitchen, and she gasps as she walks into the room, with everything in it, walls, appliances, crockery and furnishing stark white.

"This is really nice!" she remarks, before smiling at me. "I can also tell you don't do much cooking here though."

I chuckle. With my cooking repertoire limited to fixing Luna's sandwiches and popping ready meals into the microwave, she's right on the money.

She places the takeout bag on the kitchen island and smiles at me, a smile with a thousand meanings. "We could eat now… or maybe later?"

Her meaning isn't lost on me, and I walk to her just as she strides a few paces to where I stand. Our lips meet as I pull her closer, and as she covers hers with mine, I am immediately reminded why I don't enjoy kissing her. Her tongue darts around my mouth like it's playing tag with mine. Trying not to be undeterred, I lead her out of the kitchen and back to the living room, wanting to restrict our tryst to that part of the house, so she can leave with Luna being none the wiser. I undress her as she undresses me, and program my mind to ignore her sharp nails as they tug and scratch my body as they always do, or the vice grip her hand forms on my penis, squeezing it like it's a tube of toothpaste, or the heady fragrance of strawberries when I slip off her underwear, a fragrance I have since realised is being used to unsuccessfully mask a less pleasant smell. I do everything to ignore all these, determined to get the release from sex that evening, no matter what. But then, a visual of the naked Greta on my bed flashes in my head, and I know Roman Junior will not be participating tonight.

Itunu does everything she can to get me excited, but it is a lost cause. My libido has left the building and will not be returning anytime soon.

"I'm sorry," I say as we lie on the couch, panting after spending over an hour on the longest foreplay in the history of the world. "I think I'm just tired. And the incident with the Au Pair... "

"I understand. That would be enough to mess with anyone," she says, stroking my chest, her nails leaving red lines in their wake. "I'm also exhausted. Maybe we should eat, nap and try again?"

The unappealing Italian food is the last thing I want to get up for. "Maybe we could eat after we nap?"

I don't even hear her response before I fall asleep, weary from the physical and mental rigors of the day. We are both still sleeping when I hear someone calling me in the far distance.

"Daddy. Daddy."

My eyes fly open, and the rays of the early morning sun hit me through the blinds. It's morning and Luna is up. I balk at the sight of Itunu and I lying naked and push her off me like she has a contagious disease.

"My daughter is awake. Get dressed!"

Itunu rubs her eyes as she struggles to come awake. "Isn't she just a baby? She won't understand anything."

I spare her no response as I throw on my clothes. "I'm coming, sweetheart," I call out to Luna. "I'll be right up."

I rush to the stairs and see her already making her way down.

"I want to watch telly," she says as I reach over and carry her.

"In a minute, sweetheart," I say, standing on the stairs but using the corner of my eye to make sure Itunu is getting dressed. A muscle clenches in my jaw as I see how leisurely she is doing that, not caring that I have a child I'm trying to spare that visual.

"Where's Greta?"

I frown, unhappy about the difficult conversation I'm going to have with my daughter about the Au Pair I have fired. It also dawns on me that, with Greta gone, I no longer have reasonable childcare and will, again, have to scale back at work.

"Hi, there," Itunu says, walking over to the foot of the stairs when she is dressed, waving.

Luna stares at her confused and I am so angry, I feel like rushing down to choke my unwanted guest.

"Sweetheart, this is a friend of Daddy's," I say, glaring at Itunu. "Itunu, this is my daughter, Luna."

Itunu waves again, but her disinterest in my daughter is evident as her eyes remain on me. "We didn't get to eat… or even try again."

She winks and I'm furious over the impropriety of it all.

"I'm hungry," Luna says, brightening at the mention of food.

"Trust me, you won't like this at all. I'll fix you a bowl of cereal in a minute, sweetheart. Let's go downstairs first, so I can turn on the telly for you," I say, walking down the stairs and past Itunu.

Settling Luna on the sofa, I tune the TV to the Cbeebies channel and am relieved when she squeals with the delight as *Hey Duggee* comes on. Satisfied she's distracted enough, I drag Itunu to the corridor.

"What the hell was that? I told you to wait!"

"It's just a baby, Roman," she laughs. "We could even be having sex in front of her, and she wouldn't know what we were doing. Chill."

51

"*It* is my daughter," I sneer before taking a deep breath to swallow back the words my mouth is desperate to spew. "You need to leave now."

Her face falls.

"Come on, Roman. I'm sure she'll soon take a nap or whatever it is children do. I'm already here, don't be a spoilsport."

"Itunu, you need to leave," I repeat, stretching each word to drive home what I'm saying.

This time she gets it. Frowning, she walks back to the living room and grabs her handbag, not even casting Luna another glance. Thankfully, Luna is too engrossed in her TV show to pay her any mind. Itunu storms past me to the kitchen, grabs the bag of takeaway and leaves, slamming the door.

I shake my head and chuckle. I didn't even want to eat the overpriced muck in the first place.

Seven

Open Door, Closed Door

Ugachi

After a couple hours of fitful sleep, my eyes open. My heart crashes as I remember the events of the previous night; witnessing Nedu's sex show with his girlfriend... right before giving them one of my own. I sigh and swallow back yet another lump that wants to form in my throat. No, there will be no more crying. This is the situation, and it's either I swim in it... or sink.

Getting off the bed, I walk to the bathroom to brush my teeth. I look at the unspectacular woman staring back at me. With small A-cup breasts and a stomach more rounded than it should be, my wide hips almost help to salvage the situation. Almost. With skin coloured the same brown as a cut apple left standing for too long, an odd brown that is neither classified fair nor dark skinned, a forehead a good inch or two wider than it needs to be, and a ridiculously wide gap between my two front teeth, I know Ukpono, Josephine, Chioma, and the very many people puzzled by our coupling, are right. Mezie can do a whole lot better. So, rather than act like a spoiled brat because things aren't to my liking, I better be grateful and do everything I can to keep him happy.

I make my way to the kitchen to see what I can put together for him and his friends. I need to make him see that my coming over was not a mistake. I need to show him what a wonderful partner I can be. I might not look like a queen, but I darned well can treat him like a king.

I look through the cupboards but only find old, some even expired, condiments. Opening the fridge, it is the same story, with half drunk boxes of milk and juice the only things waving me hello. It's slim pickings.

"Hey," comes a voice behind me.

I look back at the dark skinned, burly guy who walks in, and I do a quick scramble in my head to remember his name. Ah yes. Eche.

"Hi, Eche," I answer, smiling politely. "Good morning."

"Good morning, my sister," he grins. "I hope you slept well."

I try not to remember the events of the night and instead nod. "I did, thanks."

I return my attention to the fridge, and he walks up to me. "You won't find anything in there o. This place is dry!"

"So I see," I remark. "When Mezie wakes up, I'm going to ask him to take me to the... "

I don't finish as Eche's hand grabs my buttock. I let out a yelp before slapping him twice across the face, front and backhand.

"Are you crazy? Are you out of your mind?" I yell, scandalized.

"*Nne*, relax," he chuckles, grabbing the leftover pack of juice and sauntering out of the kitchen, as casually as if he'd done nothing but shake my hand.

And I am livid.

"How dare you touch me? What kind of girl do you take me for? Are you crazy?" I am yelling so loud as I walk after him, my voice is quivering.

It is loud enough to awake the other occupants of the house.

"*Wetin dey happen*?" a drowsy Alex asks, as he sits up from his sleeping position on the couch. Diran emerges from the other room, the frown on his face indicating he doesn't appreciate being roused at this time either.

"No mind this yeye girl! I just greet am small, na why she come dey shout," Eche chuckles.

"He grabbed my ass!" I shriek. "What kind of stupid greeting is that?"

Mezie and Nedu emerge from our bedroom, and they are both surprised to see me standing there, shouting like a banshee.

"What's happening?"

"He grabbed my ass, Mezie," I cry. "This foolish fat fool grabbed my ass."

"*I just dey greet am. I no do anything*!" Eche says, throwing his hands up in false surrender.

Mezie glances from Eche to me, and then to Diran who gives an almost imperceptible shake of the head.

"Babe, let's go inside," Mezie finally says.

My mouth drops open, shocked by his reaction, or lack thereof. "Did you hear what I said, Mezie? This guy not only disrespected me but you as well. He grabbed my ass!"

"I said come inside, Legachi!" Mezie thunders.

I look from Diran, to Nedu, to the woman he was sleeping with, to another one that has emerged from Diran's room, and I realize I am wasting my time. Not one of them is going to do a single thing about what has just happened.

Not even my own boyfriend.

"How can you be here less than twenty-four hours and you're already fighting?" Mezie barks when we're in the room. "What kind of behavior is this, Legachi? Do you know Eche is the one who pays the bulk of the rent here? Do you know he and Diran could have kicked me out months ago, but didn't? What the fuck!"

I stare at him, too dumbstruck to even say a word in response, too devastated to hear that I am expected to accept this assault with nothing more than a courteous smile. Mezie walks out of the room, and I don't even follow him.

I sit there, staring into nothing, even as Nedu and his female companion walk in and out of the room at various intervals. And I realize one thing is for sure; I cannot live in this place.

Mezie returns almost an hour later, holding a plate of buttered slices of bread.

"I'm not hungry," I say, and I'm truly not.

"Legachi, you need to calm down," he says, placing the plate on my lap regardless. "Eche jokes a lot. He was just fooling around. You shouldn't take him that seriously next time."

Oh, there sure won't be a next time.

"I know you said there isn't much left of the money, but just give me whatever is remaining," I say, looking at him, eyes wide and imploring. "I can't stay here, Mezie. Please, I'm begging you."

He frowns. "I told you the money is gone, Legachi."

"You told me not much is left," I repeat what he said yesterday. "Whatever it is that's left, I'll find a way to make it work. Maybe if I combine it with what I brought with me… "

"It's all gone," he snaps. "I had to repay the boys for months of back rent, and then there were a few other things I needed to sort out… " he sighs and sits next to me on the bed. "Babe, just eat and lie down. You'll feel better after you've rested a bit. What happened this morning was a misunderstanding. Diran has spoken to Eche, and he won't do it again. Promise."

He places his hand over my shoulder, but I am too shell-shocked to react, stunned speechless by what I have heard.

I have jumped out of a pot of oil straight into the blazing furnace.

I am still dazed as I make my way to Middlesex University the next morning. Not only am I still reeling from the events of the previous day, but as I sit in the train from Angel to Hendon Central, the last leg of a journey that began with me catching a bus for a thirty-minute ride to the train station, I realise with dismay that the school is a whole hour away by commute.

"The school isn't even far." That was what Mezie told me before I left Nigeria.

But as I walk from the bus stop to the campus, I am seething over the realisation the school isn't just an hour away, but an hour *and* ten minutes. Not far indeed!

Bracing myself, I find my way to the Admin Office, from where I am redirected to the Accounts Department to get a fee confirmation slip, as my tuition is already fully paid. My heart breaks when the woman there directs me to the Accommodation Office to register and collect my room keys, and I tell her that I won't be staying on campus. I'm redirected back to the Admin Office for the registration process, where my picture is taken for my ID card. I am walking out when I am greeted by a loud shrill.

"Legachi!"

I turn and see the familiar face of a thick-bodied, light-skinned woman. For the life of me, I don't remember where I've met her before.

"*Abi* you've forgotten, Legachi?" she laughs. "It's me, Nonye. We met at the exam centre."

Oh, of course! I remember the obscenely loud person I met when writing the *Skyline* scholarship exam. Seated behind me, she hadn't been able to keep her mouth shut, not even when the exam was in full swing. Thinking about it now, she'd mentioned also wanting to go to Middlesex, but I'd been too impatient to get as far away from her as possible. I'd also thought there was no way she'd possibly pass the exam. But, well, here she is.

"Hi, Nonye," I say as we embrace, no longer irritated by her but actually glad to see a familiar face. "I'm so glad you made it."

"*I'm* so glad I made it, my sister. That exam was hard *ehn*, I thought I was going to fail for sure," she chuckles. "How now? I heard you were coming, and I was looking for you this weekend. Which of the halls are you staying at?"

Again, the hollow feeling in my stomach. Envy consumes me as I look at someone who has what I too could have had; comfortable school lodging all to herself.

"I'm not staying on campus," I answer, with a tight smile. "I'm staying with my boyfriend in town."

This news seems to impress her, as her eyes widen. "My dear, you're so lucky. I had to leave my fiancé back in Nigeria. *Nne*, I hope *conji* doesn't destroy me before next year."

She intertwines her hand with mine as we go to the School of Business, where we familiarise ourselves and get our course timetable. Seeing the classes, lecturers, and the new and returning students milling around, my excitement starts to return. While my living situation might not be the best, I still have been given this golden opportunity of a scholarship in a prestigious university. That has to count for something, if not everything.

But when I walk into Nonye's room in Ivy Hall, I am devastated anew. Small and with a narrow single-bed, she has already personalised the space with framed pictures on her table and a brightly coloured floral comforter.

"Very tiny room," she actually grumbles. "And I was too late to get an en-suite one, so I actually have to share a bathroom with three other people."

She makes a face, and it is on the tip of my tongue to tell her that I am sharing a bathroom with a number I'm not even aware of.

"And this weather! *E fear me as everybody dey say cold neva reach.* I'm already cold *o!*" she quips.

I laugh. "My dear, me too!"

We hang out in her room for a short while, after which we venture back to the main campus.

"*Biko*, I need to register at the Employment Centre," Nonye says. "I need to have extra pocket money. After paying for accommodation, what's left of the money from the *Skyline* allowance isn't a lot."

My ears perk up as I hear this, the answer to my prayers found. If I can get a job and earn some money, I just might be able to pay for campus accommodation for myself.

We walk into the Employability Hub, where we are interviewed by a pleasant-faced woman and fill a form.

"You're aware you're only allowed to work a maximum of twenty hours a week, aren't you?" she asks, kind eyes looking at us.

It's news to me, but Nonye nods emphatically. Once out of the office, she giggles. "*Abeg*, all that one is story. Let them get us the job first. *Na the money I dey find.*"

And that is what I am thinking as I make my way out of school. *Na the money I dey really find!* At 3pm, there is still too much of the day for me to have to endure the torture of Mezie's flatmates, so instead of heading the way I came via Angel Station, with the aid of my tube map, I head instead to Warren Street, switching there to the Victoria Line and getting off at the next stop, Oxford Circus. I've heard so much about it, and it is the one place I want to mindlessly wander around while I think about my life.

Emerging from the underground staircase, I am overwhelmed by the human traffic traipsing in all directions. Headed east, headed west, headed north, headed south, people are walking in singles and in pairs, some laden with shopping bags and others with the determined look of heading to or from work. It is intriguing and disturbing at the same time. Clutching closed my denim jacket, I cross the road in the direction of the brands I am more familiar with; *Nike, Mango, Zara, GAP*. I have bought some overpriced clothes with those nametags back in Nigeria, and hopefully should be able to buy some warm clothes that won't be as overpriced. But walking into the *GAP*, seeing the prices on the clothes, and equating this not only to their converted naira value but also to how much I have left after buying a travel card that morning, I am unable to bring myself to make any purchase. Instead, I walk out of the shop with heavy feet and an even heavier heart. More than ever, I need a job... and quickly.

"Who is this I'm seeing? Legachi Onyema?" comes a shrill voice, making me look up.

I smile as I recognise Alero Giwa, an old friend from secondary school. Dressed in a thick sweater over jeans, I am glad to see someone else who isn't finding the weather quite as temperate. With a wide smile on her face and her hair in Bantu knots, she is just as eccentric as I remember. Squealing, I rush to her, and we embrace as people shove past us.

"I don't believe it!" she exclaims, pulling away to look at me. "I haven't seen you in ages! Since 2003 or something like that!"

"It's been so long! You look great!" I beam at her. We weren't particularly close in school, but standing there, so very far from home, we could as well have been BFFs. "I didn't know you were in London."

"I moved here about eight years ago. When did you get here?"

"Just on Saturday."

"Ah, you're still a JJC!" she cackles. "You never get London initiation yet."

My smile wanes as I think about just how much of a 'London Initiation' I have already gotten.

"I'm here for my Masters," I say, wanting to steer the conversation to more pleasant waters. "I got a scholarship."

"Oh, well done you!" she says, clearly impressed. "What school?"

"Middlesex University."

"Nice one! I once had a friend there. Are you at Ivy, Pratt, or Writtle Hall? Or the other one, what's the name *sef*? Or you're staying in private accommodation?"

It's a simple question but as I start to answer, what comes out of my mouth is a sob.

"*Osanobua*!" she exclaims, tilting up my head. "Girl, what's going on?"

And then seated in a nearby patisserie a few minutes later, I tell her of my awful experience with Mezie and his flatmates. She listens with rapt attention and from the thin set of her lips, I can tell she isn't impressed by this boyfriend of mine.

And I'm right.

"You never should have sent him all your money. What were you thinking?"

I wipe my eyes, shaking my head over the same question I have asked myself several times. What on earth was I thinking?

"Hackney is even too far to commute all the way to Hendon from every day," she goes on. "You will just break down."

Don't I know it!

"Listen," she says, leaning forward with her elbows on the table. "I can offer you a place, but only for short while. My fiancé just travelled to Paris on an academic exchange program, so I have our place to myself. Our flat is in Golders Green and that's only a single bus or train ride to Hendon. But you have to be gone by the time he gets back on December 24th."

My eyes widen, the first ray of hope I've had since landing in this blasted country. December 24th will give me three whole months to sort myself out. That should be more than enough time.

"Oh my God, Alero! Would you really?"

"My dear, what is FEDIBEN sisterhood for, if not for times like this?" she smiles at me. "And I'm not judging you. I know the kind of sweet mouth our Nigerian brothers have. That's why I ran far from them when I got here."

"Your boyfriend isn't Nigerian?"

She hisses. "*For where*?! He's a nice Welsh guy, my sister. A good man that is giving me peace."

Thinking back to the animals Mezie is co-existing with, I understand her sentiment now more than ever. Speaking of the animals, a smile returns to my face over the realisation that I can leave them, that I can leave that zoo forever!

"I'll clean up when I get home and you can move in tomorrow or the day after, anytime you're ready," she says, whipping out her phone. "Let me give you my number, so you can call me when you decide."

When I decide? At that point, I burst into tears, but this time, happy, grateful tears. When I decide? She clearly isn't aware what kind of lifeline she is giving me. Reaching over, she places an arm around me and allows me cry, allows me let it all out.

It feels like I have just been set free from a cage full of wild, rabid beasts.

Roman

Monday evening, as I walk Luna home from the bus stop, I realise I am back to square one. With two back-to-back Au Pair disasters, I am unwilling to even go that route again. But if not that, then what?

It's a little past 5pm, so I fix Luna a peanut butter and jam sandwich for her tea. As she eats, I contemplate what to order in for dinner, Chinese or a good old pizza, the only kind of Italian delicacy I like. Before I can decide, my phone rings. I frown when I see Itunu's name on the display. I am tempted to ignore it like I used to, but I decide to put us both out of our misery and end this nonsense once and for all.

"What do you want?"

"Roman, I'm so sorry about how I behaved yesterday. I don't know what got over me," comes her voice, sounding breathier than normal. "I was so disappointed not to spend more time with you, but it's no excuse to have acted like a spoiled brat. I'm so sorry."

That she makes no reference to Luna is even more of a red flag. "Listen, Itunu. You're a nice girl… "

"No, please. Not that 'you're a nice girl' line," she cuts in, sounding panicked. "You can't just end things over a little misunderstanding. Please, Roman."

I exhale. "Itunu, I don't think we're very compatible."

"We are, Roman. We are! It's because we don't spend enough time with each other. If you give us a chance, you'll see how good we can be together."

I shut my eyes and shake my head, wondering why she is making this more difficult than it needs to be.

"I know you're angry, and you have every reason to be. I'm going to give you space for a while, to get it out of your system."

"Itunu… "

63

"I'll call you in a few weeks. If you still feel the same way, then I'll leave you alone."

She gets off the phone before I can even argue, and I wonder why she has decided to delay the inevitable. There's no way I'm going back to her.

—

"What do you do about childcare, Boma?" I ask my colleague, another Nigerian doctor, as we have lunch the next day. "I'm sinking. I've had two awful Au Pair experiences, and I honestly can't even stomach the thought of another one."

"I hear those Au Pairs can be very risqué," she chuckles. "And fine boy like you, *they no go fit commot eye*."

I roll my eyes in my exasperation. "Seriously, Boma."

She shrugs as she takes a sip of her iced tea. "My mother-in-law has been with us since I had the twins eight years ago," she chuckles again. "Why do you think I've tolerated her for so long?"

I am deflated to hear this, wondering once again if I should just accept my mother's offer to have Luna move in with her. But after everything Luna and I have been through, I'm not ready to release her to anyone, not even my mother.

"I'll ask a few of my friends. A few of them might have agents you might want to talk to."

I let out a deep sigh. "I don't want another Au Pair."

"These aren't Au Pairs, but more standard types of nannies. Thing is, they might be less flexible when it comes to time and will cost a whole lot more," she giggles. "Posh white nannies *o*. Modern day Mary Poppins. Well, then again, my friends can afford them. Jumoke, you've met her, is married to the son of an *Oba* or something."

I can only stare back at her. That isn't going to solve my problem.

"Don't worry, I'll keep an open ear for you," she says, taking another sip of her drink.

At this point, I have no choice but to make do with that, and accept that, until further notice, my hours at work must remain scaled down.

Eight

Grounded

Egachi

ezie doesn't share my excitement as I tell him how I fortuitously ran into an old friend willing to accommodate me.

"So, you want to leave me? We've been apart for a year and now that we're finally together, you want to leave?"

But I will not be made to feel guilty for doing what I know is better for me... for us... in the long term. Living with his animalistic flat mates will not only be dangerous for me, but for our relationship.

"Babe, I know this isn't the best of situations, but it's not something we can't manage," he prods. "If we both put our heads down and save, we'll be able to afford a place of our own in a few months."

"I can't survive a few months here," is my firm answer. "Apart from the fact I hate your flatmates, the commute to school will kill me. It will drain the life out of me, and I won't have any strength left to study, much less get a job."

He is silent for a few minutes, and I can't help but wonder if he has seen the sense in the arrangement. Surely, even he has to hate the fact that he is housing his girlfriend in such a communal environment.

"Who is this Alero girl anyway?" he eventually asks. "What's she doing in London? What does she want in exchange? Because nothing goes for nothing in this town."

"Her fiancé is away for about three months, so she's only offering the place until Christmas. And no, she doesn't want anything from me."

"*Na so!*" he scoffs. "Mark my words, you'll get there and she'll demand that you chip in for bills and groceries."

Honestly, even if she does, I'd much rather do that than remain in the Hackney boys' hostel.

"She lives only fifteen minutes away from my school, Mezie," I say, already feeling weary of the interrogation. "That has to count for something, doesn't it?"

"Call her so I can talk to her myself," he demands, the look in his eyes bordering on doubt.

I stare at him, dumbfounded he would think me capable of making up such a story. Does he think I've suddenly met a guy to cavort with? With a resigned shrug, I dial Alero's number, not minding that it's only been a few hours since we parted on the northbound Victoria Line train, with her getting off two stops before me at Euston. But I'm not bothered by how soon I am calling her. I don't need time to think about her offer.

"Hey, Leggy," comes her high-pitched voice as the line connects. "*I hope you don reach house and neva lost for London.*"

I laugh. "Very funny. I've been home over an hour." I pause and cast a look at Mezie, who is watching me with rapt attention. "Alero, thank you so much for your offer. I'm so grateful."

"Girl, don't mention. It's the least I can do to assist you, even if only for a short while."

"I'm really grateful," I repeat, nodding as Mezie raises his brows in reminder that he also wants to speak to her. "Um, my boyfriend wants to talk to you. Is it okay?"

"Nigerian guys will never disappoint *sha!*" she cackles. "*E wan make sure say no be man house you wan go. No wahala.* Put him on."

I hand the phone over to Mezie, whose frown has deepened as he accepts it.

"Hello... Hi, Alero. Oh, really?" he looks up at me, his brows knotted. "You've heard a lot about me? That's strange, because tonight is the first time I've heard about you." He nods. "Yeah, she said you went secondary school together. But that was a long time ago." He chuckles as he turns to look at me. "Oh, yeah? She's just the same way you remember her? I don't find that hard to believe." He leans back in the pillow, and I am happy to see his body language has softened. "Me? A little over a year." He shrugs. "It's okay, I guess. I can't complain. We're still hustling. What do you do?" His brows lift, and I can see he is impressed. "You're an IT Manager? Nice one." He nods as he listens to whatever it is she's saying before he smiles again. "Good stuff, Alero. I look forward to meeting you when I help Legachi move." He lets out a loud of roar of laughter. "Of course, I won't turn down a glass of beer! In fact, I'm looking forward to it now."

He hands me the phone when they have finished talking, his smile showing he is fully appeased and at ease with the person with whom I will be spending the next few months with. Seeing his mood has improved, I know this is my chance to get some answers to questions I have been dying to ask.

"Mezie, when are your PMP exam preparation classes?" I ask. "The money you paid was to cover the classes and exam, right? When do you start?"

His eyes flicker. "Um, I reckon they'll start sometime in January or something."

"All the way next year? You don't know for sure?"

"Babe, what's this *nau*? Why are you interrogating me? You think I'm lying or something?"

Not wanting to have yet another argument, I decide to back down. "Of course not. I just thought it would be earlier, that's all."

He is appeased and as he goes to the living room to hang out with his friends, I lie on the bed and try to force myself asleep. After the last forty-eight hours I have had, I crave a decent night's rest, even if only for the last time in that God-forsaken apartment.

I am drifting in and out of sleep when he returns to the room and gets on the bed. I have my back to him and expect that he too will fall asleep or fiddle with his phone as Nedu is doing with his on the floor. But I am horrified when one of his hands draws me closer, just as the other reaches into my pyjama bottoms. My eyes widen in my alarm. Surely, he can't be serious.

"Nedu is still awake!" I whisper, my hand reaching to stop his as it tugs at my underwear.

"So? Nobody is a child here," is his own gruff whisper, flipping my hand away and shoving down my pyjama bottoms and panties in one deft movement.

"Mezie!" I whimper, not wanting to rouse Nedu's attention by shouting. But it might even be too late for that. "Please!"

Ignoring me, he mounts me. "Is this how it's going to always be here? Are you going to complain every time I want us to have sex?"

He doesn't wait for me to answer as he shoves himself into me, and as he pounds away, his hands pinning mine, I want to yell that this isn't sex. This is rape. But I don't yell. Instead, I squeeze my eyes shut to keep from crying, bite my tongue to keep from screaming, as the man I love transforms the beautiful union of body and soul we used to have, to this ugly, ugly thing. Time grinds to a halt as he ravages my body for what feels like an eternity. Finally, he gets his release, rolls off me and is snoring lightly mere minutes later. I look on the floor, and see Nedu is still scrolling on his phone, seemingly unperturbed by what has just happened. And I am sick to my stomach.

The next morning, I am up at the crack of dawn, gathering my things. I will not spend another day in that house. Watching Mezie's sleeping form, I realise that he and his revolting flatmates are all the same. They are all animals!

"Babe! Babe!" he calls, as I am struggling with my boxes down the street thirty minutes later, having managed to get them downstairs myself. "Wait up!"

The logical side of me wants to quicken my steps and leave, never to ever look back. But the emotional side of me turns, wanting to lash out at him for what he did to me.

"Get away from me, Mezie!" I snap, wide eyes glaring at him. "You better get away from me before I scream."

"Babe, don't tell me you're angry about last night?" he says, smiling as he pulls me closer. "I just wanted you so bad. I waited for you a whole year, so you can't blame me *nau*."

Again, the reminder of his fidelity is enough to soften me, and I put up no resistance as he hugs me. Maybe I am being unreasonable to label what happened last night as rape. Maybe I should have been more understanding of the situation. It wasn't his fault Nedu was in the room. It isn't his fault he doesn't have space of his own.

"*Na so you dey vex?*" he chuckles, tilting up my chin. "You were going to leave without even telling me."

He takes my heavier box and travel bag, and I am happy he's there to help me. I'd already sent a frantic text to Alero before leaving the house and she gave me the green light to move in this morning.

Mezie and I take the over-ground train to Camden Road, walk over to the Camden Town tube station from where we take the Northern Line train to Golders Green. Alero's apartment is less than five minutes from the station. When she buzzes us in, Mezie grunts as we squeeze through the narrow staircase, not at all impressed.

"Isn't this a step down?" he mumbles, as we struggle with my luggage. "Our place is way better than this."

I ignore him and drag my box down the corridor till I get to Apartment 6, her place. At this point, I don't even care if her place is a literal shit hole. Nothing will ever make me go back to that awful Hackney commune.

"Leggy baby!" Alero exclaims as she opens the door. She smiles at my companion. "And you must be Mezie. Come in, please."

As we enter her apartment, I cast Mezie a smug look. Though small, it is a lovely, *clean* apartment, brightened with multi-coloured furniture and wall portraits. A vanilla scented candle burns on the mantelpiece, and I smile at the several pictures of her and a large, red-haired, red-bearded man, her fiancé from the look of things.

"This is our humble place," she says, throwing her hands wide in declaration and home pride. Turning to the couch, she smiles. "And that's you. Don't worry, it's a sofa-bed, so you can convert it at night."

It is Mezie's turn to cast me a smug look, one I can read as saying at least in his place, I had a proper bed, even if it was one I shared with him. But I turn to smile at Alero, the sofa-bed sounding like a suite at The Ritz.

"It's awesome. Thank you so much, Alero."

"Enough with these thank you's, please!" she giggles. "You can keep your boxes over there," she points to a corner of the room where several coats and jackets hang.

"How very gracious of you!" Mezie says, and I hope she doesn't hear the sarcasm in his voice.

If she does, she doesn't show it. "I'm going to have to rush off. I have an appointment I'm already running late for but was just waiting for you to get here." She smiles at Mezie. "We'll have to have that beer another time, I'm afraid." Then turning to me, she throws me a bunch of keys. "We can talk later tonight when I get back. In the meantime, get comfortable and make yourself at home."

When she is gone, Mezie lets out a scornful laugh. "And in your mind, this is better than staying with me?"

I sit with a plop on the couch. "Even if for the mere reason it's closer to my school, yes, it is."

He sits beside me on the couch and, like me, his eyes rove the apartment.

"Aha, I knew it. She's with a white guy," he remarks, as if that is supposed to explain things somehow. "I'm disappointed. She sounded like a girl with sense."

I try not to roll my eyes, understanding with even more clarity why my old friend has gone the Caucasian route. We sit in silence for some minutes, the only sound coming from the quirky clock mounted on the wall facing us, an oddity with inverted multi-coloured numerals on a bright silver background. The flat is indeed full of oddities, starting from the coffee table before us, designed to look like it has gold dripping from it, to the life-sized brass snails on the mantelpiece, paired paradoxically with ornate white fairies on either side, to the large Buddha flower pot with an even larger cactus plant, to the Ankara throw pillows strewn on the sofa on which we sit, and figurines of Ishan *Igbabonelimhin* dancers on the window sill, the place clearly reflects the quirkiness of its owners. I cast another look at a picture of Alero and her Welsh fiancé, and even though they couldn't look more different physically if they tried, with her skin shiny black and his, porcelain, it appears that they are indeed kindred spirits.

"They don't have a TV," Mezie remarks.

So it seems, if the figurine-populated mantelpiece is anything to go by. But to be honest, I don't even care.

"You didn't pay for that exam, right?" It is more of a statement than a question. I look at him, expecting him to deny it, but he says nothing, his gaze fixed ahead. I return my own gaze to the wall clock, my heart heavy as my worst fear is confirmed. "It was £8,000, Mezie. How could you have blown £8,000 in two months?"

He sighs deeply. "I told you I had to pay the guys for back rent and sort a few things out."

"What things?" I shriek. "You've been here only a little over a year! People who have lived here all their lives don't even have that kind of debt! What could you have spent that money on without having anything to show for?"

"Diran also needed a loan, okay?" he yells back. "He needed some money, and he's been so good to me, I couldn't say no."

I shut my eyes and count to five under my breath, to stop myself from saying the vile things my mouth wants to or, worse, throwing my hands around his neck to strangle him.

"He'll pay it back when he's ready. I can't rush him. I'm sure you can understand why," he says, before reaching for my hand. "But don't worry about a thing, babe. I'll make sure I start saving most of what I earn, and pretty soon, I'll be able to pay for the exam and get us a nice flat near your school. It will all be sorted, I promise."

I look at him. While that addresses one issue, it hasn't addressed the other. "And after we get our nice flat, what next? When are we getting married? By December next year, I'll be done with school. I think we should fix our traditional wedding for that month, and our white wedding shortly after."

He hisses and drops my hand, rising to his feet. "How about we walk first before we run a fucking marathon? Heck, how about we crawl first?"

I purse my lips and stand, pulling one of my boxes to their designated spot.

"Babe, you need to be patient with me," Mezie says, holding my hand as I walk back to get the other one. "I've been offered another job at a lounge on the West End, Monday to Thursday. Combined with my weekend gig, I'll be able to raise some good money."

"Another night club job, Mezie?" I say, not even recognising the man I am looking at. "Was that why you came here? Was that what you gave up your job in Nigeria for? Is it what you shut down your life to come all the way here to do? To be a nightclub bouncer? You with your Sociology degree?"

"Legachi, fuck all that! My Nigerian degree means fuck all over here. Over here, it doesn't mean shit!" he sneers at me. "And you better get that into your head, if you're thinking your degree and hundred years of work experience will get you anywhere here because, newsflash, they won't!"

Our eyes lock and even though I am angered by his words... I can't help but wonder if there is any truth in them. What if he's right? What if, even after my Master's degree, I can't aspire to any more than a random blue-collar job here?

What if?

Roman

I watch Luna squeal as she is chased by other children in my cousin Ihidie's backyard. It is his youngest daughter's 10th birthday, and the kids are enjoying a pool party on this sunny afternoon in September. If the weather outlook is anything to go by, we won't have a lot more of these before the cooler weather arrives. A child I recognise as Esohe, Ihidie's sister's 8-year-old daughter, helps Luna into the colourful inflatable pool set up for younger children, and I smile as she giggles and splashes in the water. Looking at her, my daughter, it still feels surreal that this perfect cherub is mine. Despite everything we've already been through, in spite of how much this journey of fatherhood has upended the other parts of my life, I wouldn't change it for anything.

"Still playing Mr. Mom?" Ojie, Ihidie's older brother, teases as he takes a seat next to me.

I chuckle and shake my head, used to the nickname most of my cousins have given me. "Yes, I am. I've had the rottenest luck with childcare, you wouldn't believe it. My last Au Pair... " I think twice about sharing the sordid story. "You don't even want to know."

"I don't think he's talking about childcare," Ihidie winks at me.

"When are you going to get yourself a girlfriend?" Tosan, Ihidie's wife, asks, joining us where we sit, with her friend, Bisi. "Sekani has been gone a long time. If you get yourself a nice girl, all these problems would be a thing of the past."

"That too has been a total disaster," I answer. "The last bird I was with actually called Luna 'it'!"

I am satisfied by the collective horrified gasp of everyone around me, all of them parents.

"I kid you not," I go on, buoyed. "It was a Friday night and I invited her over. She spends the night and we're still lying in the living room, naked, when we hear Luna's voice."

"Why were you lying naked in your living room?" a bewildered Bisi asks.

"He didn't want the kid to see her," Ojie answers. As a man, he understands.

"So, I tell her to wait for me while I try to distract Luna," I continue. "And I'm doing that, thinking this bird would get up, dress up and, I don't know, leave? But instead, she walks over, waves, and confuses the poor thing. When I get upset with her for doing that, you know what she says to me? *'It's just a baby, Roman'*!"

"Wow!" Bisi exclaims, shaking her head like someone who has just beheld a gory sight. "Just wow!"

"When you too will be out there picking shallow girls," Tosan retorts, unimpressed. "I'm sure she was serving looks and hot sex. I bet you didn't remember Luna when you were in her pants."

"The sex was also bad, actually."

Now that gets the guys' attention.

"Then that was the real disaster!" Ihidie laughs along with Ojie.

"Apart from that, dating is the last thing on my mind right now," I cut in, the joke now wearing thin. "I've had to scale back a lot at the hospital, and that's thrown off any plans I have of finishing this specialization program I've been on for too long." I sigh and shake my head. "All I want is good childcare. Is that too much to ask? You guys are lucky you don't have to worry about that anymore."

With their three older children in their late teens, Ihidie and Tosan no longer have to worry about childcare for their 10-year-old. Ojie, on the other hand, is divorced and his ex-wife lives in Aberdeen with their kids.

"The best and most reliable nannies are these Nigerian aunties and grandmas in England, either on holiday or stranded with no papers," Bisi remarks, taking a sip of her cocktail. "My friends swear by them."

I frown. "Is that even legal?"

"Be there looking for legal," Bisi laughs. "Clearly not. But they're effective, cheap, and frankly your best bet."

"I agree, especially with your mom all the way in Chelmsford," Tosan chimes in agreement.

I rub my eyes, the suggestion worsening my anxiety over my predicament. The thought of employing an illegal Nigerian immigrant isn't giving me any comfort at all.

"Maybe my mom is right. Maybe I should just send Luna to her," I say, my voice sounding as weary as I feel. "Heck, maybe I should quit my job and get one with a hospital over there, so all this can be over."

"So, what will happen to that overpriced house of yours? The one you spent a fortune decorating?" Ihidie taunts, never giving up the opportunity to make fun of me for spending so much on my new place.

"He spent a fortune doing it up?" Bisi asks.

"He spent just as much doing up the place as some folks spend on their entire mortgage!" Ojie chuckles.

I glare at him. "No need to exaggerate."

"Please, leave my in-law *o*!" Tosan says, but I know her better than to think she's defending me. "The only posh in-law I have."

"This one, posh?" Ihidie cackles. "With that accent? Don't make laugh!"

Even though also born in England, Ihidie, Ojie and their siblings returned to Nigeria in their teens, coming back only after completing their first degrees. Since then, it has been a running joke between us; they tease me about being too Essex, and I tease them about being too Naija.

"Thank God for medicine, or else he would have been a cast member of TOWIE for sure," Ojie joins the jibing.

"Who says he still can't join them?" Tosan laughs. "Fine boy, white teeth, natural tan, flash clothes, big watches, swanky pad, saying *'you know what I mean'* every five seconds, he even looks and sounds more Essex than the people on the show."

"Or is it these skinny trousers he wears all the time?" Ihidie is laughing so hard by now, his eyes are watering.

"You're a proper clown!" I chuckle. "Don't you know the difference between fitted and skinny?"

Laughter rings as they continue taking cracks at me, but I am happier to exchange colourful insults with them than to be reminded of what lies in wait for me when the party is over and Luna and I return to our reality; the reality that, for the foreseeable future, this will remain our situation.

"Don't worry, I'll get you a link," Bisi says before she leaves a few hours later. "My friend has an agent, and I'll have her send me his number. Just call the guy. You don't have anything to lose by talking."

And she is right. I don't.

Nine

Worker Girl

Legachi

"So, Bryn and I have a few ground rules for the flat," Alero says as we sit on the couch later that evening, eating takeout fish and chips. "This... " she raises the Styrofoam pack, "is as far as spicy meals go in this house, and it can't even be cooked in the kitchen. Bryn is allergic to a lot of spices, so you can't cook any Nigerian food or any other kind of elaborate meals. You can pretty much only make simple sandwiches or oil-free meals in the kitchen. Also, no Chinese or Indian takeaway."

I nod, trying to digest this piece of information, pun intended. No cooking. While that will be hard, it's not something I can't live without.

"You also need to be out of the flat between the hours of 8am and 4pm. I work from home and need the privacy," she shrugs. "Today was an exception because of my meeting."

I nod again, reminding myself of a lizard as I do. That also isn't something that can't be done. On the days I don't have early classes, I could always go to the library or something.

"Bryn is very wary of having strangers here. I had to do a whole lot of convincing for him to be comfortable with you moving in. So, I'm afraid you can't entertain any guests. Maybe Mezie a few times a week, but no longer than an hour each time."

My mouth goes dry as I respond with another nod. No visitors? Only restricted visits from Mezie? Hmmm.

"Of course, you'll have to buy your own groceries," she continues. "I'll do us the favour of labeling mine, so there is no confusion. Is that okay?"

I force a smile and nod. Not even with Chineme the psycho did I have to label my food.

"You can't increase the thermostat beyond 21 degrees. That's what Bryn and I have agreed as our hard number. Nothing more than that."

"What if it gets very cold?" I ask, unable to contain myself.

"Then you wrap yourself in a warm cardigan!" she giggles, hitting my arm.

I force myself to laugh along, when inside I'm dying, wondering how on earth I will cope in a chilly apartment in the colder months, if I'm already freezing in September.

"Let me see, am I forgetting any other thing?" she says, tapping her chin with her index finger. "Ah yes, Sundays. My dear, my weekdays are so busy, Sundays are sacred for me. I have a zero noise before 10am policy, so I can sleep in. And by zero, I mean zero." She makes a circle with her finger and thumb for emphasis. "No movement whatsoever in the flat, not even to the kitchen. If you must leave the house, it has to be after 10. If you have to be somewhere before then, you might have to sleep out."

This time, I don't even bother to nod. Instead, I gape at the stranger sitting next to me, not believing what I have just heard.

Never in a million years would I have thought I'd miss my shared self-contained flat back in Lagos the way I now do. I miss it so badly, I have a physical ache in my chest.

"I'm so excited to have you here," Alero says, squealing as if she hasn't just issued the most draconian house rules ever. She pulls me into a hug, as she bobs up and down in her excitement, excitement I don't even attempt to share. "I've been so lonely since Bryn left. It'll be great to have company!"

Company. Is that what she calls it? It sounds more like incarceration to me... willful incarceration on my part.

And lying on the lumpy sofa-bed later that night, with it squeaking and creaking with my every movement, all I can think of is how much a disappointment London has been so far.

The short commute to campus the next day significantly cheers me up. It is only a three-minute walk to the bus stop, and a fifteen-minute ride on the 183 bus to school. As I find my way to my class less than thirty minutes after leaving the flat, I am reassured that leaving Mezie's place wasn't a mistake.

Standing in the large lecture theater, waves of nervousness and excitement course through my body at the same time. Taking in the cosmopolitan mix of Caucasian, Asian and African faces, my main reason for being in the country is staring at me in literal black and white. And it is a beauty to behold. I smile when I see Nonye waving me over from the other end of the hall, and make my way over to her, my smile just as wide.

"Babe, how now? I didn't see you yesterday," she remarks. "I thought you were going to come so we could job hunt together."

"Long story, I'll fill you in later," I answer, my eyes still darting around the bustling room. I am so excited, goose bumps have formed on my neck. Suddenly, everything I am going through seems worthwhile.

"Meet Tayo," Nonye introduces a dark-skinned girl sitting next to her, with perfect bright white teeth that almost look like veneers. She has multiple piercings on her ears, nose and eyebrows, but, in the oddest dichotomy, the kindest eyes I have ever seen. "Her room is next to mine."

"Hi. I'm Legachi," I say, smiling as I shake hands with Tayo. "Are you also here on the *Skyline* program?"

"Hi, Legachi. Good to meet you," she smiles, revealing deep dimples. "At all *o*. I paid for it myself from my share of the sale of my late father's property."

"Oh, I'm so sorry for your loss," I say, immediately empathetic.

She and Nonye exchange a look and laugh, showing they have not only talked about this but that it is already a private joke.

"My dear, don't be. Firstly, he's been dead six years, and the will has been under contention, with his several wives and concubines splitting hairs over it. Secondly, I'm child number seventeen or eighteen and hardly even knew the dude. Thirdly, girl, if he hadn't died, where would I have seen the money to come here?"

"That is what they call *God don butter my bread* inheritance!" Nonye chimes in.

"*On both sides, come add tea on top!*" Tayo roars, as they slap hands.

I smile as they laugh. I like her.

"You have to leave the flat between 8am and 4pm?" Tayo repeats as we have tea and cake at the *Costa* coffee shop on campus, just as bewildered as I was when I first heard it. "What kind of job does she have that she has to be alone in the flat? Is she on *OnlyFans* or what?"

I almost spit out my tea in my laughter, amused by the mental image of Alero stripping for the camera to entertain online 'fans'.

"And you can't cook there, or even have visitors?" It is Nonye's turn to retort. "When it's not boarding school."

"But she's given me a roof of my head now that I need it most," I say in Alero's defense. "I'm just going to have to work and save as much as I can by Christmas, so I can get a place of my own."

Nonye and Tayo exchange a look.

"I hope you haven't forgotten it's a maximum of twenty hours we're allowed to work o!" Nonye says. "This one you're calculating your money in thousands."

"Yes, but at £14, £15 an hour, that will be about £300 a week, and £1,200 a month," I answer confidently.

My companions burst into laughter, and I find myself beginning to lose my patience. What the heck is so funny?

"Who is going to pay you £15 an hour?" Nonye cackles. "And even if you do get paid that, you think that's what you'll get as cash?"

"I read they don't tax below a certain salary band." I counter.

"True, but you still have to make a National Insurance contribution from your earnings," Tayo explains. "If I were you, I'd estimate about £180 per week, max."

I sit back in my seat, deflated. That is half of what my mental math has computed for me.

"That's still about £700 a month," I say, finding my voice. "I can work with that. School accommodation is between £150 and £180 a week, right?"

"But you have to pay for at least a full term," Tayo says, to my dismay.

"And won't you eat, move around, or even buy yourself clothes?" Nonye rubs salt into my open wound. "You think you can use everything you earn to pay for accommodation?"

"I won't lie, it's going to be a stretch to save money for an apartment," Tayo says, empathy in her eyes. "Even if you decide not to get school accommodation, for a flat share in London, you'd also be looking at, at least, £750 per month. A studio apartment would cost you a minimum of £1,200. And that's not including the deposit you'll have to pay."

I look at her so despondent, I want to burst into tears. What on earth am I supposed to do? I think about the £8,000 I lost to Mezie and my blood boils, hating him for the situation he has put me in.

Tayo soon excuses herself to meet up with some friends in town, and when we are alone, Nonye gives me a quizzical look.

"Why don't you want to stay with your boyfriend? Isn't that a better option than all this *yigi yaga* you want to do? Schoolwork hasn't even started but see how you already look haggard from stress. Take it easy *o*!"

Not wanting to divulge too much, I tell her about Mezie's nasty living arrangement and how uncomfortable I was there. But none of it impresses her.

"And so what, if many of his friends live there? And if they don't mind *straffing* their babes in each other's presence, what's the big deal? *Nne*, you have to be wise! I'm already engaged *o*! No dey look me *o*! Babes in this town aren't playing at all. Hold on to your man and never allow him walk around with a full tank in this London."

I have this on my mind as we venture out of campus, walking the nearby streets to see what we can find by way of employment. I wonder if I was too quick to react to Eche's assault and the lack of a reasonable response from the other flatmates. I replay the first night I unwillingly had sex with Mezie while Nedu and his girlfriend were sleeping, and the second time when Mezie forced himself on me when Nedu was wide awake and wonder if I am somehow to blame for how unpleasant both situations were. I wonder if both events would have been better if I'd just given in to the pleasure of being with my man again. I wonder if, maybe, Nonye is right after all.

Before the end of that week, one of the plethora of friends Nonye has made in the one week of being in London hooks us up with a job, and a juicy one at that.

"Obida says all we have to do is talk on the phone and convince people to buy windows," a delighted Nonye squeals. "And we'll be paid on commission, 15% of everything we sell, which would come to about £300 for their cheapest windows! Imagine if we sell three or four of those a week!"

I am already doing the math and can barely contain the joy bubbling inside me. This is going to end all my money troubles for sure.

"And he's sure they'll hire us?" I ask, the voice of reason in my head yelling that this sounds too good to be true.

"He says all we have to do is show up. He says they're always looking for people to hire and that they'll even be the ones begging us *sef.*"

Well, they aren't exactly 'begging' to hire us when we show up at the office. A ten-minute bus ride away in Finchley, the telemarketing company is a cramped, open plan space with so many tables and chairs, they almost seem to be piled one on top of the other. And the furniture arrangement isn't the only chaotic thing. With so many people on the phone at the same time, all of them doing what it is we are also keen to do, it is so loud and anarchic, all I can think about is the Tower of Babel. And that isn't good at all.

Gigs, the young hiring manager, with cropped, platinum blond hair, doesn't seem quite as impressed with us either.

"You say you're at the university?" he asks, looking at us with something between cynicism and doubt.

"Yes, we're both studying for a Master's degree in Global Supply Chain Management," Nonye answers, thrusting forward our school identification cards.

He accepts the cards and scrutinises them, looking at us intermittently as if to make sure we are the same people in the plastic cards. When he looks at me, I smile back nervously, desperately wanting to make a good impression. I need this lifeline more than anything.

"Noni?" he repeats Nonye's name. "Is that how you pronounce it?"

I have to bite my lower lip to keep from laughing at the flash of anger on Nonye's face. I haven't known her long, but I know one thing she hates is the mispronunciation of her name.

"It's Nonye," she answers. "Non-yeh."

The exaggerated emphasis of the *yeh* makes it sound a whole lot more complex than it should.

"You're going to have to simplify that. There's no way your customers will be able to say that," he mutters, handing her card to her. "These people like to chat, they like to be able to call you by your name. There's no way they're going to be able to pronounce that."

Without waiting for her to answer, he turns to me.

"And you're Le-ga-chi?" he pronounces it like he's saying the word *legacy*. But at that point, I don't even care what he calls me. "Did I get it right?"

I smile and nod. "Yes, you did."

From the corner of my eye, I see Nonye throw me a scathing look, but I don't care. There is no way I'm going to allow something as little as a name be a showstopper.

"Noni is fine," Nonye says to Gigs, with a defeated shrug.

"Great!" he says, pulling out two sheets of paper from one of the several piles on his desk. "Here's a script with the summary of the products and pricing. On your screen is a list of over twenty thousand phone numbers. The plan is to call as many of these as you can and, even better, sell as many windows as possible."

I take the sheet handed to me and frown as I read it. *Worcestershire Glazing.* I am tempted to ask Gigs how to pronounce it but quickly decide against it, thinking that will be enough reason for him to throw us out. I glance at Nonye, who is smiling as she reads the material. If she's even a little confused, she doesn't show it.

"It's a starting 10% commission, rising to 15% and even 20% as your sales increase," Gigs says, leading us past rows of operators, to vacant seats on the far side of the room.

While 10% isn't exactly what I'd hoped for, it's a better start than nothing.

"Is there any other salary? Like an hourly wage?" Nonye asks.

Gigs looks at her with a raised brow, and that is all the answer we get. So then, no, there will be no hourly wage. But with a 10% commission, I can live with that.

"This here is Kyle," Gigs taps a guy on a chair next to mine. "He'll help put you through today." Pointing at another guy sitting across Nonye. "And that's Jack. He'll be with you, Noni."

As Gigs walks away, I smile at my tutor, Kyle, a young boy who looks no older than 17. With pale skin and a gel-enhanced coif, he couldn't look less interested if he tried. He doesn't smile back.

"Just pick any number from your screen right here, dial, and sell the windows. It's as easy as that," is his cavalier go at teaching me.

I look at him, waiting for him to say more, but when he spins his chair away, I realise I've just been given as much tutoring as I'll get. I turn to my screen and there are so many phone numbers there, it triggers parallax. Deciding to start from the top and work my way down, I wear my headphones, look around the room one more time to see if there is anyone, anyone at all, willing to help me, and when I see there isn't, I turn to the phone box on my table and dial the number. My heart is thumping violently against my chest as it rings.

"He-llo!" comes the hearty voice of what sounds like a male senior citizen.

I clear my throat. "Hello… " I glance at the screen. "Keith. Hello, Keith, this is Legachi," I adopt Gigs' pronunciation of my name. "calling from Wor… " I pause and look at the name again. "Worcestershire Glazing… "

"You what?" Kyle exclaims, spinning his chair around.

"Wor what?" Keith on the other end of the phone asks, clearly confused.

The realisation of my goof makes me unable to say another word. With an irritated click of his tongue, Keith disconnects the line.

"She pronounced it Wor-chester-sheer!" Kyle announces to the people seated around. "As in 'war chest!'"

Heat rushes to my face in my embarrassment as they laugh. I cast a doleful look Nonye's way, but she is already rattling on the phone, talking away to her first customer. I haven't even been able to go past the company name.

"It's pronounced Wu-stuh-shuh, love," a middle-aged woman on a nearby seat offers.

Wu-stuh-shuh *ke*? How can Worcestershire be pronounced Wustuhshuh?!

Now with a grasp of how to pronounce the name, I make another call, and I am able to go a bit further. But only a bit, as I am held up by yet another name; mine.

'Legachi? That's such an interesting name.' 'Very exotic name! What does it mean?' 'Could you say your name again, luv? Oh my, it sounds like you're singing!' 'That's a foreign name, innit? Blasted foreigners coming here and stealing all our jobs!'

I smile through the pleasant and even the not-so-pleasant reactions to my name. But as frustrated as I am about not making one sale that evening, I am further disheartened by the fact that everyone on my list sounds elderly. I realise the company's strategy is to prey on this demographic, most of whom are lonely people desirous of any form of conversation. But as disgusted as I am by this approach, I am not disgusted enough to quit.

"*Nne*, did you sell anything?" a deflated Nonye asks as we wait for the 143 bus. "None of the people could even hear me o! *Na so so 'Pardon?', 'Sorry?'* they were saying all night."

I chuckle. "And I was there thinking you were on a roll!"

"I wasn't on any roll! And to add insult to injury, that stupid, small boy was now telling me to talk slowly, to pick my words as if *na just now I start to dey talk.*"

"My dear, *na now o!*" I can't help but chortle.

She glares at me. "I don't blame you. You're laughing because your own was smooth *abi*? I saw as you were *shining your 32* all night. I'm sure you sold something."

"Babe, *shishi I nor sell!*" I cackle, as the bus pulls up. "It was my name they couldn't get over."

"Anyway, it was the first night," Nonye shrugs as we board the bus and flash our travel cards at the driver. "Tomorrow will be better."

As we take our seats, all I can do is pray that she is correct.

She isn't.

Both of us continue to struggle and neither of us makes any sales at all. While Nonye's thick accent proves itself the ultimate showstopper, I'm unable to bring myself to do the heavy coaxing I overhear the other operators do to get the senior citizens to buy windows they really don't need. Even after I have shortened my name to 'Leggy' to avoid the long-drawn-out conversations about it, I am unable to convince anyone, not even myself, of the benefits of double-glazing.

"If we were in Naija, *I for say they don jazz us o!*" Nonye says, as we walk to the bus stop at the end of our third week, our third straight week of zero sales... and zero pay. "How will we be coming here every day, suffering for four hours, talking till our mouths are dry, and not earn one single penny?"

She is echoing my thoughts exactly.

"Babe, *e be like say we go bounce!*" she looks at me and I nod in agreement.

Yep, it's definitely time to bounce. If I've learned one thing, it's that a telemarketer I definitely am not.

Getting back to the apartment, I kick off my shoes and stretch out on the couch. With Alero visiting Bryn in Paris that weekend, I have the place to myself. I contemplate doing something as deviant as cooking myself something nice and spicy, but that plan is quickly thwarted by the reminder I haven't grocery shopped in a while and have nothing to even throw together. Reaching for my phone, I dial Mezie's number, hoping to catch him before he leaves for the club. In the last few weeks, with him working at the West End lounge in addition to the nightclub, he has been busy most nights, which has resulted in our phone conversations getting more and more sporadic.

"Hey," comes his voice when the line connects. "Back from work?"

"Is that what you call work?" I chuckle. "Isn't work a place you go with the aim of getting paid?"

"Well, I would have told you that for free if you'd bothered to ask my opinion before you started that job," he mutters. "Telemarketing isn't for everyone."

"You sound tired," I remark. "Have you had a stressful day?"

"I've just not been resting a lot."

I don't know if it's me or if he is sounding very short tonight.

"What time do you have to leave for the club?" I ask.

"In another hour or so," he answers, before sighing. "What about you? What are you up to tonight?"

"Nothing. The flat is grave quiet. Alero has gone to Paris to see Bryn."

"You're alone in the flat? Why didn't you tell me?" he says, his voice livening. "I'll come over after my shift so we can... you know... do some catching up."

"Ah, no oh!" I exclaim, sitting up. "You can't sleep here. You know her rules. You know you're not allowed here longer an hour, and you want to spend a whole night?"

When I told him about Alero's house rules, it had caused a major row and he'd been so enraged to hear of the restrictions to his visits that he'd sworn never to come there under those limitations.

"But she isn't there, Legachi. She won't know if you don't tell her."

I shake my head. "No, Mezie. I can't risk it. She'll know I brought someone here. If one of these her nosy neighbours don't tell her, she'll probably smell your scent. The woman is like a Bloodhound. Please, I don't want her trouble at all."

"The girl is with her man, enjoying her life, and you're here still pushing me away!" he retorts. "I haven't seen you in almost two weeks. What benefit is it having you in London anyway?"

"Whose fault is it, Mezie? I wanted to come see you last Saturday, but you chose a lad's trip to Blackpool instead."

"You wanted me to miss my friend's stag weekend? Are you even listening to yourself?"

I sigh deeply and shut my eyes. As much as I want to tackle him on all the things he has done to thwart our communication, I remember Nonye's words and decide to try my best to steer our ship away from the stormy waters it is currently sailing in.

"Babe," I say, in my calmest, most soothing voice. "I'll come over tomorrow. I'll stay till Monday morning, if you like. I'll cook you anything you want and pamper you silly. How about that?"

"I'm working tomorrow. There's a party at the lounge, and I've been asked to work an earlier shift."

"No worries. I'll come on Sunday."

"Nedu and I are going to see friends in Luton on Sunday."

Deflated, I say nothing, waiting for him to make a suggestion of his own, any suggestion apart from him coming over to spend the night here. He doesn't.

"Okay, then," he finally says. "We'll talk later."

The line disconnects before I can even say anything in response. Holding the phone in my hand, I realise with a heavy heart that we are even worse off than when I was still in Nigeria.

–

Having thrown in the towel with the telemarketing gig, Nonye and I resume our job search the following week.

"You don't know how lucky you are to only have to come for lectures and then go back to your room to sleep," Nonye tells an amused Tayo as we are seated in class.

Tayo's inheritance largesse is enough to keep her nice and comfortable without having to lift a finger.

"You guys are just being greedy," she teases. "Didn't your scholarship come with some upkeep? Aren't you only working just to have extra change? You don't have to if you don't want to, you know."

All I can do is offer a tight smile in response, unable to tell her what happened to the upkeep element of my scholarship money. It's easier to let her believe I'm being greedy.

Later that week, we are notified of vacancies at *Poundyard*, a variety store chain where most items are sold for £1. But it turns out Nonye does have her limits when it comes to a part time job.

"I'd rather die!" she exclaims. "Me? *Poundyard*? So my fans in school can come there and see me working the till? *Tufiakwa*! Kill me first!"

Well, with the month of October already whizzing by, I do not have the luxury of choice. So, when I am offered the job, at the less than charming wage of £10.50 an hour, I accept it.

On my first day, wearing the branded black and teal green t-shirt makes my heart sink. I can't believe I have become one of those who have left a decent white-collar job back in Nigeria, in exchange for a blue-collar one in London. And I am in for an even worse surprise when, instead of manning the till as I'd anticipated, I am assigned to the shop floor, restocking shelves and cleaning as shoppers traipse from aisle to aisle. A walking distance from campus, there is a steady inflow of not only familiar faces from school, but also people from Hendon, Mill Hill, Edgware and Finchley, all looking for bargain buys. Even though, in line with my 20-hour workweek requirement, I'm only there between the hours of 5pm and 9pm on weekdays, it is as soul crushing as ever every time I am called to clean up a spill on an aisle or am shoved around by shoppers as I try to load items to a shelf.

But I just have to keep my eye on the big picture. Hopefully, it will be all worth it in the end.

Ten

The Nannies

Roman

I am apprehensive when Bisi sends me the contact information of her friend's agent. His name is Mr. Lekan and there are all sorts of alarm bells ringing in my head as I dial his number. While one part of me likes the idea of a less expensive child minder with the added advantage of the maternal care from an older woman, I worry about the wisdom of hiring someone illegal. But it's true what they say about beggars having no choice. Right now, after having exhausted all my other options, this is the next best thing.

"Ah, we have plenty nannies. Plenty, plenty good nannies," the Mr. Lekan raves when we talk, his feigned British accent a thin coating over his thick Yoruba one. "You will like them, I can promise you that. Is there any particular tribe you prefer? You like Yoruba? Hausa? Igbo?"

He pronounces the last two *Awusa* and *Yigbo*, and it takes me a few seconds to understand what he's said.

"Umm, no. Not really," I answer, not having given it any thought.

"I trust you British Nigerians," he chuckles. "You guys don't understand the importance of these things. Can I ask you where you're from?"

"Edo State," I answer, with an eye roll. What has that got to do with anything?

"Ah perfect! I have the right person for you!" he exclaims. "A nice, lovely woman. Your shidren will love her."

Shidren? Oh, children! I don't even bother correcting him that I have only one.

"Her name is Lucy, Lucy Omokhodion. I'll send her over later today," he continues. "One look at her, you'll hire her on the spot, and Bob's your uncle!"

He pronounces uncle 'huncle' and this make me chuckle. I need the humour to force down the rising apprehension I feel about doing anything that could get me in trouble.

"Is she here legally?" I just have to ask.

"Of course!" he exclaims in response but doesn't bother to provide any further information.

I sigh and say a prayer. The last thing I need is to dive headlong from one problem to an even bigger one.

True to his words, Lucy shows up an hour before I need to pick Luna up from day care. She looks to be in her late 50s and I am immediately set at ease by her large smile. She reminds me of my mother and looks the sort that would pamper children silly, while retaining a firm hand. I smile as I let her into the house. This might not be a mistake after all.

"How long have you been in England?" I ask when we're seated.

"Probably longer than you've been alive!" she laughs. "I have four children and they were all born here. We returned to Nigeria in the 1994, but I've been going and coming ever since."

"So, your kids are back in Nigeria?"

"Just one of them, my youngest. My first three are here, all of them married with beautiful kids," she beams. "I have eight grandchildren and I helped take care of all of them."

I nod, impressed. With eight grandchildren, she's definitely had enough experience. I'm about to ask her about her grandchildren when her phone rings.

"Hello?" she answers it after casting me an imploring look. "*You mean am? Abeg, help me collect my own. I go call you later.*" She throws me a wide smile as she places the phone back in her bag. "Sorry about that."

I shrug. "It's fine."

"Lekan says you're a doctor," she asks. "Do you work long hours? Are you usually on call?

I'm momentarily taken aback by the directness of the question. "Not right now, but I hope to. Why?"

"I have to close by 6pm. 7pm at the very latest," she answers, her wide smile still on her face. "The West End isn't too far from here, right? I need to be able to get there before the shops close. I'm going to Nigeria this Christmas, and I still have a lot of shopping to do."

My mouth parts as I look at her, not even knowing what to say in response. Her phone rings again and she answers it without even bothering with any feigned regret.

"You don reach there? I dey come, I dey come," she giggles. "Wait for me there, I dey come na na!"

Is this woman for real?

"So," she grins at me. "When can I start?"

How about never?

Mr. Lekan is surprised when I tell him I don't think Lucy will be a good fit for me. Not wanting to scuttle her employment chances elsewhere, I don't tell him it is because I find her extremely flighty and would probably be more interested in talking on her phone than watching my daughter.

"Serious?" Mr. Lekan sounds genuinely surprised. "And I thought she would be perfect for you, especially as she's from your state."

"About that. I don't think that matters. You don't have to send me only people from Edo State."

"In that case," he says, his voice sounding considerably perkier than a few seconds before. "I have the perfect person for you. Her name is Madam Comfort, and she is a retired nurse from Yimo State."

Yimo State? I might not know much about Nigeria, but I can swear that isn't one of the country's 36 states. Or could he mean...

"You mean Imo State?"

"Yes, that's what I said. Yimo."

Whatever you say, bruv.

Madam Comfort is knocking on my door at exactly a minute before our scheduled 4pm meeting. Looking at her from the door's peephole, I am immediately intimidated by the frowning elderly woman at my doorstep. A ball of sunshine she doesn't appear to be.

"Good evening, Madam," I say as I open the door, my parents' warning of always properly greeting older people ringing in my head.

"Good evening, Doctor Isibor," she says, walking into the house, the unmistakable smell of lavender wafting in with her. By God, she actually smells like my late Grandmother.

"Please, tell me about yourself," I say when we are seated, smiling to make her more comfortable. Actually, I lie. I smile to make myself more comfortable. With the thin set of her lips and furrow of her brows, she looks so stern, I feel like I'm the one that needs to make a good impression.

"I retired as a Senior Matron after thirty years at General Hospital, Lagos Island, back in Nigeria. I came to London to join my children after that. That was seven years ago."

I try, but fail, to compute her age from that information. If I were to hazard a guess, I'd peg her at 63, 64 years old.

"Your children are here?" I ask.

"Yes," she answers. "If you're trying to ask if I'm here legally, the answer is yes. I'm a permanent resident."

I nod, very happy to hear that I won't be doing anything illegal after all. I ask her questions about her grandchildren, eleven in number, ranging in age from 3 to 19 years old, after which I'm more than convinced that I have found just the person I'm looking for. And her phone hasn't rung even once.

"I might work long hours," I say, trying my luck. "Will that be a problem for you?"

She shakes her head. "Not at all. I can be available from 7am to 7pm, or longer if we agree on overtime."

Fair enough.

"Do you have plans to go to Nigeria for Christmas?" After the fiasco with Lucy, it is a question I must ask.

She purses her lips, barely able to conceal her irritation. "All my children are here, Doctor Isibor. I don't have any need to travel to Nigeria for Christmas."

Well then, Bob's your *huncle*.

By the time she leaves, I have offered her the job and we agree that she will start the very next day. For the first time in weeks, I sleep soundly, happy to have finally found stable care for Luna, relieved that the tumultuous journey of juggling parenting with the demands of work is finally over.

But, as it turns out, it is too good to be true.

Madam Comfort arrives nice and early the next morning.

"Your daughter isn't awake yet?" she asks, as she hangs her coat. "I thought you said she has to leave the house by 8."

"Luna. That's her name," I smile at her, hoping to thaw her stony demeanour now that she's pretty much joining my family.

"Luna?" she repeats the name. "What kind of name is that?"

I don't bother telling her that was the name Sekani had always dreamt of giving her daughter.

"Anyway," I return to her original question. "In autumn and winter, I prefer to bathe her only once a day, preferably evenings. So, in the mornings, she just needs to get up a few minutes before, to get dressed and have her breakfast."

"You bathe her only once a day?" she repeats, looking at me like I've just doused myself with a bucket of rotting fish. "That's not healthy. A growing child needs to bathe at least twice a day. Sometimes even three, if you include after they come back from school."

"Just once, please," I say, walking ahead of her so we can drop the topic.

"And all these white walls," she remarks, looking around with disdain. "Is that wise with a toddler?"

"We've been fine so far. Besides, the walls upstairs aren't white."

She nods but her curled lip shows she is still anything but impressed.

I take a deep breath to calm my rising frustration. "Let me show you around."

I walk ahead of her into the kitchen. "I typically make Luna a sandwich to take to school, and also for her afternoon tea. But she likes cereal on occasion and even oatmeal, if done properly. For dinner, we usually have ready meals. I have a few in the freezer, so all you need to do is pop one in the microwave."

Her curled lip is still on her face, her arms crossed as she looks around my kitchen, my £40,000 smart kitchen, as if it were a dumpster full of week-old trash.

"I'm not touching anything in this place," she says, her frown deepening. "I don't understand all this your equipment."

I blink twice. She what?

"There's nothing to it," I say, willing patience upon myself, patience I typically do not have. "All you have to do is... "

"I'm not about to learn how to use any high-tech equipment, Doctor Isibor," she retorts, her voice an octave higher. "Your stove works the normal way, right? Just show me where your pots and pans are. That's all I need."

"That might work for the oatmeal, but what about the ready meals?" I ask, perplexed about this argument we are having. "You have to use the microwave."

"With all due respect, Doctor Isibor, why is your three-year-old child eating microwave meals?" she demands, making me feel like a naughty student standing before the principal.

I'm so intimidated, I'm momentarily lost for words. "That's what we have available," I finally answer. "Sometimes, we order take away, but for the most part, this is what we've got. I don't particularly cook."

"Then your problem is solved," she beams, her lips crinkling in what I reckon is a smile. "I will be more than happy to cook for you. Breakfast, lunch and dinner. But as that's not part of the original arrangement, it will cost you more."

I raise a brow. "How much more?"

"£300 extra a week," she answers, without even blinking.

This means I'll pay her *double* her agreed salary.

"Doctor Isibor, your child's nutrition isn't something you should toy with," she says, shaking her head as if disappointed by my hesitation. "If you can spend so much money on a kitchen you barely use, you should also be willing to pay for good food for your child."

"There's nothing wrong with ready meals, Madam Comfort," I retort, my patience now running thin. "I grew up on them and I turned out fine."

She sighs and shakes her head. "I actually don't blame you, Doctor Isibor. I blame your parents who didn't train you the Nigerian way. Being born here is no excuse to lose touch with your heritage and blend in with the mindless ways of doing things in this place. How can anybody give their child frozen food prepared God knows how long ago? And you say you grew up eating that? No, your parents didn't do a good job at all."

And that, my friends, is the last straw.

Having dismissed her, I call the hospital to reschedule my appointments for the day, and later that night, as I'm crouched by the bathtub as Luna splashes in the bubbles of her evening bath, I am once again at my wits end. Maybe taking my mother up on her offer and sending Luna to live with her is the right thing to do, given my disastrous quest to find decent childcare. But as a soap sud flies to my face, I turn to smile at my giggling daughter. I remember all it has taken to get us to this point and decide there is no way, absolutely no way, I'm going to be separated from her.

The next morning, I ignore frantic calls from Mr. Lekan, who has probably heard things didn't work out with Madam Comfort. I am not interested in seeing any more of his Nigerian Aunties. I guess I'm just going to have to figure out a way to live with things the way they are.

Eleven

The Agent

NOVEMBER 2018

Legachi

£405

That is what I have saved by the first week of November after working at *Poundyard* for a whole month. £405. Even with buying the barest minimum by way of groceries, and only a handful of warm clothing from clearance racks, that is all I have saved, with just about six weeks to find myself somewhere else to stay.

I'm screwed.

"Babe, remember what you suggested before?" I say to Mezie when we see that Saturday. In the weeks that have passed, I have made more of an attempt to patch our relationship by making sure we talk at least every day. After the first few weekends when he was seemingly too busy to see me, I have made a point of going to Hackney every Saturday, cleaning their flat from top to bottom, and even cooking several pots of Nigerian soups from the stash of ingredients I brought with me. This has appeased his flatmates, Eche inclusive, and earned me several Brownie points with Mezie himself. Even though I still find it unpleasant having hurried sex with him in the room before Nedu shows up, things are definitely better with us than in the first few weeks of my arrival. We're back on track. Or at least I hope we are.

"What did I suggest?" he asks, not looking up from his phone as he scrolls through his Instagram feed.

"You suggested us pooling money together to rent a flat," I answer. I very well know those were not his exact words, but I am desperate to steer the conversation in the direction I need it to go. "You said when we both start earning money, we could pool money and rent a place."

His brows are knotted when he looks at me. "Babe, you know I can't do that now. I have a lot of responsibilities. Or have you forgotten I send money to my mom."

I cluck my tongue, frustrated. "But Mezie, you're earning decent money from your two jobs and the other gigs you do on the side… "

He sits up abruptly. "I see you're calculating my money for me. I hope you also calculated my tax while you were at it. And how much I have to contribute here for rent and feeding, not to mention the cost of my travel card."

"I'm sinking, Mezie. I'm not earning much from *Poundyard* and I have to be out of Alero's place next month."

He sighs deeply. "Even if I were to starve myself and save what I can, the best we'll be able to afford is another flat share."

My heart sinks at the thought of having to share an apartment again, but with no other options, I'm glad to take it.

"I don't mind," I answer, eagerness making my voice high-pitched. "We can start there and get a better place when we can afford to."

He shakes his head. "Nah, that makes no sense. Why leave here and go live with total strangers?" He tilts up my chin. "When you leave Alero's place, come back here and we can start saving for a better place."

I blanch at the very idea of it, hearing the hidden implication in what he has said; I'll keep juggling school and work, while living in this dump at the same time. *No way o*. He can count me out of that!

"As a matter of fact, we could open a joint account," he is saying, his eyes wide with anticipation. "So we can pool both our funds."

I raise a brow as I look at him. This guy must really take me for a fool, after everything he has already done with my money. Joint account indeed.

When he sees I'm unyielding, he returns his attention to his phone. As I make my way back to Golders Green that night, I know my only option is to either get a better paying job or exceed my allowed 20-hour work week allocation. I mention this to Alero the following afternoon, as we sit in the living room painting our toenails.

"Yeah, you totally have to get another job, or you won't be able to afford your own place," she says in agreement.

"It's just this 20-hour issue... "

"That one na small thing!" she scoffs with a wave of her hand. "There are plenty undocumented jobs out there. Plenty. My former flatmate's older brother is even an agent for Nigerians in London looking to work as cleaners or nannies. I'll get his number so you can call him."

My heart crashes. Cleaner or nanny?! Is this what my life has come to?

She notices the change in my demeanour. "Either that, or you use someone else's N.I. number. But if they catch you *ehn*! Deportation straight. They don't take identity theft lightly here."

I'm all too aware of that. Just because Mezie has been able to get away with it doesn't mean I will too. It would be the biggest tragedy to be deported midway through my scholarship program for something as silly as that.

Accepting I have no other choice, I accept the agent's number and call him the very next day.

"Good morning, Mr. Lekan," I say tentatively. "I got your number from... " I hesitate, wondering whether or not to mention Alero by name. I decide not. "... from a friend. I'm interested in a job as a... " I do a mental flip, thinking which would be the lesser of the two evils. "..a nanny."

"Oh, is it?" he says, in the worst British accent I have ever heard. "You sound very young. Have you done this before?"

"Umm, not for a living, but I've helped care for my sisters' kids," I answer.

"What did you say your name is?"

I actually hadn't even told him. I ponder over whether to tell him my full name or use the annoying abbreviation I'd been forced to resort to at the telemarketing job. I go with the former. "Legachi."

"Legachi. *Omo Yibo*," he chuckles. "Come see me tomorrow, Legachi. Let's talk some more then. Cheerio!"

–

Right after class the next day, I set off for Mr. Lekan's office in Brixton, a terrace house which doubles as his home.

"You say you're studying at Middlesex Uni?"

I nod. "An M.Sc in Global Supply Chain Management."

"Full or part time?"

"Full time."

His mouth curves in a frown. "So how are you gonna do the work? Being a nanny is very demanding and could take up several hours of your day."

"I have most of my classes in the morning," I answer, having already thought that through. "After noon, I'm available for as long they require."

He nods, deep in thought. "Some people might even like the fact you're in school. Would you consider tutoring children if their parents ask for it?"

I shrug. "Sure. Why not?"

He smiles at me. "I like you, Legachi. You're bright, eager and have a cheerful spirit. That's very good. I'm sure I'll be able to place you somewhere great."

From the bottom of my heart, I hope so.

"Erm, Sir… " I know I must ask. "I'm on a student visa and can only work 20 hours a week… "

He waves his hand in much the same dismissive way Alero did. "That doesn't matter here, luv. You'll be paid directly by your employer, so it won't register in the system."

Hearing that is like a weight lifted off my shoulders. With any luck, I'll be able to keep my *Poundyard* job as well.

"My fee is 40% off your first salary," he says. "Just so we're clear."

My eyes widen. A whole 40%. But right now, I'm ready to agree to anything. So, I nod.

"Splendid!" he beams, revealing yellowed teeth held in place by a shockingly pink gum. "Give me some days to look through my files, to decide where would be the best fit for you. I'll be in touch."

Stepping out of the house, I walk the two-minute distance to the train station, the chilly autumn wind hitting me from all angles. It is only a little past 3pm, but the sun is already in descent. By the time I get home in forty minutes, it will be dark. Combined with my money trouble, the shortened daytime window has made me even more melancholy. All I can do is pray he finds me a good job that can fit perfectly into my life. And even if the hours don't comfortably fit, I'm ready to move around what I need to, to make sure they do.

This job will be a lifeline.

Roman

I look at my watch as I head for the elevator. It is already 5:40pm and it will take me more than twenty minutes to get to Luna's day care. I'll probably get there ten to fifteen minutes late, which will be how much in penalties? I'm doing the math when the elevator opens, just as my beeper also goes off. I frown and try to zone it out, but my phone soon starts to ring. Looking at the caller ID and seeing the hospital's landline number, I know I shouldn't answer it if I have any plans of leaving.

But I can't ignore it.

Stepping away from the lift and back onto the lobby, I do answer it. A child has gone into a diabetic coma and the Attending Paediatric Endocrinologist, Doctor Butcher, has specifically asked for me. Before I scaled back my hours, he was the one I worked with in my quest to specialise in the field. Saying no isn't an option, so I immediately rush two floors up to where the patient is being treated. Getting there, it is a more serious situation than I thought, and it is a battle to save the young girl's life, as we struggled to control the swelling in her brain. By the time we stabilize her, it is almost 10pm.

I don't get to the day care till 10:44pm. It is a new low for me. A stony-faced Cheryl hands over a sleeping Luna, and my heart breaks when I see tear stains on her face.

"I'm really sorry," I say to Cheryl. "There was an emergency at work... "

"Save the apologies for her. She cried herself ragged."

Cheryl hands me the penalty slip, but I don't even bother looking at it. I already know it's a hefty amount. But hefty though it may be, it's not enough to make up for the hurt I have caused my child. She doesn't stir as we journey back home, or as I tuck her into bed later. I stand over her, watching her as she sleeps. Something has to give. We can't continue this way.

And then my phone vibrates with a text message.

Good evening, Doctor! I have the perfect candidate for you.

Even though I have been deleting text messages like this from him for weeks, reading it this time is like receiving salvation. Not caring that it is almost midnight, I call him.

"Hi, Mr. Lekan," I say, breathless in my anticipation.

"Hello, Doctor. It's been a while. I was beginning to think you'd changed your number or something."

Not wanting to go into the why's and what's about why I ghosted him, I go straight to the point. "You say you have someone for me?"

"You'll like this one. I know you didn't have a good experience with the older ladies I sent before, so this one is a bit younger," he answers. "She's educated, pleasant and great with kids. You'll like her."

I shut my eyes and exhale. Honest to God, I pray I do.

Twelve

The Interview

Uegachi

itting in the bus headed to South Hampstead, I crack my fingers, my heart racing in anticipation of my interview. What on earth am I thinking applying for a job I know nothing about? There is no way any family will hire a novice like me to care for their children. But I owe it to myself, and my lean bank account, to at least try.

My stomach drops as the 113 bus stops at the Finchley Road Station stop. Exhaling, I rise to my feet and step out of the bus, shivering as I am greeted by the crisp November breeze. It's time to face the music.

Locating the address, I am relieved that it is less than a two-minute walk from the bus stop. I stand before the terrace house, one in a row of several elegant, two-storey brown-brick houses with window frames and stairs leading to each front door a gleaming white. A well-dressed elderly woman smiles at me as she walks past with a dog on a leash. As I smile back, I feel intimidated anew, and not just because I don't feel qualified for the job. This neighbourhood is worlds apart from Mezie's, and even Alero's, and I find myself feeling like a fish out of water. This Isibor family is clearly in a different league.

A bus pulls up down the street and a man and a little girl disembark. The girl, with long hair in pig tails and a *Shimmer & Shine* lunch box in her hand, reminds me of my niece, Chinasa, and I am endeared to her and homesick at the same time. Our eyes meet and I smile at her. Her eyes light up and she returns the most adorable smile ever, waving hello. The man next to her says something and she looks up at him. I do the same and marvel over what I see. I stare unashamedly at him, momentarily forgetting the reason I am standing there.

With a natural wave to his cropped hair and pecan brown skin, I try to work out if he is mixed race or not. In a black leather jacket over a brilliant white shirt, fitted black trousers and shiny black shoes, he looks too well dressed to be trekking the street. No, this man belongs in a magazine. And he walks like he knows it too, with shoulders back and a bow-legged swagger.

He looks in my direction and his intense gaze beneath thick eyebrows and the slightest hint of a five o'clock shadow remind me of the male love interests in the romance novels I read as a teenager. This man is drop dead gorgeous. His only flaw is that he stands only a little taller than my own 5 feet 7 inches, but damn, he's fine! His expression goes from indifferent to puzzled as they approach and, horrified, I realise I am standing in front of their doorstep.

He is the person I have come to see.

Roman

I am exhausted as Luna and I alight the bus, and I hardly hear any of the stories she tells me about what happened at Cheryl's that day. I haven't had a decent night's rest in a long time, and I am almost regretful of the interview I have scheduled for that evening. Then I notice Luna wave at someone ahead.

"Who are you waving at, darling?" I ask, too tired to even look in the direction of the wave.

"That woman over there. She's smiling at me."

That is enough to make me look, and I frown when I see someone not only standing in front of my house but looking at me with the same wide-eyed interest as someone at the circus. Her hair, blonde braids with black undergrowth inches long, looks a hundred years old and she wears a cheap looking winter jacket with large metallic buttons and stiff, scrawny fur lining its hood and wrists. Who on earth wears a winter jacket in early November? She's definitely new in town.

And then it occurs to me that this could be the person Mr. Lekan has sent. Surely, this can't be her! Surely, she's much too young!

Legachi

His frown deepens as they approach, further fraying my already threadbare nerves. I smile, hoping to present the outlook of confidence, but the closer they get, the wobblier my smile becomes. He is even better looking up close. My eyes drop to his full pink lips, and I impulsively run my tongue over my dry bottom one. Damn, this man is fine!

"Are you from Mr. Lekan?" he asks when they get to the house.

My smile wanes, disappointed he hasn't even bothered with as much as a 'hello'.

I nod. "Yes. Good evening."

He looks at his watch, his brows furrowed as if irritated. "You're early. I told him to send you by 6."

It's 5:45pm.

"I left a bit too early," I answer. "I thought it would take me longer to get here. I could wait outside till you're ready."

Still frowning, his eyes remain on me. My nervous smile returns as I stand there under his scrutiny, not knowing what to make of his assessment.

"Hi, I'm Luna," Chinasa's lookalike says to me from where she stands next to him.

Grateful for the distraction, I turn to her, my smile wider and more genuine. "Hello, Luna. That's a lovely name. My name is Legachi."

She smiles back at me. "I like your name too."

Another gust of icy wind blows past, and I return my eyes to the man, who is still studying me. I wonder if we're going to stand out there forever.

Roman

For the life of me, I can't imagine why Mr. Lekan would have sent someone this young. When he'd said he was sending someone 'a bit younger', I'd expected a woman in her early 50s, maybe even late 40s. The person standing before me doesn't look a day older than 30. But considering the Au-Pairs I had before were in their 20s, in all fairness, her age shouldn't be too much of a hindrance.

Luna says something that makes the woman smile at her, and I marvel at her gap-toothed smile, one that brightens her otherwise plain face.

"You're already here, so there's no need to wait," I say, walking up to the door and opening it. I'd really hoped to have a few minutes to at least unwind with a cup of tea.

Luna rushes into the house when the door is open and I stand by the door as the woman walks in, her eyes wide. She looks like a deer in front of headlights, and my earlier doubts return.

"You can hang your coat by the door," I say, walking into the living room where I switch on the TV for Luna, who is bobbing up and down on the couch. I frown as I realise she's on a sugar high and make a mental note to tell Cheryl not to give her any sweets after 2pm. Turning to the woman, I beckon. "Come with me."

I lead the way to the kitchen and motion for her to sit on one of the four chairs arranged around a small table where Luna and I eat most of our meals. Apart from last Christmas when my family came to celebrate Christmas with us, we haven't had cause to use the conventional dining room adjacent to the living room.

The woman walks in behind me and I am unimpressed even further by her shabby cardigan, with its bleeding faux wool and uneven stitching. One thing is for sure; this one needs the money.

I take the seat opposite hers. "What did you say your name is?"

She smiles again, revealing the gap between her teeth. That has to be the very best thing about her. "Legachi."

I nod, not even bothering to memorise it, or even offer mine. I'm pretty certain I won't be hiring her. "How old are you?"

"31."

Aha. I was almost right on the money.

"How long have you been taking care of kids?"

Her smile brightens. "Almost all my life. I've been an aunt since I was 10 years old, and I've helped mind my nieces and nephews ever since."

"Nieces and nephews?" I repeat, perplexed. "You don't have any children of your own? You haven't done this professionally?"

Her smile wanes. "No, I don't. And no, I haven't. I'm studying for a Master's degree at Middlesex University."

For crying out loud! Is Mr. Lekan having a laugh?

"You're studying for a Master's degree?" I repeat again. "So why are you here? How do you intend to care for my daughter if you already have school to contend with?"

"Mr. Lekan said you need someone to watch your daughter when she gets home from day care. He said what you need is someone who'll watch her in the evening while you're at work," she answers, her shaky voice betraying her nerves. "I'm really great with kids, Sir… "

"My name is Roman," I cut in. Sir? We're practically the same age!

She briefly hesitates. "Mr… Doctor Roman, I'm really good with kids. I have taken care of them from infant to teen age. I might not have practical experience, but I promise, you won't regret hiring me."

Her enthusiasm thaws me. Besides, I don't have any better option now. She'll do in the short term, until I can find someone better.

"What are your wage expectations?"

"£13 an hour."

I scoff. Doing a quick mental calculation, it is more than I paid the Au-Pairs who worked even longer hours. She wishes!

"I can pay you £600 a month for five-hour weekdays, 5pm to 10pm," I counter. "With an extra £60 for any extra day you work, and £10 for every hour you have to work after 10pm."

I am expecting her to haggle, and I am surprised when she brightens and nods.

"It's fine by me."

I pat my inner self on the back. I have gotten her for a steal.

Legachi

I can't believe my ears. Not only has he offered me the job, what he has offered is much more than the maximum £500 a month I'd been told to expect. I also can't believe he has bought my story about taking care of kids since I was 10-years old. While it's true my oldest sister started having children when I was that young, and it's also true that I love my nieces and nephews dearly and dote over them when we see, what I failed to add is that, save for my sister, Lotanna, and her kids who live in Lagos, I only get to see the others once a year when we converge in Umuahia for Christmas.

God has been on my side today. But after so many false starts, I think I deserve one break.

"When can you start?" he asks, and I force myself off the Cloud 9 I have floated to and return my attention to him.

"As soon as you need me," I answer, still smiling so wide, my cheeks hurt. Heck, I can start that very evening if he wants.

"Does Monday work for you?"

"Monday is perfect."

"Great!" he says, rising to his feet. "Let me have your phone number so I can send you the address of Luna's day care. You'll meet me there on Monday, so I can introduce you to Cheryl."

"Cheryl is the owner?"

He looks at me and, again, I see impatience flash through his face. "Yeah."

I nod, also standing. That works.

"I know Mr. Lekan runs background checks, but I'm going to have to see your passport and school ID."

I reach for my bag and bring them out. I came fully prepared. He examines them for so long, I wonder what he's looking for.

"Global Supply Chain Management," he says, as he hands the documents back to me. "Interesting."

Minutes later, as I make my way to the bus stop, I feel like dancing a jig. If I can get an earlier shift at *Poundyard*, say from noon to 4pm, I could fit this new job into my daily itinerary easily. Most days, my classes end before noon, and even on the one day they don't, Thursday, I'll find a way to make it work.

My money worries are about to be over.

Thirteen

High Expectations

Legachi

I am a ball of nerves as I make my way to Avenue Road on Monday. After Friday's encounter, I'd hoped to at least look decent and more presentable for my first day of work. But having successfully secured an earlier shift at *Poundyard*, I only had enough time to throw off my work uniform and throw on my jacket over the sweater and jeans I left home with in the morning. I try not to feel intimidated as I remember the posh neighborhood and my even posher employer. God knows the Doctor Isibor I was expecting was a much older person, not that hot, sexy man. I wonder if I'll get to meet Mrs. Isibor anytime soon and if she's anything like her husband.

It is an eight-minute walk from the bus stop, and I arrive just as Dr. Roman does. I look at my watch in a panic and let out a sigh of relief when I see it's still 4:53pm. Being early is way better than being late. I smile at him, but his face is expressionless.

"Hi, em… "

"Legachi," I offer, knowing he's forgotten it.

Again, he doesn't try to repeat it.

"I bring Luna here by about 9 every morning, and the agreement is to pick her up by 5pm," he says instead. "Cheryl has been kind to give a grace hour till 6pm, but after that, she charges £2 for every minute I'm late."

My eyes widen as I do the math. £2 for every minute? Good Lord!

"Thankfully, you won't need to pay that again," I giggle.

He doesn't laugh.

Cheryl soon lets us in, and I look around the room of a little over a dozen children, hoping I'll be able to recognise Luna again. When I see those pigtails, I beam as I wave at her. How could I ever forget a cute munchkin like that?

"Legachi!" she calls out as she waves back.

I am tickled that she remembers my name.

It is a short bus ride to their house, and when we are let in, the place takes my breath away all over again. Tastefully furnished, it is markedly different from everything I have come to expect from London housing. With its excellent play of monochromatic colours, it looks like the spectacular 'afters' of the home makeover shows I watched on BBC Lifestyle back in Nigeria. The place is simply stunning.

Walking behind him into the equally stunning kitchen, its stark, all-white colour intimidates me. I wonder if I'll also be expected to clean.

"Here are the sandwiches I made for her tea," he says, bringing a plate out of the microwave. He points at a frozen, branded plastic container on the counter. "And that's her dinner. All it needs is four minutes in the microwave."

I nod, my eyes flitting from the container to the said microwave.

"She has her tea about now, and her dinner at 7:30 after she's had a bath," he continues talking. "Between now and then, she watches TV. She likes Cbeebies and Nick Junior. On occasion, Disney Junior, but never, ever Cartoon Network. I don't understand their shows."

Frankly, neither do I.

"By 8, she should be in bed," he finishes.

I nod. "Got it," I try to sound convincing, even though I'm so nervous about messing up, my palms are sweaty.

"Great," he says. "You have my number. Call me if you need anything, okay?"

I force a smile. "Sure."

I watch as he walks over to the living room and kisses Luna on the forehead. He reaches for a messenger bag on the couch, slings it over his shoulder and makes for the door. Before opening it, I see him hesitate, and my heart races as I worry that he has realised I'm really not the right person for the job. I worry that he has seen through my bullshit and will turn around to march me out of his house. But when he finally does open the door and walks out, I let out a sigh of relief.

Thank God!

Roman

Once out the door and on the street, I turn to look back at the house. What the heck am I doing, leaving Luna alone with someone who is clearly a novice? In a rush of panic, I dart back and open the door, ready to tell her it's been a huge mistake and she has to leave.

But sitting on the couch with Luna, both of them giggling over God knows what, my fears are allayed.

"Did you forget something?" the new nanny asks, her eyes wide with expectation… or is that fear?

"I thought I left my phone, but I've just found it in my pocket," I lie in response.

She smiles and nods, but I'm not sure she's convinced. I notice again the high undergrowth beneath her braids and the bulky sweater she is wearing. With how high Luna likes the heating in the house to be, it's only a matter of time before the nanny starts to swelter. I consider turning the heat down, but decide not to. I grin as I walk out of the house, knowing the odds of her figuring out how to adjust the temperature herself are zero to none.

Legachi

As Luna eats her sandwich, I walk up to the large portrait hanging in the living room and smile at the picture of the beaming couple on their wedding day. I look at the beauty in Doctor Roman's arms, and I nod and smile. But *of course*, this is the kind of beauty he would marry. She is the darker version of the supermodel, Iman, and all I can think is what a beautiful couple they make. Looking at the gorgeous woman, I feel a tinge of inadequacy but quickly reprimand myself. Not only is the man waaaay out of my league, I am this close to being engaged myself.

Walking around the living room, I see other pictures of the couple, and the love they share is clear for anyone to see. There are also pictures of Doctor Roman and Luna, but none with all three of them together. Then realisation hits me, and I gasp. She is probably dead. That is why there are no pictures of her with her daughter.

"Aww, how sad!" I remark, truly dismayed. What a tragic end to what looks to have been a beautiful love story.

"Finished!" Luna hollers from the sofa, brandishing her empty plate.

Walking to her, I start to feel quite hot. I adjust the neck of my cardigan, my eyes darting around for the thermostat, hoping that, unlike Alero, he doesn't have a set 'hard number'. But there is no thermostat in sight.

I take the plate to the kitchen and as I wash it, sweat courses down my back. I am equal parts amazed that I am actually hot in London and increasingly desperate for some respite from this heat. Once done, I scan the walls, from the kitchen to the hallway to the living room to the dining room, everywhere, looking for the damned thermostat, but without any luck. I pull at the neck of my sweater again.

This is going to be one long night!

Watching TV with Luna, I fan myself with an old TV guide I find on the wood and velvet coffee table. At 7, I take her up for a bath and by 7:20, we are back down for her dinner. I take the ready meal from the counter and walk over to the microwave to warm it. But, for the life of me, I cannot figure out how to use the device. I can see it, a mere hint of glass on the stark white wall, but there are no buttons or knobs to press or pull. I wave my hand in front of it, but it does not respond. I tap on it, bang it a little, and fall short of dropping to my knees to beg it to open. I'm sweating even harder, but less as a result of the heat now. It is almost 8pm, and the child hasn't even had her dinner, talk less of prepare for bed. With resignation, I reach for my phone to call her father.

Roman

As I'm not on duty today, I have chosen to go to the library to do some reading. Doctor Butcher and I have agreed that I will ease myself back into the specialization routine, so I am trying to refresh myself on some of the basics, as well as catch up on new research in the field.

I am flipping through a medical journal when my phone vibrates. A frown creases my face when I see the word *Babysitter* flash on my screen, and I wonder why she is calling me already on her first day. Rising to my feet, I walk out of the quiet room.

"Yes?"

"Hi… good evening," she stutters. "I'm trying to warm Luna's dinner, but I can't figure out how your microwave works."

I feel a rush of irritation. If she can't work a simple home appliance, how will she be able to manage with an actual child? This is just further proof that hiring her was a mistake.

"Don't worry, I'll handle it," I say and terminate the call.

Logging into the app for my home security camera, I chuckle at the sight of the exasperated nanny, standing in front of the microwave, chewing her nails. Her face is shiny with sweat, and I see she wasn't able to figure out the temperature adjustment either. Opening another app, but this time the one that controls my smart kitchen, I tap a button for the microwave to open.

"Just put the meal pack inside it," I say, when I call her again. "I'll take it from here."

Uegachi

I jump when the microwave door pops open, startled. And then Doctor Roman calls back, telling me he'll 'take it from here'.

And I am beyond livid. Livid and embarrassed!

I place the pack in the microwave as he has asked, and purse my lips in anger as it shuts, is scheduled for four-minutes, and as it rotates. My anger simmers alongside the meal. Surely, telling me what to do would have been more straightforward than this act of show-off. Yes, he has a fancy kitchen. But did he really have to make me look like a fool?

I am not impressed.

I dish the macaroni and triple cheese to a plate and I am even less impressed as Luna toys with her food, clearly not happy with the meal. I coax her into eating a few mouthfuls and I am finally able to put her to bed at 8:35.

Doctor Roman does not return until 9:55pm. As he walks into the house, my initial infatuation has dissipated, and I see him as nothing more than an asshole. An arrogant asshole.

"Is Luna asleep?" he asks.

"Yes," is my terse answer, as I reach for my jacket, holding it in my hand as the heat is still stifling. "Good night."

"Good night."

He has a hint of a smile as I walk past him and if I didn't need the job so much, I would have slapped him hard across the face.

Arrogant bastard!

Fourteen

Blinking & Ringing

Legachi

My Supply Chain Analytics class is still on when I start scouring the Internet, watching YouTube video after YouTube video, desperate to find out how smart appliances, smart kitchens, smart thermostats, heck smart homes, work. Watching these videos, I am amazed by how simple household machines have evolved over time, and I balk when I see how much they cost. But it makes me even more determined to learn. I am not going to make a fool of myself again.

After my shift at *Poundyard*, I head to pick Luna from day care. Seeing her face light up when she spots me is enough to make me feel whole lot better. Apart from the money, the little cherub makes everything worth it. She chats all through the bus ride to their house. Her father isn't there, so I open the key with the set he gave me.

After settling her with her afternoon tea, with *Gigglebiz* playing on the CBeebies channel, I go looking for the thermostat where one of the YouTube videos said smart ones like that are usually installed.

"Aha!" I exclaim, a broad, triumphant smile on my face when I see the white panel by the staircase, so nondescript it blends into the wall. No wonder I missed it yesterday. A screen comes alive when I wave, and I place my hands on my hip, very satisfied that I can finally regulate the temperature as I like. I frown when I see it is set to 27 degrees. No wonder I was roasting yesterday. But just as I am about to reduce it to a friendlier 23, I look in Luna's direction as she laughs over Justin Fletcher's antics on the show she is watching and realise the temperature must have been set that high for her benefit. And her comfort definitely supersedes mine. Walking away from the thermostat, I take off my cardigan, having come prepared with a cotton t-shirt I got at *Poundyard* on sale for 50p, underneath. Without the cardigan, I feel much better than yesterday, and I join Luna where she sits, laughing along with her as she enjoys her shows.

At 7pm, I give her a bath and when we're back downstairs, I strut confidently to the kitchen. Sure enough, there it is on the kitchen island, the control panel I'd mistaken for Doctor Roman's tablet yesterday. I chuckle and shake my hand as I lift it from its stand.

"So, you're the thing that did me *yeye* yesterday, *abi*?" I scold the inanimate object. "Well, *I'll* be the one to show you today!"

It is easy to identify which button operates what, as each has an icon of its related device. Pressing the button with an image of a microwave, I beam when its door pops open. So, this is what Doctor Roman was using to feel cool from wherever he was yesterday? *Shior*!

I slide in the ready meal, press the button that shuts the microwave, and program the timer, just like my YouTube video instructed. This is actually very easy and something my dear employer could have taught me in less than five minutes. For the first few seconds, there is no activity from the microwave, and I figure I need to press another button to get things going. My eyes scan the panel for whatever looks like a *Start* or *Play* button, and when I don't find one like that, I press a large red button at the top right corner of the remote.

Big mistake.

All of a sudden, everything in the kitchen starts blinking and beeping in a frenzy; the said microwave, the fridge, the oven, the coffee maker, the toaster, the dish washer and even the soap dispenser. I stand there, immobile, looking around as everything goes to shit around me.

Things have gone from bad to horrendously worse.

Roman

I'm reviewing a patient's file with Doctor Butcher when my phone lights up, my kitchen app's distress lights making it blink. I frown, irritated yet again by the very antithesis to Mary Poppins that I have hired. I dismiss the notification and return my attention to what Doctor Butcher is saying. Except my mind can't focus.

Luckily, his attention is soon called by another doctor, so I use the opportunity to check the home security camera. Sure enough, there she is, looking hapless and rushing from appliance to appliance, as all of them blink and beep in alarm. Realising she must have set off the crisis button, I switch to the kitchen app and deactivate the alarm.

Legachi

I am considering biting the bullet and calling Doctor Roman again, when everything suddenly stops. The blinking lights and beeping sounds, all of them stop. I heave a sigh of relief, thinking the alarms simply ran their course. But when the microwave starts to rotate, warming the meal, I realise Doctor Roman is the one who has come to my rescue. And this infuriates me. My face is flushed as I wait for the meal to be ready, the longest four minutes in the history of the world.

The nerve of that man!

Roman

I walk into the house a few minutes before 10, and from the sitter's reddened face, I can see she isn't pleased. I struggle to contain my amusement for the second night in a row. It appears Little Miss Poppins doesn't like being shown up.

"Why on earth did you press the crisis button?" I ask her, truly wanting to understand why. Not once in the year I've had the kitchen installed has it even crossed my mind to do so.

"I didn't know it was a crisis button," she answers.

Is she actually glaring at me? I struggle not to laugh.

"If you didn't know how to use the control, you could have simply asked," I say, managing to keep a straight face.

"Well, you could at least have shown me!" she snaps.

My brows shoot up, surprised by her tone. Oh no, she didn't.

Legachi

The words are out of my mouth before I can control them, and my eyes widen in my horror.

"I'm so sorry. I didn't mean that," I quickly say, in a desperate attempt to save my job. "I'm truly sorry. I've never seen a kitchen like this, and I didn't want to have to call you a second time, disturbing you with questions. Please, I'm really sorry."

He regards me for a full minute, a brow still up. I wring my fingers in my anxiety, not knowing how much I really should grovel to make up for my goof. Gosh, Legachi, what were you thinking?

"It's fine," he finally says, walking away. "You can go now."

I stand there like a statue, watching him disappear into the kitchen. That's it? I'm dismissed?

"Good night," I call out as I wear, first my cardigan and then my jacket.

But he doesn't even care to answer.

Feeling small and sheepish, I walk out of the house. As I make my way to the bus stop, and all through the ride to Golders Green, I chid myself for talking out of turn and school myself on the need to control my temper. With only six weeks to find myself somewhere to stay, I can't afford to play with this job.

No matter how arrogant Doctor Roman is.

Fifteen

Desperation

Legachi

I don't know if it is the mental and physical trauma arising from microwave-gate, or the fact that I have been studying late into the night, working on several essays at the same time, but the next day, I can barely keep my eyes open in any of my classes.

"*Nne*, you better take it easy!" Nonye says, as we file out of the International Logistics Management class, the last for the day. "You slept through most of that class!"

"At one point, I was tempted to throw a ball of paper into your mouth," Tayo cackles. "I hear you're working round the clock. Girl, you need to slow down."

"Exactly! *This life na only one!*" Nonye chimes in. "After that silly job where they baptised me with the name my parents didn't give me, I've decided I will just be managing myself like that. I don't need any *yeye* job that will make me so tired, I can't even pay attention in class."

I purse my lips. It's easy for them to say, but alas, I have neither a fat inheritance to live off nor the *Skyline* upkeep allowance. What I do have is a timer that is already counting down to my being evicted from my current accommodation. So no, I can't afford to 'take it easy'.

I make an excuse and hurry off to *Poundyard*, getting there five minutes late. I endure a telling off from my supervisor and struggle through the next four hours. As I restock a shelf of discount deodorants, I catch myself nodding off a few times.

God help me.

Before I set off for Swiss Cottage to pick Luna up from her day care, I wash my face with freezing cold water from the tap in the toilet. The last thing I need is to arrive at Doctor Roman's place tired. That would just worsen an already bad situation.

I pick Luna at the very dot of 5pm, and we are at their house before 5:30. Opening the door, my heart crashes when I hear music. Doctor Roman is home. And there I was, hoping to be able to avoid him for as long as I can manage.

He is in the kitchen, bobbing his head to Cam'ron's *Hey Ma* as he spreads peanut butter on slices of bread, making what I can see are Luna's sandwiches for her tea. He is wearing a fitted polyester t-shirt over a pair of joggers, and I have to keep my eyes trained on his face to prevent myself from ogling his insane body, his firm, well defined body moulded perfectly by…

"You alright?"

I snap right back to attention, heat rushing to my face over the realisation he has caught me staring at him. As if I need another strike against me.

"Yes, thank you," I say, forcing a smile. "You're not working today?"

He shakes his head but doesn't offer anything else in response. Regardless, I am determined to make up for running my mouth last night.

"Can I help you with that?" I ask, walking closer to where he stands. "I can finish the sandwich for you."

"Cheers, but I got it," he answers, not looking up.

Though disappointed by his refusal, I am undeterred, desperate to get into his good books.

"I know how to bake," I declare, still smiling. "I make great cupcakes and scones especially. I could make them so Luna can have them for her tea, instead of the same sandwiches she has for breakfast?"

I have been in this country long enough to know 'tea' doesn't refer to the popular aromatic beverage, or even hot chocolate as my country people like to call it, but actually a light meal or snack eaten anytime from mid-afternoon to early evening.

He looks up at me and seeing I have his attention buoys me.

"I can also make some alternatives to the ready meals. Luna struggles to eat them, so I don't think she's a fan," I continue. "I can make rice and potato dishes, or whatever else she might like."

I watch him in anticipation, trying not to get carried away by the spicy, woody notes of his perfume. But instead of getting the long-awaited smile from him, or even just a nod or any other gesture to show his gratitude for my offer and alignment with what I have proposed, I get instead that notorious raise of his brow.

Grateful and aligned he doesn't appear to be.

Roman

I look at her and I know I am doing a bad job of concealing my irritation. But heck, why conceal it when I can show her? My mind flashes back a few weeks to Madam Comfort, and I am angered that another opportunist now stands before me. Is that the common gimmick these Nigerian nannies pull out of their hats? Offer to cook and get paid double? Give me a break!

"Cheers, but Luna is more than fine with what she eats," I say, putting the sandwiches on a fresh plate. "There'll be no need for 'cooking' or 'baking'."

Her face falls and I feel a momentary stab of guilt. She looks genuinely disappointed, and I hate that I am presenting myself as a bad guy, but after everything I've been through with child minders, I don't think I can be blamed.

"Sure," she says, her smile no longer quite as wide. "I'll take her sandwich to her."

As she reaches for the plate, I notice a sprinkling of freckles on her nose and that her eyes are a very light brown. Who knows, maybe beneath those *minging* braids and God-awful clothes, there is a nice-looking woman.

"I've left a guide for how to use all the appliances here," I call out to her as I leave for the gym. "But if you're stuck, call me."

Without bothering with a goodbye, I walk out the door. Why on earth would I notice the colour of her eyes anyway?

Tegachi

I continue to struggle with sleep as I watch *Gigglebiz*, *Sarah & Duck* and *In The Night Garden* with Luna.

At 7, I manage to give her a shower, and as I microwave her dinner, I take several swigs of the glass of water I've been nursing to stay awake. I dish her food and sit opposite her as she eats.

Pulling out my tab, I decide to use that time to skim through some research resources I intend to reference for one of my papers later tonight. I'm only able to read a couple of pages when I am hit with a horrible headache. I place my head on the table to get a bit of relief, hoping a few seconds of rest will be give me the rejuvenation I need.

Roman

I am high on much needed endorphins as I walk up to the front door at 9:30. After a long time away from it, I am happy to have spent quality time at the gym. Hopefully, I will be able to do this more often now.

I hear the blast of the TV as I open the door and frown as I wonder why on earth Luna is still up and not in bed at this time. Walking past the living room with *Ben & Holly's Little Kingdom* blaring from the Nick Junior station, I'm surprised to neither see nor hear her nor the nanny. Where the hell are they? And why the hell did they leave the TV on?

I find my answer when I walk into the kitchen.

Luna is fast asleep, her head thrown back and her plate of food barely touched. And the nanny, blimey, the nanny has her head on the table, and she is also asleep. By her head is a tablet, and I frown as I realise she was studying while she was supposed to be watching my daughter. The so-called nanny doesn't stir as I lift Luna off the chair, carry her upstairs and tuck her into bed. She is still asleep even when I return to the kitchen. Angered, I tap the table.

Legachi

I am startled awake and sit up, horrified I actually fell asleep. As my eyes struggle to make sense of what is happening, I gasp when I see Doctor Roman standing before me, looking anything but pleased. I shoot to my feet, wanting to rush to Luna but he raises a hand.

"Don't bother. I've already put her to bed."

Shit.

"I'm so sorry," I stutter, hating that all I seem to be doing since getting hired is apologising. "This never happens. I don't know how I fell asleep… "

"But you did, yeah," he cuts in, wide eyes my confirmation that he not only isn't pleased, he is livid. "I don't even know what's worse. You studying on my paid time or having a bloody kip on my bloody table! My daughter could have choked while eating, you know that?"

I lower my eyes, completely ashamed of myself. To think this is the one time, the one and only time, I have brought schoolwork over. "I'm really sorry. It won't happen again."

He exhales and shakes his head. "This isn't working. Hiring a student was a mistake. Luna is the most important thing in my life, and I need to be rest assured that she is in the best of hands when I'm away. And with you, she clearly isn't. These last few days have been nothing short of a disaster. I think it would be best for me to pay you off for the time you've already spent."

My eyes widen with the realisation of what he has just said, the realisation of what is about to happen to my job, and I drop to my knees in a panic.

"Please, I beg you. Please, don't fire me, I beg you," I plead, my hands clasped. Tears have pooled in my eyes, and I make no attempt to stop them from falling. "I can't afford to lose this job, I beg you. I'll do better. I promise, this will never happen again."

Roman

Looking at her, I see past her tears. As her hands tremble and a vein pulses in her temple, I see fear. I recognise the trepidation she feels over the prospect of losing her job, realising for the first time how important this job is to her.

And it takes me back eighteen years.

I have a vivid flashback to the summer of 2000. As a young, sixth-form teen growing up in inner-city Harlow, I was well aware of the sacrifice my mother was making, saving money in preparation for me to go to university the following year. With my good grades, we weren't worried about my getting accepted into a decent school. But being recently widowed after my father died after a long battle with debilitating diabetes on Easter Sunday of 1999, I wasn't too young not to be aware of the heavy financial burden she was now facing, raising four children on her own. And at 17, all I wanted to do was help her. So, I got a job at a local pub, to raise enough money to not only help out with my fees, but also with my younger siblings.

And I worked as diligently as I could. I kept a smile on my face, even when the punters got rowdy and abusive. I not only worked the bar, but also did most of the cleaning. I worked overtime and took on as many shifts as I could to make more money. I had a target and was desperate to meet it.

Which is why, when after a rowdy fight between rival supporters of Harlow Town FC and Bedford Town FC led to extensive damage to the pub, and the Landlord, Gavin was his name I'll never forget, decided I hadn't done enough to curtail the raucous so had to be let go, before I felt any sadness or devastation, I'd felt fear, a crippling fear, a fear of not meeting my financial goal, a fear of not going to university the following year, a fear of not being able to help my mother, a fear of letting everyone down.

So, I too had dropped to my knees to beg for my job. And Gavin had given me another chance.

Looking at the nanny, I see it is my turn to pay it forward.

"Don't do that, please," I mutter looking away, emotional from the memory and uncomfortable to have her, or anyone for that matter, kneeling because of me. "Get up, please."

She scrambles to her feet, her hands still clasped and tears now falling freely down her face. "You can cut my wages if you need to. You can choose not to pay me for today, or even this whole week. But please, don't fire me."

I raise my brow and smile. "Don't tempt me with the wages, Leg… " And I realise I don't even remember her name.

"Legachi."

"Legachi," I say, taking the smile off my face for her to see that I'm only being lenient, not foolish. "I'm giving you one more chance. The next strike, you're out."

She places a hand on her chest and holds a chair with the other, clearly relieved. Tears are still pouring from her eyes as she looks at me, the rigid chords in her neck showing just how terrified she was.

"Thank you," she sobs.

I shrug, my own discomfort rising. Why is she still crying after she's gotten her job back?

"It's past 10," I mutter. "You can go now."

She wipes her eyes, takes her tab from the table, and walks to the cloakroom to get her coat and bag. I watch as she slips her device into her bag and walks out of the house, still crying.

And I wonder why I have been left to look and feel like the villain.

Sixteen

Striking Dust, Striking Gold

Legachi

I cry the entire twenty-minute bus ride home, completely broken. That I have been reduced to a teary, begging mess by the prospect of losing a babysitting job has broken my spirit. I am crushed by the reminder that keeping this job is the difference between my getting decent accommodation or returning to Mezie's flat. I think back to when I gave away my entire allowance, a whopping £8,000, and I feel like going back in time to give that foolish girl a resounding slap across the face.

But it is too late to cry over spilt milk.

Thankfully, Roman isn't home the next day when Luna and I get back from day care, or even today. Just like yesterday, he doesn't get home till a few minutes before 10, and also like yesterday, we exchange only a terse greeting as I leave, with him reminding me to be there tomorrow, Saturday, to watch Luna. I'm unable to even look him in the eye, the memory of blubbering and pleading for my job too vivid in my head.

Leaving the house that Friday evening, I walk past the bus stop and head to the Finchley Road & Frognail Rail Station instead, Hackney my destination, hoping to catch Mezie before he leaves for work. We've barely spoken this whole week and I believe this has been what even allowed my mind wander and start to fixate on my employer, noticing things about him I have no business noticing. Spending time with my boyfriend should be enough to cure me of whatever silly infatuation I have for Doctor Roman. But the awful episode of two nights ago might just have done that already.

It is a twenty-two-minute ride on the overground train, and when I emerge from the Hackney Central station at 10:39pm, I am completely exhausted. I barely manage the ten-minute walk, trudging up the stairs like I have lead in my boots. As I round the corner of the hallway leading to their apartment, I see a light skinned girl with bright red lipstick walk out the door. She is carrying a bag and I can tell she has been there a while. Our eyes meet as we walk past each other, and I can't help but wonder who she was there to see. In the months since I have been in London, I could have sworn I've met all the women, significant others and otherwise, of Mezie's four flatmates. For some reason I can't explain, seeing this one unsettles me.

"Ah, our wife!" Diran calls out as he opens the door, and I notice his eyes dart down the hallway as if looking for something. "*How you dey?*"

"Good, thanks," I answer in response as I walk in, smiling at Eche and Alex who are sprawled on the couch, the former watching TV and the latter on his phone. "Where is Mezie?"

"Babe, I wasn't expecting you," I hear his voice as he emerges from the bathroom.

I smile at him, relieved he hasn't yet left. With a small towel round his waist and his skin still damp from a shower, he stands tall and sexy, his well-defined chest and biceps commanding attention. With this fine specimen of a man that I can call my own, I have absolutely no business lusting after another.

"You didn't tell me you were coming," he says as we walk into his room.

"I wanted to surprise you," I wink, dropping my bag and getting on the bed. "We barely spoke all week."

He nods. "We were both busy. How's your new job going? The nanny job."

My smile wanes and I decide against telling him all that has happened in the short space of time. "It's okay. The money is okay, so I guess that's all that matters."

"You got that right," he says, wearing his briefs and an undershirt, before buttoning on a crisp white shirt. "It's a Nigerian family, right?"

"Yeah, a Nigerian doctor. He's a single dad."

Mezie glances at me. "A single dad. How old?"

"Early or mid-thirties, I think."

He stops buttoning, his full attention on me. "You didn't tell me that before."

I scoff. Like Doctor Roman would even give me a second glance. "The guy is only Nigerian by name. He's such a snob, and very mean too. I literally count the hours when I'm there. The silver lining is that his daughter is so adorable. She reminds me of Chinasa."

"Who is Chinasa again?"

I frown. "You've forgotten? Chinasa is Lotanna's daughter." Before he further upsets me by forgetting who even Lotanna is, I decide to remind him. "My sister in Ajah."

"Oh yeah."

It's been less than two years and he can't even remember my family members anymore.

"Who was that girl I saw leaving the flat?" I ask.

"What girl?" he asks, slipping on a smart black jacket.

"That light skinned girl wearing a purple and black dress. She had a big bag with her, like she'd been here a few days."

He shrugs. "Probably one of Diran or Alex's visitors."

"*Ehn*, but you should know which, if she was here for so long."

He shrugs again. "There are so many people in and out of this place, I can't even keep up."

Fair enough.

"Do you have to go to work tonight?" I ask, my lips curling in what I hope is a come-hither smile.

He gives me an incredulous look. "I know you didn't just ask that."

Considering I can now comprehend how valuable even a single pound is, I completely understand.

"Wanna come with me?" he asks.

The mere thought of doing anything but curling up in bed makes me exhausted.

"I couldn't even crawl to the living room if you asked me to," I say, stretching on the bed for emphasis. "I'll wait for you."

He nods and reaches for his perfume. As he sprays it, I hear a crinkling sound underneath the pillow. Lifting it, I frown at the sight of a pack of condoms.

"Who owns this?" I demand, inspecting the half-empty box.

"It's for Nedu."

"Why is it under your pillow?"

"Because when I'm at the club, he sleeps on the bed," he retorts. "Or is that a difficult thing to believe? Why would I let him sleep on the floor when the bed is vacant?"

I want to yell that it means Nedu is also having sex on the same bed, but I choose instead to let it go. I didn't come there so late at night to start a quarrel.

Mezie soon leaves for the club and, comforted that Nedu is away with his girlfriend that weekend, I get myself comfortable. I have a bath, slather on some coconut body butter I splurged on from *The Body Shop* and change into a lacy red slip that was also a splurge. Lying on the bed, I wait in anticipation for when Mezie will return.

But it is a long wait as I fall in and out of sleep as I wait for him. He doesn't walk into the room until almost 7am.

"Welcome back," I purr, trying to sound sexy even as sleep fights for prominence.

He grunts something in response before crashing on the bed. By the time I look at him, he's already fast asleep. I tap him on the shoulder, but he doesn't even stir, clearly very tired. I exhale in my disappointment and lie back in bed, hoping my alluring smell or the feel of my moisturised body sheathed with lace will be enough to rouse him, but neither is. By the time it is 8, I have no choice but to accept that it is a failed mission. Hannah, my supervisor at *Poundyard* has approved me for a Saturday shift that day, from 10am to noon, which will give me just about enough time to make it to the Isibor's for 1pm.

Swinging my feet off the bed, I go and have another shower, but this time a less luxurious one. Dressed, with my bag in hand, I cast another look at Mezie's sleeping form. Something just doesn't feel right.

As I journey back to Hendon, and all through my shift, thoughts of the mystery girl and the condoms weigh heavy on my mind. Was she there to see Mezie? And did those condoms belong to him?

It is all I can think of on the bus ride to South Hampstead, and even as I walk down the street headed to the Isibor residence.

Roman

That Saturday, I finally make out the time to hang new wall murals in Luna's room. It has been painted a light pastel pink since we moved here, but after a play date with one of her friends from day care a few months ago, her heart has been set on the *Tinkerbell* decorations that designed her friend's wall. I made the promise to get her the same, and actually did, but haven't had the time to put them up. Until today. With Legachi expected to mind Luna from 1pm till whenever, I have the whole day to myself. Finally.

I am standing on a chair, placing the stickers that go above the window, and I spot her in the far distance. She is walking with her head down, clearly deep in thought. I pause and chuckle as I notice for the first time her walk; part stomp and part strut. I also notice the flare of her hips beneath her jeans.

"There's Legachi over there!" Luna cries, rushing to the window and waving. "Legachi!"

A megawatt smile appears on Legachi's face when she hears Luna's voice, and I am again amazed by how much it transforms her face. She looks up in the direction of Luna's voice, and her smile dims when our eyes meet. She quickly averts her gaze as her pace quickens in the direction of the house. Since the incident the night I tried to fire her, she has tiptoed around me like a mouse, unable to even look me in the eye. As much as I was trying to put my foot down, the last thing I meant to do was frighten her.

Deciding the rest of the mural can go up another time, I step off the chair and head downstairs with Luna.

"Hi. You alright?" I ask, making a point of smiling at her when she walks into the house.

She gives me a quizzical look in return. "I'm fine, thank you. Good afternoon."

"We were upstairs decorating Luna's room," I say, before turning to my daughter. "Weren't we, darling?"

"We were! With *Tinkerbell*!"

"Oh, that's lovely!" she says to Luna, the gap-toothed smile again on her face. "You finally have your *Tinkerbell* room!"

"Let's show her!" Luna says, this time to me.

"In a minute, dear," she answers, before looking up at me, the smile completely gone. "Do you need me to heat up her lunch?"

"We actually just ate. I made us some ham sandwiches," I answer. "So, she's good until tea."

She nods and takes off her jacket.

"How did it go with what you were studying the other day?" I ask, as she's about to walk away, suddenly eager to prolong our conversation. "Was it for a test, a paper, or something like that?"

"A paper," she answers, her brows furrowed.

"Global Supply Chain Management, right?" I ask, surprising myself by remembering her course. "That's impressive. Pretty much every industry has a supply chain, so you can work anywhere."

She nods, not saying anything in response.

"I also worked part time when I was in medical school." God, I'm still rambling. "I had all sorts of jobs back then. I waited tables, delivered pizza, cleaned up after punters at my local. But I kept my eye on the big picture and that was what saw me through. Don't worry, it'll be all worth it in the end"

She nods again. "Thank you." She couldn't be more dismissive if she tried.

"About what you offered the other day," I continue, like someone with absolutely no vocal brakes. "About Luna's meals. You say you bake nice scones, cupcakes and all?"

She nods, those light brown eyes narrowing suspiciously. "Yes."

"Cool. Just let me know what you need, and I'll pop by the shops tomorrow, so we can get you cracking."

I really am not that keen on changing my daughter's meals, but I find myself eager to undo the damage losing my temper the other night has caused.

Uegachi

It feels like I'm in some sort of alternate universe, thrown by his chattiness. I listen as Doctor Roman rambles on, talking about the odd jobs he had in school, but when he accepts my offer to bake and cook for Luna, I brighten.

"That'll be great, thank you," I answer, trying not to smile as wide as I want to, still very cautious in his company. "I'll make the list before I leave today."

He smiles. "Great. Just let me know how much extra you'll charge for it."

"I'd never charge for that," I blurt without even thinking about it first.

He looks at me with a raised brow. *Ehen,* this is the Doctor Roman I know.

"You're sure?"

I hesitate as I think about it, wondering if I'm blowing the opportunity to make some cool extra cash. Cooking is a no-brainer for me, and it would be great to be able to make even more money, solving my financial problems even quicker. But I know my conscience would never allow me to be that much of a shyster.

"My food isn't worth paying that much for," I answer with a nervous laugh. "Besides, it would be my pleasure to do that for Luna."

He smiles again. "Brilliant. Anyway, I'll leave you two while I go have a shower. You're here till 10 tonight, yeah?"

I nod. Like I have a choice. It's what I signed up for, after all.

He turns and heads to the stairs, and I exhale when he's gone, feeling lightheaded. Why does being in his presence make me so nervous? I probably can count how many times I breathed while we were talking. This insane infatuation must end. Shaking my head, I walk over to the living room where Luna has since scurried off to, joining her to watch *Tinga Tinga Tales* on the Cbeebies channel.

We are still watching TV when his perfume announces his return. Headier than his normal one, with stronger aromatic notes, I can't help but wonder if he's going somewhere or seeing someone special. Looking up, in a blue Ralph Lauren shirt tucked into jeans, he looks just as delicious as he smells. I quickly look away. For someone who only a short while ago was worried about her boyfriend cheating, this admiration isn't just inappropriate, it's downright silly and infantile.

"I'll try to be back before 10," he says to me, walking over to where Luna sits and kissing her on the forehead.

I fight off the very many images colliding in my head of what he will be doing the whole time. He is not dressed like he's going to the hospital, that's for sure. My eyes follow him until he's out the door.

Legachi, you are one confused girl!

Roman

Walking out of the house, a glance at my watch confirms I am a few hours too early for the meet up with my friends this evening. But after rambling like a fool, I needed to leave the house, and quickly. Clearly, it's been too long since I was with a woman. That has to be the reason why my daughter's nanny, of all people, is making me feel some type of way. The very thought is an absurdity as she is nothing, absolutely nothing, like the kind of women I go for.

I reach for my phone and scroll through, looking for any number to call for a much-needed hook-up. As I scroll, I hesitate over Itunu's name, but shudder at the thought of calling her. It has been almost two months since our last encounter, and I absolutely do not want to awaken that beast. No, Itunu should remain boxed in the *Never Again* pile. By the time I get to the station, I have not found anyone of interest to call, and resign myself to the reality that there will be no hook-ups tonight.

"Where you at?" I ask, as the line connects with Sean, hoping he doesn't remind me we're not to meet up till 7.

"We're at *Carlsberg*, watching the game," he answers, referring to the sports bar in Leicester Square we occasionally frequent to watch football matches, something I haven't been able to do with them in a long, long while. "We're waiting here till it's time to meet up at *Dirty Martini* later."

"I'm on my way. Is the Leicester City and Burnley game still on?"

"Na, mate," he answers. "That just ended. Goalless, if you can believe those gits. The Crystal Palace, Tottenham game just started."

I grin. Even better.

"I'll be right there," I say, heading in the direction of the southbound Jubilee line trains.

Finally, I am getting my life back!

Twenty minutes later, I walk into the bar just as the second half of the game is starting, and I have a blast laughing with my mates, yelling at the screen and at the Crystal Palace lads who go on to lose the game. But regardless of how much fun I am having, I check my home camera app intermittently, to see what Legachi and Luna are up to. When they are not watching TV, they're playing games and I can't help but smile as they play a game of *Peekaboo*, and also when Legachi pretends to pass out as Luna tickles her, loving to see my daughter laugh so many times in such a short space period. Even when my friends and I set off for *Dirty Martini* later, I can't keep my eyes off my phone, watching Luna and Legachi until they are all played out, seeing the tenderness with which Legachi takes Luna up to have her bath and prepares her for bed. My heart melts at the gentleness with which she tucks her in and, contrary to everything I thought days ago, I realise I couldn't have hired a better nanny.

"You've been looking at your phone all night," Chuka teases, adding a wink. "A new bird?"

"Nah, no new bird," I answer him, a smile still on my face as I watch Legachi turn on the night star lights in Luna's bedroom. "I just struck gold. I hit the nanny jackpot."

Sean's eyes widen. "Another Au-Pair?"

"Way better," I say, as a group of curvy girls, friends of Chuka's from the look of things, approach our table.

The tallest, slimmest one catches my eye and as she leans in for conversation, I set my phone down, all thoughts of Luna and her nanny gone, happy there could be a hook-up tonight after all.

Seventeen

Monikers

Legachi

ou know those condoms probably belonged to him, right,"
Tayo states, as we sit in the coffee shop after our first class on
Monday.

Nonye nods in agreement. "And that girl you saw, I'm sure she
was there to see him."

"Why else would he have been acting clueless when you
mentioned her? Someone that was in the house at the same time he
was?"

I sigh deeply, crushed to hear them echo my suspicions.

"But it's your fault!" Nonye reaches over to smack my arm.
"Why did you move out of that place?"

"Nonye, Hackney isn't exactly next door," Tayo says in my
defense. "Not exactly where she can come and go from."

"*Ehn* but look at *nau*! Now that she lives where she can 'come and go from', see what is happening!" Nonye retorts. "I told you these London girls aren't smiling. Hold your man, Legachi. I've told you before, hold your man!"

Tayo rolls her eyes, and I can see she isn't exactly on the same page as Nonye, but rather than say so, she takes another sip of her coffee.

"And you said he asked you to go with him to the club and you said no?" Nonye continues her rant, clapping her hands in amazement. "In fact, whatever happens, you deserve it."

Tayo nods, looking at me. "Yeah, you should have gone if he asked."

"You better hear word, Legachi," Nonye says, pulling her right ear. "This Friday, even before he asks, you will dress up and go there. Show all those foolish mice that the cat has returned. The owner of the food has come for it."

"True, you need to go," Tayo nods. "We can even go with you for moral support."

I wince. I have never been one for nightclubs at all. But they're right. I have been careless with our relationship and, even though it rankles to think he has cheated on me, I accept that I haven't done enough to make him not. So, reluctantly, I agree to go there on Friday.

Getting to South Hampstead that evening, I am pleased to see Doctor Roman has bought everything I asked for. From flour, to eggs, to white and brown sugar, to fresh tomatoes and peppers, to frozen steak and chicken, everything on my list is there. But when I spot the green bunch of plantains on the counter, I can't help the look of disdain on my face. If I have learnt anything in the two months I have been in this town, it's that you can only get reasonable plantains from African shops that source African produce. I make a mental note to stop at one in Hendon tomorrow.

Footsteps down the stairs let me know Doctor Roman hasn't left for work. I straighten in anticipation of his appearance in the kitchen, feeling less tense about seeing him again. After how chatty he was on Saturday, I am no longer quite as anxious about being in his presence again.

"Good evening," I say, smiling at him.

But he doesn't even look my way. "Hi there," is his distracted answer, as he scrolls through his phone.

I should have known it was too good to last.

"So, I got everything you asked for," he says, finally looking up, but without the smiles and kind eyes from Saturday.

I nod in response. "Thank you."

"I made a sandwich for her tea today, as I reckon it might take a while for you to bake whatever," he says. "Please don't take your eyes off her even while you do."

"Of course."

I watch as he kisses Luna goodbye, a smile on my face as I shake my head. The old Doctor Roman is back.

I set about mixing batter and blending tomatoes, all while keeping a keen eye on Luna. By the time it is 7pm, the scones and cupcakes are baked and cooling, pots of steak stew and *jollof* rice are ready, and the chicken is just out of the oven. After her bath, I tentatively dish Luna a plate of rice and chicken, worried it might be too spicy for her, but I am surprised when she not only eats everything on her plate, but also asks for more. By the time she is done, it is no surprise that she falls asleep even before I take her upstairs, clearly fully sated. Making my way back downstairs, I feel like pumping my fist in triumph, happy that the meal has gone down a treat.

I clean the kitchen spotless and, not knowing whether or not her father will be interested in eating what I made, I proceed to dish the rest of the rice, stew, and chicken into Tupperware containers, stashing the rice in the fridge and the rest in the freezer. I slide the cupcakes and scones into the fridge, more than satisfied with everything I have achieved today.

Maybe I should have charged him after all.

Roman

I'm so tired when I get home, I am barely able to respond properly to Legachi's greeting. It isn't until she's gone that I remember she was supposed to have cooked something for Luna's dinner and wonder how it all went.

Walking into the kitchen, it is as bare and sparkling clean as it was before I dumped all her requested groceries there. It almost makes me think she changed her mind about cooking... almost. The lingering smell of cooked tomatoes is enough of an indicator that some cooking did go down in that space. I smile at the memory of that smell, remembering how it was what I needed to know my mother was about to throw it down in the kitchen. Opening the fridge, I see, first the cupcakes and scones, and then the Tupperware bowls of rice. Out of curiosity, I take a cupcake and bite into it, pleasantly surprised by the delightful confection, rich and moist, with a vanilla and strawberry flavour that feels hearty and solid. My interest piqued, I reach for one of the Tupperware containers of rice, grab a spoon and take a mouthful. Despite it being cold, the melody of the fiery flavours in my mouth, the perfect blend of spice and heat, is enough to make me do a happy dance, taking me way back to the kind of food I ate as a kid when visiting relatives, and not the gentrified version of *jollof* rice people of my generation now make. I dish a generous portion to a plate, take a couple more cupcakes, and sit there in the kitchen for a nice, hearty meal, the best I have had in a long time.

I am home the next day when Legachi and Luna walk through the front door.

"Compliments to the chef for yesterday's meal," I remark, with a small salute. "It was a spectacular spread."

Her face, her whole face, lights up with a smile that goes all the way to her eyes. "Really?"

I nod and chuckle, surprised she looks genuinely shocked to hear it. "Really."

"I was surprised Luna liked it so much. She cleared her plate and asked for more!"

I laugh. "Yeah, I have my mom to thank for teaching her the joys of spicy food. If it's not burning the tongue, my mother isn't satisfied."

She laughs and I see she is more at ease than she was on Saturday. I notice the bag in her hand.

"The plantains I got were rubbish, right?"

"Just not what would have tasted nice," she smiles, setting the bag on the counter. "I had to get these from a market near my apartment."

"Yeah, those definitely look a lot better," I remark, as she pulls out the fleshy, spotted yellow tubes. "Luna loves them, so she might like them for dinner."

"You read my mind."

"I'll be home today," I say as she makes for the kitchen. "I want to catch up on a bit of reading, and I don't feel like going to the library. I hope I won't be in your way."

Legachi

He says this with a cheeky grin, and I almost laugh at the very insinuation. In my way how? In his own house? I manage a smile in response and, thankfully, Luna calling out to him from where she has already settled herself in the living room, in front of the TV, soon distracts him.

I make my way to the kitchen to heat up some scones and as I return to sit with her, I remain all too aware of his presence, even when he has returned to his study. His perfume is lighter than what he wore on Saturday, but its vanilla and cinnamon notes hang in the air long after he has left. I try to remain focused on episodes of *Clangers* and *In The Night Garden* but fail miserably. Intermittently, his voice reverberates from the study as he talks on the phone, and anytime he laughs, I find myself wondering who he is speaking to, imagining a beautiful, leggy woman like the one whose picture is scattered all over the house. My eyes wander to the large portrait of the doctor and his late wife, and I am surprised by the overwhelming feeling of inadequacy I feel as her perfect face stares back at me.

This is madness.

It is soon 7pm and I am grateful for the chance to break away from Doctor Roman's intimidating presence as I take Luna upstairs for her bath. Back downstairs, I settle her in the living room and go to the kitchen to make her dinner. The busier I keep myself, the less likely my brain is likely to wander. Rather than fixate on whom he is or isn't talking to on the phone, I should be more focused on fixing things with my own man.

Roman

The smell of frying plantain lures me out of the study. Luna is watching TV when I peer into the living room, and when I walk into the kitchen, Legachi has her back to me as she spoons fried plantains from the pan to a waiting colander. My eyes are drawn to the curve of her hips, more pronounced than ever in an ash grey fitted jersey dress. Even though her waist isn't particularly narrow, hers is almost a perfect hourglass figure. The ping of the microwave jolts me, and I quickly look away.

"Oh, I didn't hear you come in," she says, smiling when she sees me.

"The smell of plantain shut my brain down." And it's the truth.

She smiles as she dishes leftover *jollof* rice to Luna's plate. "I never would have placed you as a plantain lover, Doctor Roman. You don't even look like someone who eats Nigerian food."

"Are you kidding? That's what I grew up on," I remark, sitting on one of high stools by the kitchen island. "Plantains are the best thing in the world."

She nods and smiles, forking the fried plantain to Luna's plate. "They sure are." Then looking up at me, she asks. "Should I dish you a plate as well?"

"Yes, please."

I watch her as she reaches above for a plate, and as she proceeds to dish me a plate as well, noticing the same freckles on her hand as the ones on her nose. She hands me the plate and then goes to the living room with Luna's, settling her in her highchair there, where she insists on eating if she likes what's showing on TV.

"You should also dish yourself a plate," I say to her when she returns to the kitchen.

She casts me a wary look and I almost think she will decline, but a slow smile forms on her face. "I won't say no. Thank you."

She dishes herself a small fraction of what she served me and takes the high stool opposite me. "This angle gives me the best view of Luna over there."

"She's fine. You and I are no match for *Sofia the First*," I chuckle and I am enamored when she laughs as well. I don't think I have ever heard her laugh before. It sounds like a child's. Almost musical.

We eat in silence before I ask her. "Why do you always call me Doctor Roman?"

She stops eating for a second, before shrugging. "It's the right thing to do to address you by your title."

"Not unless we're at the hospital or you're one of my gushing relatives, ever proud to boast about having a doctor in the family," I smile. "Roman will do nicely."

There is a look of uncertainty on her face, but she finally smiles and nods in acquiescence.

"Can I ask you something?" she asks, after a few minutes. "And please, don't hesitate to let me know if I'm overstepping."

Now, my interest is piqued.

"What happened to your wife?"

Aha. The million-dollar question.

"My wife, Sekani was her name, is dead. Cervical cancer."

She shakes her head, her empathy evident. "I'm really sorry about that. That must have been devastating for you."

I shrug, not wanting to be submerged with the grief that comes when I talk about Sekani's illness and subsequent death. "Yeah, it was."

"Sekani, that's such a beautiful name," she remarks, after a brief pause. "Where was she from?"

"Malawi."

"That doesn't surprise me. She was a real exotic beauty. Was she a model or something?"

"She was a doctor, actually. We met in Med School."

"You don't say!" she exclaims, and I chuckle at the reminder of the mistake people commonly made when Sekani was alive and the look of surprise on their faces when they found out the truth.

She is quiet for a few seconds, as if contemplating her next question. "What inspired the name Luna?"

"It was the name Sekani picked for her daughter as far back as when she was a little girl. It's the Latin word for moon, and she always associated it with beauty."

"It's a beautiful name… and she's a beautiful little girl."

"Speaking of names," I say, leaning forward on my elbows. "Yours is pretty unique as well. I've heard a lot of Nigerian names but I never heard that one."

"It means 'look at God'," she answers. "I'm the youngest of five girls, so I don't know if my parents meant that in awe of God, or if they were just plain angry with Him."

I let out a loud chortle, not having seen that coming. "I'm sure the last thing they were doing was wagging an angry finger at God when they named you."

"By the fifth girl, the average Nigerian man would," she chuckles in response. "What about you? Roman. Is that short for Romanus?"

"That might have actually been easier to explain as a kid," I laugh. "My dad, my late dad, was really random with our names. He says he named me Roman because it's supposed to mean strong and powerful in ancient Hebrew. But he went on to name my younger brothers Reagan and Kennedy, and my sister, Paris. So yeah, very random."

She smiles and crosses her arms in her interest. "He must have been a very interesting man. Did he grow up here?"

"Nope. He came here in his 30s so was already very set in his stubborn, patriarchal ways. And don't be fooled, choosing our names was the only 'exotic' thing about him. He was a typical Edo man and raised us with a very firm hand," I answer, nostalgic over my father's memory. "Back then, I thought he was mean and awful, but in hindsight, I'm grateful for it. Growing up in Harlow, if it hadn't been for his discipline, God knows how I would have turned out."

She raises an inquisitive brow and I smile.

"Harlow is supposed to be the roughest, most dangerous part of England. Growing up as a black boy there, I very easily could have ended up a different person. My dad died when I was 16, and not a day goes by that I'm not sad he didn't get to see me become the man I am now."

"I'm sure he's proud of you, wherever he is," she remarks, her eyes glistening. "I'm sure they both are. Is your mother still alive?"

I smile, warding off my own rising emotions. "Yeah, my old girl is still very much around. She lives in Essex. Chelmsford to be precise. As soon as we were able to, my siblings and I moved her out of Harlow and got her a house there."

"Is she... " she seems to hesitate with this question.

But I already have an idea what she wants to ask. It's a question I am still asked a lot.

"Is she Nigerian?" I complete for her. "One hundred percent. She's just really light skinned."

She nods, the slight furrow of her brows showing she is still grappling to accept my answer. And she wouldn't be the first. For as long as I can remember, my naturally wavy hair, especially, has always had people questioning my racial combination.

"I'm sure she brags about you like no man's business," she says, smiling. "Your parents did a great job with you, Doctor Roman."

"It's Roman, Legachi."

Our eyes hold and her light brown eyes remind me of a blend of wood and the brightest summer sun, like polished amber in the first rays of dawn.

"Your parents did a great job with you, Roman," she says. "Just like you're doing a wonderful job with Luna."

Her words are enough to make me snap out of my trance. Yes, I am doing a wonderful job with Luna, one that doesn't involve flirting with her minder. I reach for my phone, and she takes that as her cue to rise and clear the table.

As she loads the dish washer, I return to the study, wondering why on earth I let my guard down like that. I hear her carry a sleeping Luna to her bedroom and I remain in the study until she knocks on the door, announcing her departure. I return her farewell greeting without even opening the door, remaining there long after I'm sure she's left. But even as I try to return my attention to the journal I'm reading, I chuckle intermittently as I remember our discussion, surprised that she has such a mischievous sense of humour.

And lying in bed later that night, as I remember her twinkling eyes and disarming smile, I realize one thing.

I am fascinated by her.

Legachi

Walking to the bus stop, I can't wipe the smile off my face as I think about the conversation with Doctor Roman... Roman. Apart from it being the most words he has ever said to me, I am intrigued by the part of himself he has shared, the part of being the son of working-class Nigerians who did all they could to make sure he turned out right. It is such a far cry from the mindless snob I'd thought him to be, and I almost feel guilty for ever seeing him that way. All through the bus ride, I laugh when I remember something he said, or how he ate the meal I made with undisguised gusto. I am still laughing as I walk up the stairs leading to Alero's apartment, stopping only to reach for my ringing phone. The laughter evaporates when I see the name on the caller ID.

Mezie.

My faces flushes in my guilt, guilty about the reminder of the person, the only person, that should be tickling my fancy like that. Grateful for the prompt, I answer the call.

"Hey, babe."

"Babe, how now?" comes Mezie's sleepy voice. "I said I should call you, so you won't complain the way you were complaining last Saturday."

I smile. "I wasn't complaining. I was just sad we don't get to talk often."

"Well, I'm not working tonight, so this is me calling. I had to wait till 10, since you said that's when you get off work."

"That was very thoughtful of you," I answer, smiling. This is more like it. Maybe if we talk more often, we won't start to disconnect to the point that I start noticing men I shouldn't. "Hey, I was thinking of coming to your club this Friday."

"Oh yeah? That'll be great! I'd like that very much. I can't wait to introduce you to all my mates there."

Beaming, I let myself into the apartment.

Roman who?

Eighteen

Liquid Nitrogen

Roman

I glance at my watch as I step on to the platform from the train. It is 9:53pm on Friday night and I'll get home just in time for Legachi to leave at 10, which is exactly how I've timed it all week. After over-sharing on Monday, I've tried to put as much distance between us as possible. I blame the aroma of fresh plantain and that enticing *jollof* rice for my loose tongue and mush brain. Eyes like the summer sun indeed! I shake my head and chuckle. What a load of bollocks!

Getting to the house, as I let myself in, I prepare myself for her muted greeting and prompt exit. She has been just as willing as me to keep some distance between us, and that has been just as well.

But walking in, I am surprised to see her standing there, dressed in a fitted black velour turtleneck top tucked into fitted blue jeans. She has a full face of makeup, complete with bright red lipstick, and her braids even look passable in a topknot. One thing's for sure; she definitely isn't dressed like that to watch Luna.

"I see you're out on the town tonight," I remark, unable to help the smile that forms on my face. This girl is full of surprises. Never in my wildest dreams would I have pictured her the type who hits the town on a Friday night.

She smiles, looking at me for the first time in days. I notice how even more pronounced the gap in her teeth is beneath the fiery red lipstick and think, once again, how nice she looks when she smiles.

"Something like that," is her scant answer.

Ah well, it really isn't any of my business.

"Do you need me here tomorrow?" she asks as she slips on that ridiculous looking thick jacket of hers.

I shake my head. "Nah, I'm expecting my sister any minute. She'll be here with us this weekend."

My younger sister, Paris, is in London after weeks on a project in Dundee. She is a freelance videographer and has been working on a documentary with an Indie filmmaker, who also doubles as her boyfriend. Come to think of it, she should have gotten here by now.

"Okay then. Have a good weekend," Legachi says, smiling again as she opens the door and walks out.

I hesitate to shut it behind her, watching her stomp this time to the train station and not the bus stop. I see she is wearing heeled boots instead of the trainers she typically does, and I can't help but wonder what exactly she'll be doing that night... and with whom. I shake my head to brush off those recalcitrant thoughts. Whatever she does is absolutely none of my business.

My phone rings as I lock the door.

"Where you at?" comes Sean's voice. "We're waiting for you."

"Don't get your knickers in a twist! I literally just walked through the door," I chuckle. "I need at least an hour to shower and get ready. Besides, Paris is meant to watch Luna and she isn't here yet."

"Just get yourself over here. If you don't get here in fifteen minutes, you'll have to meet us at Shoreditch."

"Why all the way over there?" I exclaim, not believing they want to go all the way across town for a few pints. "I can't guarantee I can come all that way."

"Oh, don't be such a knob!" Sean retorts. "Dotun says there's a great place near his place and he wants us to check it out."

I frown, my interest in hanging out diminishing with every word. It's bad enough I'm already exhausted after a long week. As I don't like to use public transport when I'm out late, I shudder at the thought of driving forty-five-minutes just to check out a new club.

"No worries. See you soon," I say, more to get Sean off the phone than anything.

With the call disconnected, I head to the kitchen and smile when I see refilled Tupperware containers of *jollof* rice. Legachi must have made a fresh batch that evening. Dishing a generous portion to a plate along with some stewed chicken, I sit at the kitchen island, happy to tuck into a good meal and probably retire to bed shortly afterwards.

The doorbell rings before I can even take my first forkful.

"I'm so sorry!" Paris exclaims, when I open the door. "We got into London at 2 this afternoon but Declan has been dragging me all over town checking out camera lights. Apparently, we'll need to fill lots of shadows when we start filming in Bath next month."

I smile as I let my sister into the house. Typical Paris, ever talkative, never allowing anyone get a word in edgeways. With only two years between us, we grew up very close and have grown closer still as adults. Physically though, we couldn't be more different, as she is the only one of us four who got our father's stocky build and dark colouring. Standing an inch taller than me, even though she looks intimidating, she has the heart of an angel.

"Oh my days, is that *jollof* rice?" she asks, racing to my plate as she walks into the kitchen. Without asking, she takes a forkful and looks at me wide-eyed. "This is amazing! Where'd you buy it?"

"Luna's nanny made it," I beam, more than happy to take credit for it. "I got a Nigerian nanny."

"Get in!" Paris exclaims, wide eyes even wider still. "And she cooks? Tell me there's more of this rice where it came from."

"There's loads in the fridge. She bakes too."

She is soon sifting through my fridge and grabs the Tupperware container I have just dished from and a tray of still-warm pound cake.

"I thought you'd be dressed and ready to be out the door when I got here," she remarks, popping an overflowing plate into the microwave. "It's almost 11. You're not going out with the boys tonight? You're not going to take advantage of me being here to go get sloshed with your mates?"

"They want to go all the way to East London," I mutter, returning to the island. "There's no way I'm going to drive all that way to go to some dodgy club."

"Don't be such a snob!" she cackles, smacking me on the arm. "If your mates want to go there, then you should go with them. You're only young once, and I know you haven't been able to get out much recently."

Her words give me cause to rethink. Apart from having a few beers, it has been a long time since I've been able to properly hit the clubs with my friends. So what, if the one they want to go to tonight wouldn't exactly be my first choice? It's all about the camaraderie, isn't it?

"Okay, you convinced me," I say, reaching for my plate. "But not until after I finish my meal."

As we tuck into our plates of *jollof* rice, hers steaming hot and mine now tepid, she tells me stories of her filmmaking adventure in Scotland.

Legachi

I am a bit unsettled as I walk down the street in the direction of Finchley Road Station, disconcerted after the short exchange with Roman. After making up my mind to stay focused on Mezie and not giving in to any schoolgirl fantasies about my employer, I was glad that Roman also went back to being his cold, unfriendly self; not home when Luna got back from day care, returning minutes, sometimes even seconds, before I was to leave. Even though sometimes I would wonder if I'd imagined our chat on Monday, wondering if my overactive imagination hadn't just conjured it all, other times, I was just happy he hadn't continued with the anomaly that was his friendliness. Because if he had, I'm not sure how easy it would have been to keep my mind focused on Mezie. And this evening was evidence of that; one smile from him and I already had knots in my stomach.

This weekend, Mezie is going to remind me why he is the one, the *only* one, my heart should beat for. I'm going to make damn sure of that. Starting with hanging with him at his club tonight, this weekend, our love will be re-ignited, so help me God.

But all that is forgotten when I get off the westbound Metropolitan train at Liverpool Street, and immediately spot Nonye and Tayo, dressed to the nines and there to support me. A wide smile breaks on my face. Maybe tonight won't be that bad after all.

"Na wa o! Aren't you cold?" I exclaim, as I take in their skimpy outfits; a leather jumpsuit and a flimsy sequined jacket for Nonye, and a tiny black dress with fishnet tights for Tayo. Beside them, I could pass for their chaperone or, worse, mother.

"It's not that cold," Tayo says, putting out her cigarette. "Wait another few weeks and you'll see cold."

"Me, I'm cold *o*, but I know the sight of fine, sexy men at that club will warm me up!" Nonye hoots, interlinking her arm with mine as we make our way out of the station.

"What about your fiancé in Nigeria?" I just have to ask.

"E dey there na," she grins. "But just the way he dey catch im fun, me sef go catch my own!"

Okay then.

It is a ten-minute walk and, even though we are talking and laughing as Nonye imitates some of our course mates, it is a struggle for me to endure the biting cold and the ache in my ankles from the heels I am no longer used to wearing. But as we approach the club, *Liquid Nitrogen*, and I spot Mezie at the entrance screening people as they file in, looking handsome in his black suit, I'm so proud I want to burst.

"That's him," I declare to my friends, loving the wide-eyed looks on their faces as they take in my sexy, bodybuilder-looking man. I'll bet they didn't think he'd be that hot.

"And this is the man *you dey take do yeye!*" Nonye replies in a stage whisper. "Are you serious at all?"

"Mezie!" I call out to him, waving from where we stand on the pavement.

He looks in our direction and smiles when he sees me, beckoning us over. I beam as we cut the long queue but the smile on my face starts to wane when I see a frown has taken over his.

"You wore a turtleneck?" he retorts when we walk up to him. "You wore a turtleneck to a nightclub? Did you think you were going to church or what? Do you think this is Nigeria? Even in Nigeria, you wouldn't wear this nonsense. It's your first time here, and you decided it would be best to make a fool of me?"

Nonye and Tayo exchange a glance and I'm so embarrassed, I want the ground to open and swallow me whole.

"You know I have a problem with the cold, Mezie," I manage to answer.

"She looks amazing!" Tayo quickly comes to my rescue. "See how the top and jeans emphasise this banging body of hers."

"As in!" Nonye jumps in. "*She set die!*"

Mezie shrugs and pushes us through the barricade. "Go in and ask for Lateef. He'll sort you out."

And with that, he returns his attention to the burgeoning queue. My heart is heavy as I walk behind Nonye and Tayo, in search of this Lateef who'll 'sort us out'. So much for wanting to spend the evening all loved up with my man. Tayo soon spots the guy, and we are soon led to a section slightly elevated from the common side. The room is a rainbow of lights, and the music is so loud, it sounds like a heartbeat on a loudspeaker. I take one look in the direction of the door and see a buxom redhead whispering something in Mezie's ear. He laughs at whatever she says, prompting her to wink at him. I search his face for some sign that he is merely tolerating the flirtation for the sake of the job, but if his dancing eyes and wide grin are anything to go by, he is enjoying it very much indeed.

Lateef brings us glasses of gin and tonic, and sets a bottle of whisky on the table.

"If you need anything, let me know," he smiles at us, his accent unmistakably Nigerian, giving me some more comfort.

"Not bad," Tayo remarks, looking around.

"What?" I shout back, the music making it impossible for me to hear her.

She gives me a thumbs-up sign and a forced smile, and I am not naïve enough not to know she is only doing it for my sake. She rises to her feet, glass in hand, dancing to the Davido song, *Fia*, that's playing. Nonye soon starts to bob her head as she sings along.

I look around. Even with the mix of people there, I can see that it is, if not Nigerian, an African set up. The waiters and bouncers all have the set look in their eyes of people desperate to make their way in a new country, and the DJ seems hell bent on reliving his Lagos memories, playing Naija hits back-to-back. I watch the excited people dancing, their hands in the air and their faces almost masked by the blinding strobe lights, moving their bodies like uncoiled rope. The dance floor is no longer visible, with people literally dancing wall to wall. The atmosphere is electric and menacing at the same time. I cast another desperate look in the direction of the door, wishing Mezie would come to spend time with me. I have never liked nightclubs and, only minutes in, I already hate this experience just as much.

Without warning, the DJ switches to breakneck house music, but his crowd doesn't seem to mind, their dancing picking up a frenetic pace. I imagine what Chineme would say if she were to behold this crowd, and the imagery of her casting and binding the heathens is enough to make me smile. I look again in the direction of the door, and I still when I see the person walking in.

What the hell is Roman doing here?

My mouth goes dry at the sight of him strutting in like he owns the place. He walks towards the VIP section, his eyes scanning the room like he's looking for someone. Try as I may, I am unable to look away. In a black shirt molded to his body like a second skin and fitted jeans that show off a nicely shaped ass I've never noticed before, he is every shade of sexy there is in the book.

"You know him?" Nonye leans in to ask, noticing how long I have been looking his way.

"That's my boss," I answer, smiling at the incredulousness of it all. Here I am, trying to spend time with my boyfriend, but undressing another, my employer for that matter, with my eyes.

Nonye's widen. "That fine man is your boss?" she exclaims, making Tayo's head spin in that direction, her brows shooting up in appreciation. "No wonder you don't mind going there seven days a week!"

Roman

I'm getting too old for nightclubs.

This is what I think as I meander through the sea of people dancing without a care in the world, dodging limbs as they fly around. This club in particular is rowdier and noisier than I like, and I again curse under my breath, wondering why on earth my friends have decided to meet here, of all places.

As my eyes continue to scan the room, they collide with a familiar pair of light brown ones. My brows knot as I squint, certain my mind is playing tricks on me.

What on earth is Legachi doing in a place like this?

Legachi

I swallow as we make eye contact. I see him squint, as if unsure of what he's beholding, and I realize we have passed the stage of pretending not to have seen each other. We might as well get the uncomfortable greetings over with.

Rising to my feet, I force a smile as I walk in his direction. He is already doing the same and walking in mine.

"Hiya," I say with an awkward wave when I reach him. "Fancy seeing you here."

"Fancy seeing *you* here," he smiles. "So, this is where you were headed to all dressed up. You come here often?"

I shake my head. "It's my first time. My boyfriend works here." I point in the direction of the door. Mezie by now is looking our way. "That's him."

Roman

I look in the direction of her finger and I am taken aback when I see the tall, muscular guy who let me into the place. Her boyfriend is the bouncer? She is dating a club bouncer?

The guy is now walking towards us, and I feel an alien anger building inside me, disappointed this is the kind of man she would go for... disappointed this is the kind of girl she is. I realize I have subconsciously put her on a pedestal, one she clearly doesn't deserve. The guy walks up to us and slips a protective arm around her, a visible frown on his face as our eyes meet. The feeling is mutual, bruv!

"Babe, this is my boss, Doctor Roman Isibor," Legachi says to the guy. "Roman, this is my boyfriend, Mezie."

Boyfriend. Everything about that word coming from her mouth has just blown my mind.

The Mezie's frown deepens for a split second before it is replaced by a tight smile. "It's good to meet you," he offers me his hand in a firm handshake. "I've heard a lot about you."

I can only offer a taut smile of my own, unable to lie in reciprocation. Apart from having heard nothing about him, I wouldn't say meeting him is exactly a pleasure.

"You come here often?" he asks, trying to make conversation.

"Um, no. I'm only here this one time," this one and only time, "to meet up with my mates." My eyes light up when I spot Sean, Chuka, Yash and Dotun sitting a few paces away, their table already littered with several bottles of champagne. Now *that* is where I should be, not witnessing the spectacle that is my child's nanny loved up with her bouncer boyfriend. "That's them over there. I better go join them."

With a curt nod, I walk away, heaving a sigh of relief as I do. But as I approach my friends, and as they scream and yell my name in their happiness to see me, I wonder why I am still a little pissed off.

Legachi

I am disappointed watching him walk away. What did I think he was going to do? Join us? Form an immediate bromance with Mezie? I look in the direction of the party he has joined, the well-dressed men surrounded by gorgeous women, and I am immediately reminded what his natural habitat is. *That* is his crowd. *That* is his natural habitat.

"You didn't tell me the guy is that young," Mezie retorts next to me.

I frown at him. "Don't be funny. I told you he's in his early or mid-thirties."

"He looks like a cad," he mutters, looking in the direction of Roman and his friends. "What's with those tight clothes and jerry curls? Is he gay or what?"

It is at the tip of my tongue to tell him Roman's hair is naturally wavy, his fitted clothes are *hella* sexy, and there's nothing remotely homosexual about him. But I decide against it.

"He's so cocky. Did you notice how he was feeling himself?" Mezie is still muttering. "All these *Mandem* guys that have touched small money and think they're better than everyone else."

Mandem? Dude is a doctor! Rather than give him this reminder, I just shake my head and allow him to lead me back to our table.

As the night wears on, the alcohol soon loosens me up and I am soon dancing uninhibited with Nonye and Tayo. Mezie makes several trips to our table to check on us, and on one of those times, pulls me up to dance with him. As we dance to *Lights, Camera, Action* by Mr. Cheeks, I look in Roman's direction. He is dancing with one of the gorgeous women in his group; a slim, tall one with skin so light, I can't tell if she's just fair, mixed race or even Caucasian. She has her hands crossed around his neck and his are around her slender hips as she shakes them provocatively against his. They are whispering into each other's ears intermittently, and the intimacy incenses me. I quickly look away, but my eyes are drawn back to them several times.

And then he looks at me.

Roman

I am dancing with one of the girls Dotun has invited over and she is more enthusiastic than is necessary. She has her hands around my neck, fluttering ridiculously long lashes at me. I smile politely back, wondering how soon will be too soon to make a quick getaway. She is whispering something I can't hear and as I crane my head closer to hear her, my eyes land on Legachi and her bouncer boyfriend. She has her back to him, twerking, and the visual makes me clench my jaw in anger. So, I put my hands around the waist of my own dancing companion, determined to get into the groove of things, just as Legachi has clearly done with her boyfriend.

Looking away, I don't discourage my companion as she presses her hips into mine. On the contrary, I whisper to her to repeat what she said earlier, and chuckle when she repeats her suggestion for us to leave for somewhere quiet. As if pulled by an invisible force, my eyes return across the room to where Legachi and her boyfriend are dancing.

And our eyes meet.

Legachi

I turn away and put my arms around Mezie's waist, dancing with more gusto than I ever have. Not even when he is distracted by his friends do I relent, pushing his face back to mine anytime he looks away, wanting Doctor Roman to see that I too can dance flirtatiously with my significant other.

Roman

She now has her back to me, and I am unable to look away as she dances, as her rounded hips sway from side to side, and I am surprised, angered… and aroused by her display. The realization of the last feeling forces me to look away, stunned by the realization that the hardening of my member has nothing to do with the woman I am dancing with, but the one who has succeeded in stealing all my attention that night.

The fuck!

How can my child's nanny be giving me a hard-on? It's time to get the hell out of this place.

My eyes catch Sean's, and he recognizes the lift of my brow. Thankfully, he nods and gestures in Dotun's direction. It's time to blow out of this joint.

Legachi

I watch, crestfallen, as Roman and his friends file out of the club. I am disappointed he has left with not even a goodbye. He is walking hand in hand with the light-skinned woman, and I fight off vivid images of him taking her back to the house, taking her to his room, and them continuing their very sensual dance... but in an even more sensual way.

I hiss under my breath as I return my attention to Mezie, and when he has to return to man the door, I focus on my friends who are by now having the time of their lives; Nonye giggling and laughing on a bearded man's lap and Tayo with a glass of Hennessy in one hand and a lit cigarette in the other, as she dances solo. Smiling, I join her, and as we dance, I force all thoughts about Roman and his companion to the back of my mind.

Nineteen

Strictly Business

Roman

We head only ten-minutes away to a club in Farringdon, one that is less rowdy and more like the ones I am used to. I have been able to shake off my long-lashed companion from the club at Shoreditch but sitting at the bar in the company of another even more gorgeous one, I am struggling to stay focused on what she is saying. Having driven, I am cautious about the amount of alcohol I drink, but as I continue to struggle with vivid images of Legachi and her bouncer boyfriend, all I want to do is numb myself with alcohol.

"You seem distracted," the girl I'm with remarks.

I shake my head, more to banish my wayward thoughts than to deny her statement. Taking another look at her, I wonder what is wrong with me. Tall and thin like I like them, with skin the same colour as Sekani's, a rich chocolate brown, and wavy hair I can tell is all hers, flowing all the way to her back, I sit up, forcing myself to be interested. There just might be something here.

"I'm sorry, I didn't quite get your name," I call out, leaning forward such that my cheek brushes hers, allowing me to inhale her peach and caramel aroma.

She giggles, leaning forward to answer, her cheek also brushing mine. "Fawzia."

"That's a Somali name, isn't it?" I ask, further intrigued... and relieved. The last thing I need that night is an encounter with yet another Nigerian girl.

She beams and nods, impressed I have made that deduction. We continue to chat, and I am already hoping she lives alone and will be able to invite me back to her flat with her.

"Roman Isibor!"

I look up as two girls walk up to us. I frown, trying to make out whom they are, but realization sets in too late as they both proceed to empty their glasses of wine on me.

"*Yeye* man!" one of the mutters through grit teeth.

"Goat!" the other chimes in, rolling her eyes at me before they both hiss and walk off, leaving my companion and I staring after them, stunned.

I rise to my feet, pointlessly using my hands to wipe my face dry. It has been a long time since I've had this kind of encounter and I was naïve to think enough time had passed to make them.

"Wow! Are you that much of a cad? You must be a real heartbreaker," Fawzia laughes, her eyes shining in what looks to be amusement... and heightened interest.

Alas, my own interest has diminished. I have to get out of there... and fast.

"It was nice meeting you," I say, offering a regretful smile before turning around and making my way out of the packed club.

Sitting in my car, I start texting Sean to let him know I've decided to leave early, when my phone vibrates with an incoming message.

God punish you, Roman. You haven't heard the last of me. I will make sure you pay for what you've done.

My jaw clenches and a lethal mix of anger and agitation starts to bubble in me. One thing I'm not going to take is anyone making threats, especially not someone as vile as this.

If you try any funny business, I type back, an angry thumb flying across my keyboard, **I'll get you arrested wherever you are. Try me.**

I glare at the phone after hitting the *send* button, daring the person to reply.

Watch your back is the response that soon drops.

This is the most direct message I have received, and it succeeds in leaving me shaken. My hand is quivering as I block the number, the first I've had to do in several months, all thoughts of Fawzia, Legachi, or anyone else, pushed to the back of my mind.

Legachi

I shut my eyes in the bus headed to Swiss Cottage to pick Luna up from daycare, cringing at the memory of my shameless display on Friday night. All weekend, I've felt sick thinking of coming face-to-face with Roman again after behaving like a total hussy, bumping and winding on Mezie like a sex-starved animal, all the while brazenly looking his way. He must think me a total tramp, and he wouldn't be blamed for it. I can only hope that, like last week, we hardly see each other, so I can salvage whatever is left of my dignity.

But alas, as I approach Cheryl's house, he is the first person I see, standing at the door, his face set like stone. This is going to be even harder than I thought.

"Good evening," I say, dropping my eyes, unable to look at him.

"You and Luna aren't to take the bus home anymore," he answers, not even bothering with any cordialities. "From now on, you'll use a taxi."

My brows furrow in my confusion. "A taxi? It's barely a ten-minute bus drive."

But he says nothing in response to me, instead walking into the house as Cheryl opens the door. I watch as he exchanges pleasantries with her and as his face lights up when he sees Luna. He carries her, taking her bag with his free hand, and walks past me as I stand there in a daze.

What on earth is going on?

Quickening my pace, I follow them, smiling at Luna as she smiles at me from her father's shoulder. When I see him walk up to a parked Vauxhall Vectra with tinted windows, and as we all file into it, I realize he isn't joking at all.

"This is Raafe," he says, as the car makes its way down the street. "He'll be here waiting for you every day."

The Raafe waves and smiles at me through his rearview mirror and I force myself to reciprocate, still feeling like someone having an out-of-body experience, wondering what could have brought on this unprecedented change. Surely, not my dancing from Friday night?

I decide I'm not going to wallow in my confusion and that I deserve to have answers.

"What's going on, Roman?" I ask, after Luna has dashed into the living room upon our return. "Having a taxi bring us home every day makes no sense. Apart from it being a ridiculously short distance, it's an unnecessary waste of money."

"I think I can decide what's a necessary or unnecessary use of my money, don't you think? My daughter's wellbeing takes top priority," is his icy answer. "And when you're home, under no circumstance whatsoever are you to take Luna anywhere. For no reason at all is she to even step out of the door. Have I made myself clear?"

I stare back at him, speechless. What has come over him?

"Have I made myself clear?" he repeats, his voice several octaves higher.

I swallow down the lump that is forming in my throat and blink twice to force back the tears that are threatening to fall. "Yes, you have."

Roman

I immediately feel guilty about yelling at her, especially when I see her eyes water. But as she excuses herself to go make Luna's tea, my indignation returns. I don't owe anyone any explanations, especially not her. Apart from keeping Luna safe, my opinion of her has been tainted. Gone is the innocent, wholesome girl I thought she was. After seeing her with her bouncer boyfriend, I have realised she is no different from the other opportunistic Nigerian girls on the streets of London.

"I'm frying eggs for Luna's dinner. Eggs and plantain," comes her voice as I turn around to return to the hospital. "Should I make some for you as well?"

I'll be damned if she uses food to enchant me like she did the last time. "I'll get something to eat at work."

And with that, I slam the door shut. From now on, with her, it will be strictly business.

Twenty

The Party

DECEMBER 2018

Legachi

It is another Friday night, and I am, yet again, sitting down in *Liquid Nitrogen's* VIP section, alone and cold as an Eskimo. After the first two times, Nonye and Tayo stopped accompanying me, but I have had to keep coming, in what has now been defined as my duty as Mezie's girlfriend. But I might as well not even be here, considering that he hardly ever even looks my way. After dumping me in the VIP section, when he's not manning the door, he's hobnobbing with the club's patrons, women mostly.

Fatman Scoop's *Be Faithful* is blasting at full volume from the speakers and the pulsating lights are giving me a headache. I rub desperate hands on my bare shoulders, willing myself warm. Tonight, like all the nights after that first time, I am in a skimpy top Nonye has picked out for me, considering they all think this kind of dressing more appropriate for clubbing. The irony is that the skimpier my own clothes have gotten over the weeks, the more clothed the other female club patrons now seem to be. Today, the first Friday in December, I'm pretty sure I'm the only one dressed this sparsely.

I look across the packed room and see Mezie sitting at a table with a mixed-race girl. She says something that he appears to find funny, and he throws his head back in throaty laughter. I purse my lips. How long am I going to continue like this? I wave at him, hoping to catch his attention. After trying hard not to look my way, he finally does, a small frown creasing his face. Undeterred, I beckon him over. He returns his attention to his friend, lingers for another few minutes, before finally rising and walking towards me.

"You alright?"

"Mezie, why will you just leave me here like this?" I cry. "I'm bored and freezing. Please let me wear your blazer."

He frowns before reluctantly slipping off his jacket and handing it to me. "How can you be bored in a nightclub, Legachi? With all the music and free drinks?"

"Neither means anything if you abandon me here all night the way you always do."

"In case you're blind, I'm working, not playing."

"You were working when that girl over there was tickling your fancy just now, *abi*?" I retort.

He raises his hand in dismissal and walks away from the table. I watch as he actually returns to the girl's table, smiling even before he takes a seat. I watch as she leads him to the dance floor and as they dance for almost an hour before he is called back to the door. Working indeed.

Why on earth have I agreed to this colossal waste of my time every Friday night?

I think back to the first Friday I came, how being with my friends had made it a fun experience. I remember, for the gazillionth time, the incident with Roman and, again for the gazillionth time, heat rushes to my face. I will never cease to be horrified by the way I behaved that night.

After that night, the small ember of friendship that had started sparking between us had been extinguished like a bucket of ice-cold water over a small candle. We have returned to being polite and civil, our only conversations being about Luna. Raafe still picks Luna and I up from day care, and even though I still cook and bake, Roman has never again sat in the kitchen for a meal. In hindsight, I now know I was the one reading more meaning into the very few times we conversed, realising he was probably just bored and in the mood to banter. And, of course, seeing me dancing like a two-bit hooker didn't help matters any.

I shut my eyes, not caring how much Mezie hates it when I fall asleep there. Letting me sleep would be the kindest thing he can do for me tonight. Not only will it let the four more hours before we leave fly right by, I won't have to subject myself to watching him flirt with women all night.

A rough shove on my shoulder awakens me. The club has emptied, and we can finally leave. I scramble to my feet, reaching for my small purse, eager to get the hell out of there.

"See you later, Harry," Kwame, one of the supervisors calls out to us as we leave.

Mezie waves at him, once again not bothering to introduce me. It hasn't skipped my attention that Lateef is the only person he has introduced me to in the four weeks of my coming there. To everyone else, he hasn't even introduced me as a person, let alone his girlfriend. Kwame waves at me, almost as if prompting him to make an introduction, but instead he walks out the door, leaving me trailing behind.

It is a three-minute walk to Bethnal Green Road, where we will catch a bus home. It is 5:05am and the bus service has only just begun.

"Why have you never introduced me as your girlfriend?" I ask as we stand, waiting for the 26 bus.

"Nobody there is supposed to know I have a girlfriend. I already told you that will affect my job," he mutters.

This is news to me. He has never told me that.

"It's December, Mezie. What are we doing about our accommodation situation? When are we going to put our money together and think about what we can afford to rent?" I ask, as the bus approaches. "We can't keep living aimlessly. We have to start planning for our future."

"Oh, for fuck's sake!" he exclaims, throwing his hands up. "Do you have to nag every fucking time? Jeez!"

And without warning, he starts to walk away. I am torn between following him or going with the bus, which is about to leave. I decide to go with the bus.

Disembarking at our Shore Road bus stop, I stand there for a few minutes, waiting for him. I stand there in the cold, shivering for almost thirty minutes, before I walk the seven minutes to the flat. Letting myself in, I'm surprised to see him sitting in the living room, lighting a cigarette.

"I've been waiting for you at the bus stop," I cry. "In the cold."

Icy eyes look back at me. "Legachi, go to bed, I beg you. I don't need this stress. You can see I've been working all night. All I want to do right now is sleep."

Not wanting to argue, I retreat to the bedroom, stepping over a sleeping Nedu on the floor. By now, I no longer balk at the thought of undressing when he's there and get out of my uncomfortable outfit and into warm flannel pyjamas. I lie in wait for Mezie until I finally drift off to sleep.

I awaken with a start at 9am, realising he never made it to the bed at all. I hear loud laughter from the living room and, from Nedu's vacant sleeping bag, realise most of the guys are already awake. Getting out of bed, I go to the living room, where Eche and Nedu are playing PS4, and Diran and Alex are laughing over something on Diran's phone. Mezie is nowhere in sight.

"Good morning," I say to all and nobody in particular. "Where is Mezie?"

"*E dey for commode,*" Eche answers, not taking his eyes off the screen, referring to what he prefers to call the lavatory.

I walk to the corridor in the direction of the toilet, wanting to find out if he's okay and why he didn't come to bed all night. I am about to knock on the door when the sound of his laughter from inside makes me stop. His voice is muffled but he is undoubtedly on the phone. I raise my brows, remembering how strongly he once felt about phone conversations in the toilet.

I lean on the door, wanting to make out what he's saying, but I can't hear anything but the timbre of his voice. I stand there for several minutes, before eventually returning to the bedroom, leaving the door open so I can see when he finally does come out of the toilet. By the time he emerges fifteen minutes later, twenty-five since I first heard him there, and God knows how long before I even found him, I know one thing for sure. He was talking to another woman.

He walks into the bedroom and casts lazy eyes my way. I want to ask whom he was talking to, but I know he will surely lie about it. He gets on the bed and turns his back to me, not even making any moves to touch me. It takes a few minutes, but the soft purr of his snoring soon indicates he's asleep. I reach for his phone, eager to get the answers to all my questions, but the device is now more secure than Alcatraz. Never one to password his phones, not even when we were in Nigeria, I am shocked to find it guarded by several dots, prompting a pattern password. After two failed attempts to trace it from what I see as his print outline, I put it back beside him, resigned to the fact that I will not be getting any answers from there today.

I wait a few more hours, but he remains asleep. When it is 11am, I am left with no choice but to prepare for the day. For the first time in a long while, Roman has asked me to watch Luna that Saturday. My love life might be falling apart but I can't afford to mess with my job any more than I already have, especially as I haven't been able to secure any more weekend hours at *Poundyard*.

Roman

I notice something is wrong the moment I open the door to let her in. Even though we've barely said more than we need to in the weeks since the club incident and the threats that necessitated my ramping up security around Luna, I am concerned by her downcast eyes and puckered forehead.

"Good afternoon," she mutters in her now characteristic subdued manner.

I nod in response, in what is now my own indifferent one. I watch as she goes to Luna in the living room, noticing her smile isn't as bright and her voice not as cheery. Something is definitely wrong.

Brushing it off, I head back to my study where I have been trying to catch up on some work, but I can hardly concentrate on the journal on my table. We haven't been in the same space for a long time, and I am equal parts keenly aware of the fact she is in the next room and wondering what has happened to upset her.

Convincing myself I need a glass of water, I go to the kitchen, where she is now warming leftover pasta for Luna's lunch.

"You alright?" I ask, noticing her vacant stare as she waits for the microwave to complete its rotation.

My voice startles her and she looks in my direction with wide eyes, as if wondering if I was talking to her.

"Huh?"

"Are you okay? You look rather sour this afternoon," I repeat, wondering why the heck I care anyway.

She shrugs and I am expecting her to give me a template answer, saying she's fine. But she doesn't.

"Can I ask you a question?" she throws back at me. "Would you give me your honest opinion as a guy?"

"Of course," I answer, mighty intrigued by now.

She sighs deeply before looking me in the eye, the first time our eyes have held in five weeks.

"Mezie and I have been together seven years, eight by February," she says. "He came to London last year, and he's the reason I even applied for the scholarship that brought me here. We weren't faring well long distance."

I lean forward on the kitchen island, very interested in this back-story.

"But even here, we seem to still be struggling. At the club, he's always flirting with other women. He never introduces me to anyone as his girlfriend, saying it will compromise his job if he does. He hardly ever touches me now, and this morning he locked himself in the bathroom for over thirty minutes, talking and laughing with some mystery person on the phone. As if that isn't bad enough, his phone now has a password, something he's never had before."

She stops talking and searches my eyes, as if looking for an answer there, an answer to a question she hasn't even asked. I have a fair idea what her question might be, but still need her to ask anyway.

"And your question is?"

She sighs deeply again. "Do you think he's cheating on me?"

Do birds fly? From the little she has shared, I am absolutely certain the bloke is doing just that. One hundred per cent! But something else she has said has caught my attention.

"You've been with him almost eight years?"

She nods. "We worked together at First Guaranty Bank back in Lagos. We started dating a few weeks after I joined."

I have to stop myself from parting my mouth in surprise. The bouncer was once a banker? Them bumping and grinding in nightclubs hasn't always been their norm? That puts things in a completely different perspective.

"I didn't know you worked in a bank back in Nigeria," I remark, so many questions in my head. If she is here on a scholarship, why is she working her tail off as a nanny *and* a *Poundyard* floor staff?

"Yeah, I did," she answers, sounding a tad impatient. "Well? Do you?"

Do I what? I stare back at her, momentarily confused. Ah yes, the boyfriend. There is a part of me that wants to scoff and tell her of course he's cheating on her. It's pretty obvious to me, and I'm sure to her as well.

"He actually might not be," I hear myself say instead. "It's possible his club does discourage serious relationships."

Her face brightens. "Really? You think? What about the person he was talking to on the phone in the toilet?"

"It could have been anyone. I don't think you should rush to any conclusions based on that."

"And him not touching me?"

I shrug. "He could just be tired. It happens sometimes."

For the life of me, I can't imagine why I'm spinning these porkies, when it would give me so much satisfaction to burst her and Mr. Muscle's fantasy bubble. And then I realise it really won't. I realise I'd rather see her happy than sad.

"Things have been so rough between us for a while, you know," she says, clearly still seeking reassurance that all is well with her relationship.

"He'd be daft to leave a lovely girl like you," I answer.

And I mean it.

Legachi

The compliment ignites a glow in my very core, and a wide smile spreads across my face. Less than an hour ago, he was still giving me the silent treatment and now he's telling me he thinks I'm lovely. Hearing that pacifies me even more than any reassurance he has given me about Mezie's fidelity.

"That's really sweet of you. Thank you," I say, my smile making my cheeks hurt. Deep down inside, I know Mezie is very likely cheating, and that Roman has only defended him to make me feel better, and I am touched that he has even felt compelled to do so, touched that he even took any notice of my mood in the first place, especially after so many weeks of giving, and getting, the cold shoulder.

"You're welcome," he answers, offering a small smile as he rises to his feet. "I'll be in the study if you need me."

"Why did you stop Luna and I from taking the bus back home from day care?" I ask as he makes for the door, wanting to take advantage of this cordiality, which might be as short-lived as the ones before.

He pauses by the door before turning around, clearly debating with himself whether or not to tell me.

"I just need to keep her safe for a bit," he finally answers. "I've been receiving a few threats from someone I had a run-in with a while ago."

My eyes widen in my fear. "Have you reported this to the Police?"

He laughs and I am surprised he finds it amusing.

"Nah, it's not that serious. The person doesn't have that kind of capacity. All I need to do is keep Luna out of sight for a while."

I nod, trying not to get agitated. I guess if he says there's nothing to worry about, then there probably isn't. But despite the anxiety from hearing the news, I go about my chores in much better spirits, the melancholy I arrived with completely gone. Yes, Mezie might be cheating on me, but no, it isn't the end of the world... not when Roman thinks he'd be 'daft to leave a lovely girl like me'. Even if he was just being nice, those words have made all the difference, and I know I'll be drawing on them whenever I need comfort, even after today.

As I get ready to leave, he emerges from his study.

"I'd like to ask for a favour," he says, looking uncertain. "It's my birthday in a week. Next week Saturday to be precise."

"Oh, lovely!" I grin. "Happy birthday in advance."

"Yeah, cheers," he answers, the look of uncertainty still on his face. "I usually have a few friends over on the day, and this one being my 35th, I expect quite a few people to come over. So, I was wondering if you could sleep over that day, to help out with Luna? It's not a party or anything, just a small do. I'll be happy to pay you double."

"It would be my pleasure to, and you don't have to pay me double," I answer, still smiling. "Consider it a birthday present from me to you."

His smile is just as wide as mine, and I notice for the first time the dimple in his right cheek. "Wicked. Thanks a lot."

"Would you like me to cook some rice or something?" I feel the need to offer.

"No, that won't be necessary. I typically order in when I have people over," he answers, before smiling in his appreciation. "But thanks so much for offering."

I am still smiling as I walk to the bus stop, and as I sit on the 13 bus headed to Golders Green, still tingling over how much more pleasant and congenial a day it was with him. I make up my mind to bake him a cake anyway.

187

The week goes by quickly and we remain congenial on the few occasions I see him, which is only when he gets home a few minutes before I leave. But much different from the reluctant murmuring of before, this time we make eye contact and I ask how his day went, just as he asks how things are with Mezie. Even though our answers are always brief, with him just answering it went well, and me saying things are fine with Mezie, it is much better than dreading those few minutes of interface.

That Friday, even though I go to Mezie's place from South Hampstead, I refuse to follow him to the club, choosing to wait for him at home instead. He doesn't argue, and I can almost swear he even looks relieved. But I have decided not to put myself through that torture any longer. Whatever is wrong with our relationship will not be fixed by my inconveniencing myself, week after week, tagging along where I'm not wanted. We'll just have to find another way to make things work. I wear a pair of comfortable but highly unsexy fleece pyjamas, and when he makes no move for me when he gets back at 6am, I don't even mind. The way I feel about our current situation, sex is the very last thing I even want.

Rising from bed at 8am, I head to the kitchen, bring out the baking supplies I brought with me the day before, and set about making a two-tier chocolate cake for Roman. I dance along to Tuface's classic *Grass 2 Grace* album as I beat together flour, sugar, cocoa powder, baking powder and a dash of espresso powder with eggs, milk, butter and vanilla extract, happy for no real explanation. As the cakes bake, I toy with the idea of sending Roman a birthday text message, or maybe even a call, but I quickly quash the thought. That could appear forward, and the last thing I want to do is rock our fragile friendship boat.

"This place smells goooood!" Eche remarks, walking into the kitchen. In the three months since the ugly incident on my first morning there, he now knows better than to come closer than a foot near me. "You're baking a cake for us?"

"It's not for you guys," I answer, offering a tight smile and nothing else.

His bushy brows curve in surprise, after which he shrugs and opens the fridge to see what his breakfast options are. I reach for the mixing bowl to start whisking butter, sugar and cocoa powder for the frosting. Where has slaving to cook for them in the past gotten me? Absolutely nowhere, that's where.

By the time I am frosting the cakes, the flat is bustling with activity, with pretty much everyone awake.

"What's going on?" Mezie asks, walking to where I am piping the cakes. "Who's that for?"

"My boss," I answer, not taking my eyes off what I'm doing. "It's his birthday today."

He regards me for a while before bursting into laughter. "You're making a cake for your *Oga*? That's not how they do things here *o!*"

I glare at him. "What's wrong with giving my boss a gift?"

"You think he will increase your salary or something? You think this is Naija?" he cackles, as Diran and Nedu walk into the kitchen. "This babe, you're funny *o!*"

"*Wetin she do?*" a curious Diran asks, his eyes flitting from me to the cakes I am piping.

"She dey make birthday cake for her Oga. She think say this na Naija where she fit buy favour with even one bottle of small stout sef."

"This place where they go collect the cake, come sack you on top!" Nedu cackles.

Diran is still observing me. "You're making a cake for your boss? Male or female?"

"*Na one yeye Mandem boy like that,*" Mezie answers, and when Diran raises a surprised brow, he shakes his head. "*At all! Na all these tall, fine girls the bobo like.*"

Translation, there is nothing to worry about as my boss wouldn't look at me twice. Charming.

Mezie dips his finger into the mixing bowl and his eyes light up as the chocolate buttercream hits the spot. "This tastes really good. You need to make me a cake one of these days."

"Hey, guy," Eche calls from the kitchen door. "Alex don dey go Cricklewood. E say e go branch D'Den. You want any chow?"

D'Den is our favourite Nigerian restaurant in the city. Mezie walks over to the living room to discuss what to order. No sooner has he gone does a message flash on the phone he has left on the kitchen counter.

Last night was awesome! is displayed in his notification centre. This is soon followed by several kissing emojis.

I reach for the phone, but he beats me to it, rushing back into the kitchen, grabbing it, and quickly scrolling through.

"Who sent you that message?" I ask, but even I know it is a futile endeavour. Apart from knowing I won't get the truth from him, it is pretty obvious the message is from a woman. As much as he loves his pals, I don't see any of his male buddies sending him a message with kissing emojis.

"What message?" he asks, not even looking up as he continues to scroll.

Shaking my head, I return my attention to my piping, knowing he has almost certainly deleted the message. But I'm not going to allow that rain on my parade today.

By noon, the cake is ready, and I go to the bathroom to shower, following which I wear the brand new ankle-length jersey dress I bought in a bold blue and orange tie-dye pattern. I pair it with a navy blue, bold braid wrap cardigan I have also just bought, and as I apply light makeup and wear the hoop earrings and stacked bracelets I have bought from *Primark*, I remind myself of the excuse I gave as I splurged on the new outfit. With all the people coming, I can't afford not to look my best for Roman's birthday party.

"I'm going," I call out to the guys as I make my way out of the flat, the heavy cake in hand.

A lethargic wave of the hand is the only acknowledgment Mezie has heard me. Pursing my lips, I walk out anyway, determined not to think about him or whatever he may or may not be getting up to. I struggle down the stairs with the cake and into the *Uber* I have summoned to take me to South Hampstead, as there ain't no way I'm going to hobble and wobble in trains and buses across town with that cake. Apart from it being pretty heavy, I don't want to risk smudging it and destroying the result of my hard work. I laboured too hard for it, and it looks so perfect, it is well deserving of the £30 ride. I wince as I think about how much this birthday has cost me but reassure myself that it is money well spent. I have already managed to save £1,100, so I'm not feeling quite as hard up as I was a few months, or even weeks, ago.

Forty-three minutes later, the taxi pulls up in front of the house, and, unable to reach for my keys in my handbag, I use my foot to tap the door.

Roman

I am surprised to see Legachi already at the door, and even more so when I see the large cake in her hands.

"Happy birthday!" she says, walking into the house. "I need to put this down before I drop it."

"You got me a cake?" I ask, following her into the kitchen as she sets it on the counter.

"I *made* you a cake," she declares, beaming at me. "I hope you like chocolate. Where's Luna? Having her nap?"

I nod, astonished as I take in the two-tier cake, expertly decorated enough to pass for store-bought. This is not a simple slap in the oven, bake and tie with a ribbon cake. This took time and effort, and

I'm touched she put herself through that much trouble on my account.

"Where is everyone?" she asks. "Where are all the decorations? I was expecting to meet something more festive."

"Festive? Decorations? It's just my birthday, not a jubilee," I scoff. "My mates will probably get here at about 6 or so."

She looks around, noticing the bare kitchen. "And food? I thought you said you had it covered."

"Paris will pick up some Chinese on her way here."

She raises a brow, and I can see she isn't impressed by that. "There's some leftover rice, so I'll have that nice and warm for anyone who wants it."

As she talks, I notice she has on light blue eyeliner, further enhancing those damned brown eyes. My eyes drop to her lips, glossy beneath pale pink lipstick, and all I can think is how luscious they look. As she makes her way to the fridge, my eyes skim her body. Even though her dress is about a size too big, it still flaunts her ample derriere. For someone who likes his women slender, I have noticed my babysitter's curves a few times too many. Standing shorter than I like my women, and with a waist that could lose a few inches, I can't understand why her body has caught my attention so many times.

"I hope I didn't dress up like this for nothing o!" she giggles as she continues to scour the freezer. "I thought you were having a big party."

Whether or not she is my usual type, I can't deny the fact that, today, she looks the best I have ever seen her. Her dress looks new, and even the jacket she has just removed is a welcome replacement to the tatty one she wears every day. Her jewellery is more prominent than normal, and it is clear she went to a lot of trouble to look her best today. I want to compliment her, to tell her everything about her looks beautiful; her dress, her makeup, her jewellery, everything. But I decide against it. No need to give her a big head. I still cringe every time I remember telling her that Mr. Muscle would 'be daft to leave a lovely girl like her'. That was way too much, even if I was just trying to make her feel better.

The question is, was I just?

The doorbell chimes and Paris' loud voice soon reverberates through the house as I open the door for her and Declan, both their hands laden with takeaway bags.

"Happy birthday again, darling," she says, blowing me a kiss as she walks to the kitchen. "See? I told you I'd get here early."

"Happy birthday," Declan grins at me, walking quickly behind his girlfriend.

I shake my head and chuckle, my large and boisterous sister and her diminutive, almost mouse-like boyfriend, always comical to behold.

"Oh, hello," Paris remarks when she sees Legachi in the kitchen.

"This is Luna's nanny," I quickly introduce. "Her name is Legachi. Legachi, this is my sister, Paris, and her boyfriend, Declan."

Legachi offers a shy wave, just as Paris' eyes widen with surprise.

"*This* is the nanny? The same Nigerian nanny you told me about? The same one who made… " her voice drifts as she spots the Tupperware bowls of *jollof* rice Legachi has brought out of the fridge. "The same one who made those?"

Legachi throws an imploring look my way, not knowing what to say in response to my sister. But Paris turns to me at the same time, wiggling her thick eyebrows.

"I see you, fam. I see you."

I roll my eyes at her. She sees absolutely nothing! "Declan, get your Missus out of my kitchen."

Thankfully, the chime of the doorbell announces the arrival of Sean and his wife, Lara. They are soon followed by Ojie, Ihidie and Tosan, and then Yash and Kavya, along with a few friends from work. Chuka and Dotun arrive with a few more friends, and by 7pm, the house is teeming with people. Food is flowing, drinks are a'plenty, and Luna is enjoying being the centre of attention. It's your typical house party.

Legachi

Now, *this* is what I was expecting! I am in my element as I help Paris dish food for the guests, the oddest mix of egg fried rice, sweet and sour sauce and *jollof* rice, expertly bouncing from doing that to attending to Luna. Even though mostly casually dressed, this is a posh crowd, but rather than feel insecure, I bask in the convivial atmosphere, loving every minute of it.

Justin Timberlake's *Justified* album is playing on loop, and several times as he talks to a guest, I spy Roman dancing along to one of the catchy tunes. He hasn't changed from the red Ralph Lauren polo shirt he has been wearing since I arrived, and as he moves his head and shoulders in rhythm with *Rock Your Body*, I find myself riveted, unable to look away. From his slightly overgrown hair and more pronounced curls to the way his snug polo shirt sits on his body like it was tailored specifically for him, showing off his toned biceps and washboard abs, to the glint of the thin gold chain that peeks from his neckline, he is the very definition of sexy. He smiles at something his friend says, and I feel a flutter in my stomach. What is with this schoolgirl crush that just won't go away? My life is complicated enough without having to add lusting after my unattainable employer to my long list of problems.

The party continues to pick up tempo, and I see Roman was right all along about not needing any frills or thrills for a good celebration. All it has taken has been decent food and good music, and they are having more fun than people who might have splurged a fortune on all the usual bells and whistles. I see that it is less about money, and more about good company.

I break away a few times, mostly to attend to Luna; give her a bath, dish her dinner, and finally put her to bed. But the party remains in full swing. It isn't until well past 10pm that people start to leave, but his close friends and their spouses remain, and if the way they are still pouring glasses of wine is anything to go by, they aren't leaving anytime soon.

I am walking to the kitchen to start clearing up when Paris hollers my name from the living room. "Legs, come and join us for a game of charades."

I am filled with intense dread at the mention of the game I am atrocious at, and I tell her just as much when I walk into the room.

"Then you'll be in good company. Roman is also pants at it, and he hasn't got a partner," she chuckles, beckoning me over to sit next to her brother.

I look at him, worried he will be angered by this gross over-familiarity. Hanging around the fringes as he parties with his friends is one thing, being called to join them for games is another. But rather than look annoyed, he smiles at me.

"If my track record is anything to go by, we'll be out of the game in," he looks at his watch. "ten minutes."

Okay then.

As Paris and Declan kick off the game of movie charades, Roman leans close to me. "We do this to wind down after every get-together. It's really nothing serious."

I nod, even though it does nothing to quell my nerves. I hate the fact that the hopefully good impression his friends have of me will be destroyed after I royally flop the game, because flop I will.

Chuka, Dotun and Ojie are the appointed moderators in charge of giving the teams the words a member is to mime without words, to get their partner to guess what movie it is. Seemingly simple... except if you can't act to save your life. But I am consoled when I see how hopeless Declan looks as he twists his body in a desperate attempt to give Paris hints. He is so thin that his body movements are not only comical but look exactly the same. Paris is hardly any better, as she is too high-energy to effectively communicate anything. They end the game with zero points, and I am consoled that, worst case, we'll tie with them. Sean and Lara perform much better, as do Ihidie and Tosan, but Kayva and Yash appear to be the ultimate champions, getting four out of their six assigned movie names correct.

All too soon, it is our turn.

"I'll go first," Roman says, taking the word from Chuka.

He turns to me and smiles, and I force myself to remain focused on the task at hand. I can't be the one to let our team down. He winds his right hand in a circular motion.

"Movie," I call out. Redundant, considering it's a movie-themed game.

He nods and raises two fingers.

"Two words!" I holler. Lord, why on earth am I shouting?

He motions wearing sunglasses, a big frown on his face.

"*Men in Black*!" I yell, hoping maybe the 'in' is considered a silent word.

He shakes his head and my stomach plummets. He raises an imaginary cigarette to his lips, but I just gape at him, still clueless. He then starts moving his head back and forth in a dance, raising a hand to his face and forming a horizontal V-shape with his fingers.

"*Pulp Fiction*!" I yell and almost burst with joy when his face lights up and he gives me the thumbs up sign. One down.

Next, after winding his hand in circular motion to indicate it's a movie, he raises two fingers again and stands with hands akimbo, looking around the room with as much pride as a king.

"Coming to America!" I yell.

He beckons, letting me know I'm close. He lifts his hands as if raising something, turning around the room like he's showing it to everyone.

"The fuck is that?!" Yash chortles.

I squint as I look at him, racking my brain. Until it comes to me. *"Lion King!"*

His face lights up again and he throws me a wide grin. I'm just relieved that we already have two more than Paris and Declan.

"Okay, last one from Roman before Legs takes over," Ojie says, and I am amused by how they have all taken to calling me 'Legs', almost like I actually belong in their gang.

Roman rolls his hand in a circular motion, raises six fingers and then stands bent over, walking with an imaginary cane, staggering for emphasis.

"Walking Dead!" I yell, not even sure that's a movie, and totally ignoring the fact he raised all the fingers on one hand and an extra on the other.

He frowns at me, prompting laughter from his sister.

"Like you can blame her!" Paris hoots.

He continues to walk bent over, before straightening and walking upright and regal, like someone in a pageant.

"Miss Congeniality!"

He shakes his head and then starts rocking his hands like someone putting a baby to sleep.

"The Curious Case of Benjamin Button!" I yell, connecting the dots, all six words of them.

Ecstatic, he jumps and pummels the air with his fist. Returning to our seat, I am well aware that even though we have done well to get three out of three so far, the onus is now on me for us not to come crashing down like a pack of cards.

I look at my movie and shudder. How on earth am I supposed to mime a movie named after a person? I rotate my hand in a circular motion, raise two fingers, before drawing an imaginary box with my fingers. I then act like I'm eating from the box.

"Breakfast at Tiffany's!" Roman yells.

I look at him, bewildered. For goodness' sake!

I ponder over it for a few seconds before I start to act like I'm running.

"*Forrest Gump!*" he yells, leaping off the chair when I smile and give him the thumbs up.

"These two are just as weird as each other!" Kavya remarks, her eyes twinkling.

I'm just happy that we have now tied with them, the highest scoring couple.

For the next movie, I make a circular motion with my hand again, raise four fingers, and then shield my eyes with my hands, as if looking for something.

"*Look Who's Talking Too!*" he yells, making me actually stop to look at him, wondering how he comes up with guesses so far removed from what I'm acting.

I shake my head and act like I'm pointing. I then make a wavy motion with my hands, point again and make another wavy motion with my hands.

"I'll be damned if he gets this right," Sean chuckles, watching me with something between amusement and amazement.

But Roman's gaze remains intense. "Wind… gone… *Gone With The Wind!*"

I squeal with delight, and he gets up to give me a high five. At five out of six, we have already won the game. But we decide to go for the sixth, to try for a perfect score. I flush when I see the movie name, knowing there is only one iconic scene that will make anyone know what it is. But I decide to try other clues to see if he'll guess them. I raise four fingers, then proceed to hug myself and pout my lips like I'm kissing someone, to demonstrate two people in love.

Everyone in the room, Roman included, looks back at me, confused.

I frown, wag my finger, and stomp my feet, hoping that is enough to show the two lovers getting into a fight. I sling an imaginary bag over my shoulder and lift an imaginary box as I stomp away, hoping it shows them breaking up. And then I rush back to the centre of the room and start hugging myself again and kissing the air.

Crickets.

By this time, even Roman is trying not to laugh. And I know I have no choice but to bring out the big guns.

I stand still before closing my eyes and throwing my head back as if in pure ecstacy. I caress my chest as I rock my head from side to side, my eyes still closed, opening my mouth as if groaning, the picture of the perfect orgasm.

"*When Harry Met Sally!*" Roman yells, hopping to his feet as we celebrate our perfect win.

"You're kidding me!" Lara roars with laughter. "So Roman has finally found someone with as warped a brain as he has!"

I cover my mouth with my hands as I giggle. I have never been able to get anyone to properly guess anything I've mimed in this game. Having Roman guess all three of mine, and me all three of his, maybe there is some truth in his friends saying that we are indeed kindred spirits with the same odd sense of reasoning.

An hour later, after everyone has gone, we are standing side-by-side by the kitchen island, packing up the leftover cake.

"That was amazing!" he remarks, and I know he is referring to the game. "Nobody has ever been able to guess any of my mimes before."

"Me neither," I laugh, still amazed by it all. "Getting a perfect score was really something. Even though you had me worried with that old man walk of yours."

He guffaws at the memory. "That was way better than that tribal dance you were performing for *Gone With The Wind*."

"But you guessed it in the end, didn't you?" I giggle, turning to look at him. "And how did you guess *When Harry Met Sally* anyway?"

He shrugs. "That's the movie with the most iconic orgasm scene in the history of film."

"I agree! Meg Ryan killed it," I laugh, reaching for a knife to cut another slice of cake to keep in the fridge for later. My hand brushes his as I do, and the feel of his skin on mine awakens every single one of my senses.

The energy in the room changes as I look at him, and as our eyes hold, I am so very keenly aware of his presence. He licks his lower lip and all I can think is how much I want him to kiss me.

Roman

The feel of her hand against mine is so brief, it's something I could have missed. But I don't. Soft and supple, but electric at the same time, I am not prepared for the way the rest of my body responds in reaction.

Turning to look at her, she is also looking at me, and those light brown eyes bordered by turquoise blue suck me in, making me feel like I am floating on a perfect blue sea in the sunset. It feels like all the air has been sucked from the room and my lips suddenly go dry. In my heightened nerves, I lick my lower lip and when her plump lips, lips now bare of any gloss, part in response, all I want to do is grab and her... and kiss her.

But bloody hell, this is Luna's babysitter.

The reminder is enough of a splash of cold water in my face. Apart from the fact kissing her would be terribly inappropriate, I don't want her to think that was the reason I asked her to stay over. Not to mention the very obvious fact that she *does* have a boyfriend.

"This cake was proper amazing!" I say, taking the knife and cutting a slice of cake I don't want. "You should think of making a business of baking."

"Thank you," she answers.

I'm not brave enough to look at her again, lest I lose every resolve I have barely managed to scrape together.

"I've set up the guest room for you. It's the one next to Luna's and opposite mine," I say, making my way out of the kitchen. "Cheers once again."

In the safety of the living room, I let out a puff of air and set the plate of cake on the coffee table, knowing I won't eat it tonight. I lie on the couch and shut my eyes. I don't know why my body responds to her the way it does, but whatever the reason, it has to stop.

It has to stop like yesterday.

Twenty-One

Essex Boy

Uegachi

ater that week, Thursday, I get off the bus at the Golders Green
Station. After making a fool of myself last Saturday, gaping at
Roman like a lovesick fool, I have made a more concerted effort
to remind myself how way out of my league he is. With the cloud of
confusion still hanging over my relationship with Mezie, the last
thing I should be doing is lusting after a man I can never have.
Walking to the flat, I chuckle as I remember how, for a few fleeting
moments, I'd thought he was actually looking at me with desire, and
that he wanted to kiss me just as much as I wanted to kiss him. It
must have been the high from winning the game that clouded my
mind. But I won't be making that mistake again, not even tomorrow,
when I journey with him and Luna to Chelmsford to see his mother.

That night, before I left their house, he'd walked into the kitchen.

"Will you be able to come a little earlier tomorrow?" he'd asked
tentatively. "I have to go see my mom, and I'd really like help with

Luna for the journey. Don't worry, we should be back in London before 5pm. 6 at the very latest."

I'd agreed, happy for the opportunity to make some more money. But making my way up the stairs to Alero's apartment, I find myself wishing I hadn't. Considering how long my silly bout of infatuation has stretched without any signs of abating, maybe being in such close proximity with him isn't such a good idea.

Opening the door, I see Alero decorating a Christmas tree so large, it occupies almost half the room. Okay, maybe not half, but a large portion of it. I frown when I see some of its branches hovering over the sofa-bed, sharp pines pointing downward where my face will be in a few hours.

"*Babe, you don come?*" she beams at me. "*Omo*, that's how I forgot to put up the tree *o*! I've never had to wait till the 20th before. I just realised I haven't even *Christmased* the house for when Bryn gets back on Monday."

Monday. Monday is the 24th. Monday is Christmas Eve. Shit. With all that's been going on in my life, I have completely forgotten.

"You and I haven't even *gisted* in a while," she continues talking, reaching for yet another bright red ball ornament. "With this your work that keeps you out of the house all day, I'm sure you would have saved enough dough." For some reason, that makes her chuckle. "You've found a place, *ba*? You'll be able to move this weekend, right? Saturday preferably, so I'll have enough time to get the place ready for Bryn."

Cold and heat waves course through my body intermittently, and I am momentarily tongue-tied.

She looks at me when I don't answer. "*This one wey you tanda like statue.*"

That is enough to snap me out of my trance.

"I'm still working on a few things, but I'll be able to leave on Saturday," I answer, forcing a wide smile. "I don't know how to thank you for helping me out. If not for you… "

She shrugs and smiles. "What are friends for?"

Despite her draconian house rules, living with her hasn't been as unpleasant as I'd feared. She has helped me as far as she has been able to, and for that, I'm grateful.

Later that night, sitting on my sofa-bed, I am regretful of the upwards of £100 I spent on Roman's birthday. If I hadn't, my savings would be almost £1,300 by now. Considering the requirement to pay for at least three months, I am still unable to afford my school's accommodation. And with the requirement to pay a security deposit equivalent to one month's rent, I realize with despair that I will not be able to afford even the cheapest flat share until the end of the month.

Notwithstanding, I still send emails to the renters of available rooms I see online, getting a few instant replies. To my dismay, they all respond saying the earliest I can move in is after the holidays. So, even if I did have all the money, I wouldn't even be able to get a place now. I am resigned to the fact I will have to return to Mezie's place on Saturday. And this alone feels like the biggest defeat of all.

Roman

I am relieved to hear the clinking of keys at the door. It is ten minutes past noon and as it's not like her to be late, I have been worried she will not show up at all today. In the days since my birthday, she has retreated so deep into herself, I almost expect her to give her notice any day. She is fine with Luna, but even her smiles and laughter now seem forced. Asking her to come along with us to Essex has just been my way of attempting to take things back to normal.

Even though the truth is that I don't even know what normal is.

"I'm so sorry I'm late," she says breathlessly, as she walks into the house. "I had to sort out some things."

I am filled with curiosity over what 'things' are, wondering if they have anything to do with her lowlife boyfriend.

"You alright?" I ask. "You've been a bit... distant all week."

There is a flicker in her eyes, and she shrugs. "I just have a lot going on."

"If you're in any kind of trouble, you know you can talk to me, right?" I say, meaning every word.

She looks at me for a few seconds before she finally smiles, the first real one I've seen all week. "Thank you. I'll keep that in mind."

"Legachi!" an excited Luna calls from the staircase.

As Legachi rushes to her and lifts her off her feet in what is now her characteristic way, it is with the same cheer and excitement as before. Relieved, we grab the things we'll need for the trip and head out the door.

"Why don't you like to drive?" she asks as we walk past my Mercedes E350 parked in front of the house. "I've never seen you drive your car."

"I do drive. Luna and I drive to church some Sundays. We also drive when we go visiting friends. I don't drive to work because of the congestion charge and the fact parking is a menace."

"So why aren't you driving to Chelmsford now?" she presses, her eyes glinting with mischief. "There's no congestion charge or 'parking menace' there." She actually makes air quotes, and I can see she is getting back to her old self. "Wouldn't that be more convenient than hopping from train to train?"

"I can think of a lot more useful things to do with my time than driving for over an hour. On the train, I get to do other things, like read," I answer, before winking. "If you'd like a spin in my car, all you have to do is say so."

She laughs in response, and I am gladdened by the sound. After the week we've had, it sounds to me like a melody.

We get on the eastbound Jubilee line train, disembarking thirty minutes later at Stratford, from where we get on an overground train to Chelmsford. Sitting through the thirty-minute ride, I try to keep my focus on the journal I have brought along, but I am distracted by Luna and Legachi as they marvel as the train whizzes first through the burling neighborhoods of Ilford and Romford in London, and then the suburbs of Brentwood and Ingatestone in Essex. Luna still *oohs* and *aahs* even though she has seen it several times before, but to Legachi, it is a completely new experience. I steal several glances her way, enjoying seeing her enjoy the view of London's outskirts. By the time we get to Chelmsford, I don't know if it is the sights and sounds of the trip, or just being somewhere less chaotic, but she looks decidedly more cheerful. I hail a taxi, and before 2pm, we are pulling up in front of my mother's house in the Springfield area of town. She is already opening the door before we even get out of the cab.

"Grandma!" Luna squeals, running up to her as soon as she's out of the car.

I smile as my mother lifts her only grandchild and squishes her in an embrace. After twirling her around, she smiles in my direction and pulls my cheek.

"Osareme, why are you looking so lean?"

I see a small smile on Legachi's lips and know she is amused to hear me addressed by my Esan name.

"You say that all the time," I say, leaning to kiss my mother on her own cheek. "You look gorgeous."

And she truly does. Being able to retire her was one the best things I ever did and seeing her looking healthy and well-rested is indeed the best reward. She grins in response to the compliment, and as her eyes drift to Legachi, her smile is even wider.

"This is Luna's nanny," I jump in before she starts getting any ideas. "Her name is Legachi. She's Nigerian as well."

If she is disappointed, she doesn't show it.

"Oh, lovely! Such a pretty girl," she says, embracing her. "Obehi has told me all about you"

Legachi smiles at her in response and casts me a questioning glance.

"Paris," I clarify. "We better go inside. It's brass monkeys out here." And it is. At ten degrees Celsius, it's too cold to be outside having this discussion.

We file into the house and see Paris waiting in the living room.

"I thought you and Declan left for Bath this week," I remark, embracing her.

"We did, but after a couple days filming rubbish, we decided to take a break for the holidays," she answers, before beaming at Legachi. "Hallo, Legs. Lovely to see you again."

Legachi waves, and I watch as my mother ushers her in and as Luna guides her by the hand to sit on a chair, hoping the visit won't be too overwhelming for her.

"Don't worry, we don't bite," Paris whispers in my ear, before walking into the nearby kitchen, chuckling as she goes.

I cast another glance at Legachi, Luna and my mother, before following my sister.

"What do we have here?" I ask, opening the pots on the cooker. I wince at the first one, a pot of *ogbono* soup, but the other with fried rice appeals to me. My smile widens at the cooler full of plantain, fried soft and semi-burnt like I like them. I could eat the entire cooler if given the opportunity.

"You've got me to thank for the plantain," Paris remarks. "The old bird only fried like five pieces. I told her she had to multiply that by at least a hundred."

I laugh at my sister's exaggeration and throw a piece into my mouth. Heaven.

"So, you and your nanny!" Paris beams, crossing her arms. "You're taking family trips now."

"I asked her to come so she could help with Luna."

"You know you don't need help with Luna on the train," Paris says, undaunted. "You fancy her, don't ya?"

"Don't be daft. Of course, I don't fancy her. She's Luna's sitter."

"Oh? Because she fancies you," Paris says, with a casual shrug. "I saw how she was staring at you last weekend. She could hardly take her eyes off you all night."

This piques my interest. "Yeah?"

"You *do* fancy her!" Paris guffaws, hitting me on my arm. "You wouldn't care if you didn't."

"Stop taking the piss, Paris. I do *not* fancy her. I don't need to remind you how inappropriate that would be." But even as I'm saying the words, I know they are untrue.

I do fancy her.

Legachi

I can hardly take my eyes off the beautiful woman playing with Luna; her skin so bright, it looks almost porcelain. Small and almost waif-like and wearing a beautiful cashmere sweater over a pair of jeans, she could pass for someone in her 40s. Deep dimples slice each of her cheeks into two, and I can see where Roman got his pointed nose and ridiculously long eyelashes. The woman is beautiful.

As she plays with Luna, my eyes scan the very many framed pictures on the wall. I smile at images of a younger Roman and Paris in their family portraits, and also their two brothers, as they all flank their parents. The younger Mrs. Isibor looks even more ethereal and sits in sharp contrast to the bulky, dark-skinned man next to her. The late Mr. Isibor stares unsmiling at the camera in every picture, and I can immediately see that Paris got her slightly over-spaced eyes and broad nose from him. But as unsmiling as he is, his hand is firmly interlaced with his wife's, and I can tell that she was the most important thing to him. There are a few other pictures of all six of them as a family, but as the pictures progress to college graduations and more recent family vacations, he is conspicuously absent.

I smile at a picture of Roman graduating from medical school, and of him holding an infant Luna. I look with keen interest at a few pictures of him with Sekani, one from their wedding day and another of them dressed in some kind of fancy dress; he in a Vampire's cape and she as Catwoman. In the latter, they are looking at each other like nobody else in the world exists, and I am once again intrigued by the depth of their love. He must really miss her.

"You must be so proud of Roman," I say to Mrs. Isibor. "He's done very well for himself."

"Proud isn't enough of a word to explain how I feel about my boy," she says, the word emanating from every pore of her body. "He is my backbone. If it weren't for him, I probably would have followed my husband to the grave."

I look at her, puzzled, and she nods.

"I married my husband as a very young girl," she says. "Osejie came home from the UK for Christmas, saw me and decided I was the one he would marry. When I came here to join him, I had only just turned 20. He was all I knew, so to lose him seventeen years later almost killed me. For several months after he died, I couldn't even get out of bed. It was Osareme who held this family up. He worked several jobs and held things down at home with his younger ones, at the age of just 16. Even when I finally got myself and went back to work, he was my biggest support system, holding me down anytime I wanted to crumble. He still is."

I listen in amazement as she continues to pour encomiums on her son, fascinated but not at all surprised that beneath the cool and sometimes arrogant façade, lies a thoughtful and kind man. His offer of help to me earlier today a testament to that.

"God was partial to me with my children. Six years ago, when I turned 50, they relocated me to this town, bought me this house, and retired me with an allowance almost double what I was earning as a Care Worker. Now, all I do is some small voluntary work to while away my time, take care of my flowers in the spring, and holiday with my kids in the summer," she continues, smiling as her eyes fall on a picture of her flanked by all four of them. "This was taken in Venice last year. My youngest son, Ogbeide, has always planned these holidays, but we got more intentional about them after what happened to Osareme."

I nod in understand, thinking how devastating it must have been for them as a family to be bereaved of another loved one.

"Obehi is my gossip partner and personal bodyguard, always ready to fight anyone for me, and my other son, Odianose, works in fashion and insists on sending me these ridiculously expensive clothes," she chuckles, and I have to laugh with her, heart-warmed that after facing life's challenges so early in life, she now has so much to be thankful for.

"When I arrived here so young, it was a scary experience. I hadn't even been out of Ekpoma before, and I was suddenly in this new country. I felt so awful those first few months in such an awful, cold place," she shakes her head as if nostalgic. "But I couldn't have wished for a better husband than Osejie. He took such good care of me, went out of his way to settle me in, he loved me so completely that I was soon no longer homesick. He was a wonderful man." As she talks, I notice she still wears her wedding ring, a dull brass band, a testament to the love she will cherish for the rest of her life. "And I have made sure I have raised my children, my sons especially, to be just as wonderful partners to their spouses, so help me God."

Our eyes hold, almost like she is passing me some sort of subliminal message, and I immediately look away. The last thing I need is anything that will feed the beast of infatuation I am trying to slay. Thankfully, Luna squeals, calling her Grandma's attention.

"Ejemhen, are you hungry?" Mrs. Isibor says to her grandchild, rising to her feet. "Let's go and see what your father and aunty are doing in the kitchen. Hopefully, they haven't finished all the plantain."

She beckons me as she and Luna walk to the kitchen, and I quickly rise to follow them, hungry, if the rumbling in my stomach is anything to go by. After spending most of the morning boxing my things at Alero's place, food was the last thing on my mind. But I am now reminded of the fact I haven't eaten at all today.

"Don't tell me you and Osareme have eaten all the extra plantain you just fried?" Mrs. Isibor shrieks at Paris, as she beholds the half empty cooler.

The culprits have their mouths full and can only offer shamefaced looks in response. Clucking her tongue, Mrs. Isibor proceeds to start dishing what is left of the plantain to two plates, before doing the same with the fried rice.

"Let me serve Ejemhen and our lovely guest, before you two finish everything," she mutters, shaking her head. She looks up at me and shakes her head again. "Left to my children, these two especially, they will be happy eating only plantain three times a day for the rest of their lives."

I am laughing as I turn to Roman, amused seeing him in this completely different light. He shrugs as our eyes meet and reaches into the cooler for another piece of plantain, clearly not remorseful.

"Here you go, my darling," Mrs. Isibor says, placing a plate before where I sit at the table. "Let me make some *eba* for myself to eat with the soup."

My ears perk up when I hear *eba* and soup. Because of the cooking limitations at Alero's place, and the fact Mezie and his crew devoured the soup supplies I brought with me after only a few weekends, I am longing for a taste of home.

And she sees it.

"Or would you prefer to have some *eba*?" she asks, smiling.

I am too desperate for the meal to think of playing it cool, so I nod, not caring if my wide eyes are portraying just how eager I am for it.

"Please, let me help you make it," I say, remembering my manners and rising to my feet.

She smiles at me as I walk over to where she is now standing by the cooker, and I almost want to drop to my knees in ecstasy when I sight the steaming pot of *ogbono* soup.

"I'll have this then!" Roman says, taking my plate of rice. "Mom, Legachi makes the most delicious *jollof* rice ever!"

"Yeah, Obehi already told me that," Mrs. Isibor answers, looking at me with a glint in her eyes. "You must cook it for me next time I'm in London."

I blush as I work the *garri* in hot water with a spatula, nervous not only about not messing up the *eba* I'm making, but at the prospect of one day cooking for Roman's mother. Thankfully, I don't mess up the *eba* and it turns out perfectly. Soon, we are all sitting at the table eating; Mrs. Isibor and I the most delicious meal of *eba* and *ogbono* soup ever, Roman and Luna fried rice and plantain, and Paris just the leftover plantain. So delicious is the meal that when I see Mrs. Isibor eat with her hand, I do the same. I close my eyes, on a high with every mouthful, teleported back home. Of all the meals I have eaten since coming to London, this is by far the best.

"Legachi... that's an Ibo name, isn't it?" Mrs. Legachi inquires. "What state are you from?"

"Abia State," I manage to answer, through mouthfuls of food.

"Ah, Abia State. An uncle of mine married from there," she says. "Do you go there often?"

"We go home every year for Christmas," I answer, and I realize neither my parents nor siblings have said anything about a trip this year. It hits me that, for the first time, that tradition will be broken, and the realization saddens me.

Ever astute, Mrs. Isibor must notice a dip in my disposition as she pats me on my shoulder in silent consolation.

"Do you go home often?" I ask, wanting to change the topic.

She shakes her head. "Not in a while. Everyone I know back home is either dead or has relocated. The last time I went, I knew it was no longer home for me." She looks across the table where Roman sits, and there is a strange look on her face. "But Osareme has been there recently."

I turn to him, intrigued by this piece of information. But apart from a brief glance at his mother, he says nothing in response. The conversation soon moves on to other things, with Paris recounting how one of her crew members almost plunged to his death as they filmed on the Isle of Wight, and Mrs. Isibor praising me when she hears I'm studying for a Master's degree. It is such a pleasant experience, I can't believe I'd actually dreaded it.

All too soon, it is 5pm and time for us to leave. Mrs. Isibor hands me a bag.

"I packed some soup for you to have later, dear," she says, pulling me into an embrace. "Keep it up with your studies. Your parents must be so proud of you."

I am speechless by this show of warmth and generosity and can hardly wipe the smile off my face as the taxi ferries us to the train station.

"I had such a good time," I say to Roman, as our train pulls out of the station. "Your mom is such a lovely woman. Thanks so much for inviting me."

"Yeah, you two really hit it off," he smiles back. "You had her in the palm of your hand when she heard about you studying for a Master's degree. She'd only gone as far as secondary school when she got here and was never able to further her own education, so nothing excites her more than seeing women working hard to improve themselves. It's music to her ears."

I remember everything she told me about Roman and his siblings, and I smile. "She doesn't call any of you by your given names."

He chuckles. "Not since the day we were born. It was almost like she was telling my dad she wouldn't be a part of whatever strange epiphany he'd had to pick our names."

"Osareme," I say, a coy smile on my face. "Maybe I should start calling you that."

"Don't you dare!"

"Paris is Obehi, and… "

"Reagan is Odianose and Kennedy, Ogbeide."

"She said Odianose… Reagan… works in fashion?"

He raises an amused brow. "You two *really* got chatting. Yeah, he works as a stylist in Los Angeles."

"And Kennedy, the one who plans all your family trips?" I am quite enjoying this insight into his family.

"He and his wife are vets at the Beijing Zoo."

"Beijing as in China?"

He chuckles. "One and the same."

"I'm tired," a sleepy Luna says, placing her head on the seat divider.

I raise it up, move to her seat and carry her on my lap, allowing her to nestle her head on my chest. I place my handbag on my now vacant seat. It is only after I have done that that I realize I am now closer to Roman. I glance at him, worried he will think me forward by sitting next to him, but he has his eyes shut, probably very tired himself. And so, I decide to get comfortable, leaning my head back on the headrest. We are sitting close enough for his arm to be touching mine, and I close my eyes, enjoying being so close to him, intoxicated by his perfume, content to remain like that for the rest of my life.

"When are you taking out these braids?" I hear him chuckle, forcing my eyes to fling open.

Self-conscious of my hair and any smells that might be emanating from it, I laugh nervously and sit up, no longer confident enough to have my head so close to his.

"I have more important things than hair to worry about right now," I mutter, trying to mask my embarrassment however I can.

Roman

I feel like slapping myself when she sits up, wondering why, of all things I could have said, it had to be a snarky comment about her hair. I'd opened my eyes and seen her sitting with eyes closed, her head tilted in the most acute angle in my direction. I'd seen that we were sitting so close to each other, our arms were touching, and the feel of her awakened all my senses, even through the several layers of both our clothing. Her smell wafted into my nose, a clean, minty aroma with a mild hint of berries, and all I wanted to do was smell her forever. But then, I'd opened my big, fat mouth.

Despite Luna lying asleep in her arms, Legachi remains sitting in an upright position until the train pulls into Stratford Station, and even when we are in the underground train headed to Finchley Road. Wanting so much to be in close proximity again, I place my arm on the backrest behind her, willing her to lean back. But she remains sitting at a right angle.

Ah well.

When we open the door of the house, it is 6:45pm. Luna is still asleep, so I take her up to her room, keenly aware of the disruption to her schedule that day, and hopeful she will sleep through the night.

"Have a cup of tea with me before you leave," I say to Legachi when I am back downstairs. "I could do with a bit of company."

She hesitates briefly, before taking a seat.

"I didn't even ask, tea or coffee?" I ask, offering a sheepish smile.

"Hot chocolate, please," she answers, making to rise.

I raise a hand to stop her from standing. "Two mugs of hot chocolate coming up."

Neither of us says anything as I brew the hot beverage in the espresso machine, and as I pour it into two mugs, satisfied with the frothy mix.

"So, what's up?" I say, when we are seated. "Something's on your mind."

She blinks twice before shrugging. "Accommodation issues. Mezie shares a small flat with his friends and staying there was awful for me. That, and the fact the commute to my school from there is over an hour one way."

"Where does he stay?"

"Hackney."

I nod in understanding. Not exactly next door to Hendon.

"Anyway, a friend of mine offered me a temporary place, with the understanding that I had to be out by Christmas. But even with everything I've saved, I can't afford a place until the end of the month, at best. But I have to move by tomorrow." She sighs. "I hate the fact I'm returning to Mezie's apartment. You can't imagine how horrible the place is. I can barely tolerate it when I spend a night or two there. Now I have to live there."

I have a fair idea what that kind of arrangement would be like, and yes, it is hardly ever pleasant.

"But why didn't your scholarship cover living expenses?" I ask, curious about this again. "Or is it a partial one?"

She sighs. "It's a full scholarship, and you really don't want to know."

We are quiet for a few moments as we sip our sweet, hot drinks. An idea flashes in my head, and as it takes root, I sit up.

But of course!

"How about if I hire you as a live-in nanny?" I ask. "Apart from helping Luna in the mornings, you'll only have to watch her in the evenings, the way you currently do. That way, you'll have more time for school, not have to work at *Tesco* or wherever, and have a stable roof over your head. And I'll double your salary."

Her eyes widen as she gapes at me, clearly surprised by my proposition.

"For me, I'll be able to put in more hours at work," I continue, to let her know I too will benefit from the arrangement. "With you here with her, I can take longer shifts and rotations. So, it's really win-win." I take in a deep breath, aware that I'm rambling. "Your hours with Luna won't change much, so you'll be getting paid to have more time. Not to mention that you'll be able to save all your money, since you won't have to worry about accommodation." I shrug. "Think about it. You don't have to give me an answer now."

But a wide smile has already formed on her face.

"I don't have to think about anything!" she exclaims. "I accept. I accept a million times!"

"You don't want to talk it over with your boyfriend first?" I ask cautiously.

"Are you kidding? He'll be the first person to tell me to accept it fast!" she laughs. "So, you mean I'll finally be able to quit that hopeless *Poundyard* job?"

Aha, Poundyard not Tesco.

"Thank you so much, Roman," she reaches over to hug me, her voice shaking. "You don't know what you've just done for me. Thank you."

I shut my eyes, again savoring her minty, berry smell, but she soon pulls away, wiping tears from her eyes.

"Nah, I should be thanking you," I say to her. "You'll be doing me a huge favour as well."

We agree that she can move in tomorrow evening, and shutting the door after she leaves, I am equal parts surprised by my impulsive offer and excited about the prospect of her moving in with me. With us, I quickly correct myself. Moving in with *us*, Luna and me. I haven't made the offer for anything other than what will clearly be for everyone's benefit; Legachi's, Luna's and mine.

Nothing more than that.

Legachi

All the way back to Golders Green, it feels like I'm floating. I say several prayers thanking God for this wonderful stroke of luck, still unable to believe how I have gone from being pretty much homeless, to being offered a comfortable roof over my head, and without my having to spend a dime. This is beyond lucky or fortuitous. This is a downright blessing from the Most High!

Alero is out when I get home. Settling on the couch for what will be the last time, I dial Mezie's number, but it rings off. I try a few more times and the same thing happens. It isn't yet 9pm, so it's too early for him to be at the club. Shrugging, I decide to tell him in person tomorrow. The agreement with Roman is for me to move in later in the day, so I can see Mezie earlier to share with him the great news.

But as I lie on the couch later on, a part of me nags about why I'm really so excited… and if it has anything to do with the butterflies in my stomach I still get just by looking at Roman. But I immediately shut those wayward thoughts down. My excitement has everything, and I mean everything, to do with the fact it is rescuing me from a bind.

Nothing more than that.

Twenty-Two

Flat Mates

Legachi

ith my things still at Alero's, I set off for Mezie's the next morning. It is almost 11 when I get off the 55 bus, and I am confident that he would have woken up by that time. But to my surprise, he isn't even there. And neither Nedu, Eche, Diran nor Alex is willing to give me any reasonable explanation for his absence.

"Maybe he follow Lateef go house," is Eche's lame offering.

"Abi im dey sleep for club. Maybe he too shayo last night," is Nedu's even lamer one.

But I know Mezie would never get drunk at work, neither would he follow Lateef all the way to Shepherd's Bush where he stays.

I make my way to his room and the bed is untouched, confirmation he hasn't been there this morning. I lift his pillows and peer under the bed, looking for anything questionable, anything to confirm my suspicions. But the place is clean; no condoms, no female underwear, no smell of strange perfume, nothing. I kick off my shoes and sit comfortably on the bed, determined to wait for him to return from wherever it is he has gone.

It is 1:30pm when he finally walks into his bedroom. I look up from the *Argos* catalogue I have been idly flipping through, and a look of irritation flashes across his face when our eyes meet.

"You didn't tell me you were coming," he mutters, sitting on the bed next to me and pulling off his boots.

"Is that why you don't look pleased to see me?"

He sighs deeply and shakes his head. "Legachi, if it's fight you came here for, *come and be going abeg*. This is the last thing I need now."

I stare at him, not recognizing who he is, who we are. "What's happening to us, Mezie?"

He shrugs. "You're the one who likes to stoke fires and pick unnecessary fights."

I open my mouth to respond, but I have no words. No doubt, a cancer is ravaging our relationship, eating away deeper every day.

"I'm sorry," I say, trying to do what I can to make things right. "I think we need to talk about this, so we're able to… "

The door opens, cutting me short.

"Guy, I don dey wait you!" Eche bellows. "Come parlour make we discuss that thing."

I look at Mezie, willing him to dismiss his friend, willing him to tell him he and I are having a serious discussion, but I am disappointed when, instead, he grins and rises to his feet, disappearing with Eche out the door.

I wait for almost an hour, wait for him to wrap up whatever discussion they are having, but he doesn't show up. In the end, I go to find him, and I am surprised to see him, not engrossed in discussion with Eche, but lying on the couch, scrolling through his phone.

"I've been waiting for you, Mezie."

"Why? What's up?" he mumbles, not even deeming it fit to look up at me.

What's up? We were about to have a serious discussion about our relationship, and he's asking me *'what's up'*? Deciding that's a discussion we can have later, I sit next to him on the couch.

"I have some good news about my accommodation," I say, smiling. "Can you guess?"

"There's always something dramatic about your living situation, Legachi," he grunts, still not looking up from his phone. "Has your crazy flat mate thrown you out?

I recoil, feeling like he has struck me across the face.

When I say nothing, he finally looks up at me. "You've finally saved enough to move to campus, right? You've found a room, isn't it? Is that the good news?" he chuckles and shakes his head. "Don't make a big deal out of it. There's nothing special about securing one small box room, just so you can feel good about staying on campus."

"Wetin happen?" Alex who, as usual, is playing a video game, asks.

"Na that their yeye school accommodation she don get wey she no wan make we hear word!" Mezie cackles.

I am stunned silent as his friends laugh along with him, cracking jokes about sharing kitchen and toilet facilities with Caucasian and Asian flat mates. I remain quiet as they laugh, and even when they all return their attention to what they were doing prior. My heart breaks as I realize that Mezie and I are now unable to even have a simple conversation. Something as phenomenal as me finding a solution to my accommodation problems has happened, and I can't even talk to him about it.

I sit there for another hour, all the while with him still on his phone. Looking at the time and seeing that it is almost 4pm, I concede that coming there has been a wasted endeavor.

"I need to go now," I say, my voice coming out a croak. "Please come to the room, so we can talk."

I get up and walk to the bedroom before he has a chance to complain.

"What do you want, Legachi? Can't you even allow me rest today?" he mutters, walking in behind me.

"Something is broken between us Mezie," I say to him. "Something is horribly broken."

He rolls his eyes and shakes his head. "Your stress is too much, I swear."

I regard him for what must be a full minute, but looking at him, I know there is probably no going back from this.

"I think we should take a break from each other," I finally say. "I think we need to take some time apart to decide if this," I point at the space separating us, "is worth saving."

He hisses and rolls his eyes again, before turning in the direction of the door. "Girl, do what you fucking like. *Your wahala too much.*"

And he leaves, slamming the door shut.

In resignation, I put on my shoes, sling my handbag across my shoulder, and walk out of the room. Nobody speaks to me as I make my way to the front door, or even when I stop to pick up my coat. And I say nothing to them either. Instead, I walk with my head high down the corridor and down the staircase. As I am about to exit the main door, I see the mystery light-skinned, red-lipped girl from several months before.

"Excuse me," I call out to her as she walks past me, totting a large bag.

She turns around and raises well curved eyebrows.

"You're going to the boys' flat upstairs?" I ask. "Who are you going to see?"

"Harry. Is he around?"

She pronounces it *Hairy*, and I can immediately detect an Ibo accent.

I nod and smile, the confirmation of my suspicion from as far back as then.

"Yes, he's around," I answer, still smiling.

Mezie and I are over.

As I make my way to the bus stop, rather than feel devastated, I am relieved. The worrying, the over-thinking, the mind games, not to mention the disrespect... I am relieved all of that is over. Yes, it's been almost eight years of my life, but I'd rather cut my losses now than endure another second of what I've had to, not only in the time I have been in London, but, if I'm to be honest, the last three or four years of our relationship.

It is time to let all that go.

Roman

I give the guest room another onceover, looking around to make sure everything is perfect. With brand new yellow sheets and an also new yellow and blue comforter, I hope the room is as welcoming as it is cheerful.

"It's pretty," Luna remarks, a broad smile on her face, reflecting the excitement she's had since I told her Legachi is moving in.

"Yes, darling. It is. It's Legachi's room."

"Is she living here forever?"

I want to tell her the obvious answer, which is no, but I also don't want to spoil her excitement. So, I lift her off her feet and give her a spin, laughing along with her as she giggles. We'll save difficult discussions for later.

At 7:30pm, I have started wondering if I heard Legachi correctly about moving in today, when she rings the doorbell. I smile at the habit she has of sometimes doing that when she knows I'm in the house, as against opening the door with her keys. Well, now that she lives here, there won't be any need for that.

"I'm so sorry I'm late," she pants, dragging in the last of her boxes. "I got held up."

I can't help but wonder if it was her boyfriend that 'held her up' and have to shake off mental images of them having parting sex. Nope, Roman. That is absolutely none of your business.

"No worries at all," I smile. "Let me help you with these."

I lift the heavier of the boxes and carry it upstairs, with her and Luna tailing me.

"Wow! This room looks different!" she exclaims, her eyes brightening when she walks into it.

"I made a few changes to make you more comfortable," I say. "I've given Luna a bath and ordered in some Chinese. When you're ready, you can come join us downstairs."

Coaxing Luna out the door with me, we leave Legachi to settle into her new room.

Legachi

I stare at the beautiful room decorated blue and yellow, not believing this is all for me. It's not an uncomfortable sofa-bed, neither is it a narrow bed I have to share with Mezie in a room with other people in a sleeping bag. I smile as I open the empty closets, grateful I will no longer have to live out of a box. I lie on the soft bed, spread-eagled, and start to giggle, still unbelieving of the turnaround in my luck.

Breaking up with Mezie gave my day a shitty start, but this solution to my accommodation issues has been the biggest blessing of all. No longer will I have to miss any classes that are scheduled for afternoon. No longer will I have to slave and toil on *Poundyard's* shop floor. No longer will I be too tired at the end of the day to pay adequate attention to my books. All that is over now. Yes, the end of my relationship with Mezie feels like the end of an era, but I am grateful to him regardless, because if it weren't for him, I wouldn't have contemplated applying for the *Skyline* scholarship, or even coming to London. And now that all my money drama is over, I can now settle back and enjoy the experience properly.

Roman

At Luna's prompting, we put up our Christmas tree the next day. I smile at them as they fuss over the box of ornaments and as Legachi lifts Luna to place balls and fairies on the branches. It has been a long time since I enjoyed putting up a Christmas tree and less than twenty-four hours in, I'm loving her being here more than ever.

Starting from as early as I when I walked out of my room this morning and was hit with the smell of her mint and berry body wash from the bathroom she shares with Luna, to seeing her fresh faced in the kitchen, dressed casually in a long-sleeved t-shirt and track bottoms, to when all three of us had breakfast together in the kitchen, eating the fried eggs, hash browns and sausages I made, having her here is different from when anyone else has stayed over, even my live-in Au Pair. Having her here feels… right.

And I know I haven't made a mistake.

"Does Luna have to go to daycare today?" Legachi asks as we sit at the table the next morning, both of us having cups of coffee while

Luna has her cereal. "School is out for the holidays, so I could watch her."

It is Monday, Christmas Eve, but I have some consultations scheduled for the day.

"Cheryl is throwing the kids a party," I answer. "Luna wouldn't hear anything about missing it."

"Ah, the Christmas party is very important!" she giggles. "Will it go all the way till 5, or do I pick her up earlier?"

"Cheryl hasn't mentioned anything, so I'm guessing it's the same pick-up time," I say, rising to my feet. "Besides, they're closed for a whole week after this."

She nods as she also rises, clearing both our cups and Luna's tray. I am initially tempted to ask her not to bother doing that but remind myself that's what she's being paid to do. We all walk outside, but while Legachi and Luna head to the bus stop, my own destination is the tube station.

"Call me if you need anything, okay?" I say to her, after waving at Luna goodbye.

She nods and flashes her gap-toothed smile. I have to force myself to turn around and walk away. If this living arrangement is to work, I'm going to have to learn not to react to her brown eyes, wide hips, or the gap between her teeth.

My last appointment is cancelled, so I am able to leave the hospital by noon. Sitting in the train, I decide to make a stop at the supermarket to buy some last-minute supplies for the holidays. I disembark at Swiss Cottage station, the stop before my usual one, and get on a bus to the *Tesco* at Belsize Park. Getting off the bus, I hear the rumble of what sounds like thunder and I look up at the sky, wondering if this will be another wet Christmas.

As expected for Christmas Eve, the express store, which is smaller than the standard ones in the chain, is packed. I grab a basket and head towards the fresh produce aisle, to see if I can find fruits for the trifles Luna likes, the only dessert I know how to make. But if I'm to be honest, it isn't Luna I'm looking forward to impressing this time.

I am reaching for peaches when I see Legachi down the aisle, examining two tins of canned fruit, trying to make a selection. A smile curves my lips as I watch her read the labels of both tins, her brows furrowed in a focused frown. She is still dressed in the oversized, navy blue pullover over jeans that she was wearing this morning, but even with the loose clothing masking her curves and her face devoid of any makeup, I am unable to take my eyes off her. As if sensing my gaze, she looks up and smiles when she sees me. My heart lurches as brown eyes twinkle at me, and I walk in her direction.

"Fancy seeing you here," I remark, before looking at the two tins in her hand. "Go with the *Nature's Finest*. That's the better choice of the two."

"But it's £2 more expensive!"

"It also has 10g less sugar per 100g than the other one."

She pouts and reluctantly replaces the cheaper one. "A little bit of sugar isn't that bad."

"Tell that to my patients," I chuckle. "What do you need this for?" My eyes widen when I see her overflowing basket on the floor beside her.

She laughs at my reaction. "I just wanted to get a few supplies to bake some treats for Christmas. I'm sure Luna is sick of eating my scones by now."

My face falls as I realize I forgot to tell her.

"Luna and I usually spend a couple of days in Borehamwood with Ihidie and Tosan at Christmas. We'll be leaving tomorrow morning."

The smile on her face wanes. "Oh, okay. It's fine, I can always bake them for her later."

"Maybe New Year's Day?" I offer, smiling again to goad hers.

It works as she brightens. "New Year's Day it is."

"I thought you'd have plans for Christmas Day," I say to her as we walk down the baked goods aisle. "Aren't you spending the day with your boyfriend?"

She shakes her head. "If it's okay, I'd like to just stay home. But if you'd rather have the house empty… "

"It's your house now, Legachi," I cut in. "You don't have to ask for permission to be there when we're not."

She smiles in gratitude at me, but that smile turns into a frown when we get to the till, and I insist on paying.

"I have a lot of my own personal supplies in there, Roman," she protests, referring to the contents of her basket. "I came here to pick up some toiletries and other personal items. I'm not going to allow you pay for those."

"Consider it an early Christmas present then," I answer with a wink.

She shakes her head and acquiesces, and as both our items are rung up and bagged, I have to fight the temptation not to look at these 'toiletries and personal items' she is buying. The last thing I need is a visual of what brand of body wash or maybe even underwear she favours. No, I have more than enough to feed my imagination already.

It starts to rain as we walk to the bus stop, and we have to run to catch the 31 bus, which is about to pull away. We are drenched and panting when we finally board it. It is packed, so we have to stand, holding the overhead grab handles, our bags of groceries at our feet.

"What kind of heavy rain is this on Christmas Eve?" she remarks. "Isn't it supposed to be snowing by now?"

"Welcome to London, where you're more likely to have a wet Christmas than a white one," I answer, chuckling.

The bus stops abruptly at a traffic light, and I instinctively put my arm around her waist to prevent her from lurching forward. She turns to me, and I immediately drop my hand and look away, not wanting to make her uncomfortable. But for the rest of the ride home, my body burns with the imprint of hers on mine.

The next stop is ours and we alight into the rain, which is now pouring even harder. Struggling with grocery bags, we run home, the eight-minute distance from the station seeming more like eighty. After running for what seems like forever, we finally get to the house. We huddle under the portico as I make to open the door, standing so close, I can feel her breath on my face. I turn to her, her face only inches away from mine, her light brown eyes staring back at me, and all thoughts about the keys, the door, or even the rain, are forgotten. Cupping her face with my hands, my lips claim hers... and they are luscious, soft and sweet, just like I have imagined.

Uegachi

My breath catches in my throat as his lips take mine, in the perfect climax to the tension I have felt since seeing him at the grocery store. From looking up and seeing him standing down that aisle, gorgeous in a black peacoat jacket over a navy blue cardigan and indigo blue jeans, to the feel of his body when he pulled me close to break my fall in the bus, to us standing cheek-to-cheek seeking shelter under the portico as he tried to open the door, all my senses have been heightened, and the feel of his lips on mine is an hallelujah moment, a symphony, a full-on orchestra complete with sopranos, tenors and bass. I close my eyes as I savour this kiss that has stopped my world on its axis, no longer feeling the chill of the rain still striking us. Knotting my fists in his jacket, I pull him closer, and he groans softly as his arms circle my waist, pulling me even closer still as our kiss deepens.

And then his phone vibrates, bringing us both back to reality.

He immediately pulls away and turns to the door, the hitherto stubborn key now opening it in one swift movement. Once open, he picks up the bags of groceries from the floor with one hand and reaches for his phone with the other as he walks into the house.

I stand at the doorway, stunned, wondering if I have just imagined what just happened. I pick up the bag he missed and follow him into the kitchen. He is talking on the phone as he loads what we bought into the fridge and pantry. I stand there for a few seconds, not knowing if I'm expected to wait for his call to be over, or if we're to pretend it never happened. Deciding it is best for me to at least get out of my wet clothes, I turn around and head upstairs to change.

In my bedroom toweling myself dry, my heart races as I have flashbacks of the kiss. I close my eyes as I remember the sensation of his tender lips, the taste of coffee in his breath, the subtle prickle of his stubble, and the feel of his firm chest and thumping heart when I held him, and I know that I don't want to pretend it never happened.

I want this man.

I take my time getting dressed, choosing one of my more flattering cardigans over a pair of jeans. I line my eyes and apply lip gloss, in what I hope will enhance my looks, and finish it up with a spritz of the bottle of perfume I only save for special occasions. Satisfied with the outcome, I take a deep breath and make my way downstairs.

But I am disappointed to see he has not only left the kitchen but is now in his study. I sit in the kitchen, hearing his voice as he talks on the phone, waiting for him to come out. As the minutes become hours, as the silence from the room indicates he is no longer on the phone but is still choosing to remain there, I am forced to accept that the kiss, for him, was just an unfortunate fluke that will probably never repeat itself.

When it is 4:45, I have no choice but to slip on my jacket and set off to Luna's daycare. The rain outside might have stopped but the storm inside me is raging worse than ever before.

Roman

I hear the door shut and exhale. I rub my eyes and groan, wondering what on earth I was thinking kissing her like that. I have never been one to give in to passion that way and have always been calculated and deliberate with every woman I have been with, Sekani inclusive. This wanton act of throwing all caution to the wind and kissing Legachi without even stopping to think about it, is alien behaviour for me.

But wanton thought it might have been, I can still taste her lips, smell her perfume, feel her curves. I groan in my body's response to the reminder, the reminder that I want her so bad, it physically hurts.

For the first time, I wonder if I made a mistake asking her to move in.

Twenty-Three

Christmas

Cegachi

I awake early on Christmas morning and, after speaking with my family on the phone, have a shower and go downstairs, holding the gifts I have bought for Roman and Luna, with the intent of putting them under the Christmas tree. I am surprised to meet them already down there as early as 7am.

"We were just about to come get you," Roman beams at me. "Merry Christmas."

"Merry Christmas," I say to him with a smile of my own, before lifting Luna up and hugging her. "Merry Christmas, munchkin!"

"Christmas mornings are for presents," Roman declares, beckoning me over as he walks to the tree.

I watch him go, and follow a few seconds later, holding Luna's hand, no longer even trying to figure out what he must be thinking. When Luna and I got back home yesterday, I'd expected either of two things; that he would want to talk about the kiss or he'd be so regretful, he'd become cold and aloof again. I'd been surprised to meet him nice and chatty, making me wonder if the kiss had been a figment of my imagination. If it weren't for the throb I still had in my lips, that would have been my conclusion. But if he has chosen to archive it as a non-issue, then I probably should too.

"I guess these are late," I say, putting my gifts under the tree.

"Gifts are never late," he says. "And you really shouldn't have, Legachi."

I shrug and smile. Truth is, with the stress on my finances only just eased, I'd picked them yesterday before going to *Tesco*. And sitting on the floor, cross-legged, with my boss and his daughter, I'm so glad I did. It would have been a disaster if I'd joined them for their annual ritual without any gifts of my own to present.

Luna gets her gifts first, and she squeals at the entire collection of Disney Princess dolls from her father, a building block set from her grandmother, a light-up activity board from her Aunty Paris, a Bianca City Life dollhouse from her Uncle Kennedy, and the most beautiful two-piece *Burberry* knit dress and cardigan set from her Uncle Reagan. By the time her little hands touch my own gift, I pray she isn't disappointed, and I regret her not opening it before the other wonderful gifts she's gotten. But she is excited by the musical storybooks, throwing her arms around me as she thanks me.

"Your turn," Roman smiles at me.

I am touched to see wrapped gifts from Paris and his mother and have to swallow back tears, still stunned that I have gone from being almost homeless, to not just celebrating Christmas in a lovely home, but being presented gifts as well. I smile at the self-love workbook from Paris and the scented candle set from Mrs. Isibor, but it is the beautiful, pastel blue cashmere sweater from Roman and Luna that melts my heart.

"Because we noticed you like blue," he says, smiling at me.

That I do. Our eyes hold and I search his for something, anything, any leftover sign of passion from yesterday. But there is nothing.

"Daddy's turn!" Luna squeals, bobbing up and down.

"What do we have here?" he exclaims, looking at the pack of multi-coloured, Christmas-themed socks from Luna. "These are amazing! The best Christmas present ever!"

I smile as he embraces her and as she beams, proud of the gifts her aunt has most likely helped her buy. He proceeds to open his other gifts; a Shiatsu back, neck and shoulder massager from his mother, a Bluetooth smart pen and notebook set from Paris, a wireless charging pad and organizer from Kennedy, and a *Ralph Lauren* messenger bag from Reagan. I see he has deliberately left my gift for last, and his brows raise when he unwraps my gift.

"*There Was a Country*," he calls out the name of the Chinua Achebe book I found in *Waterstone* the day before. I'd been so excited seeing it and had bought it without a second thought, certain at the time it would be a good gift.

"Because you like to read, and also because you said you wanted to know more about your country," I offer lamely, suddenly wishing I'd splurged on a nicer gift.

"This is amazing!" he remarks, and there is no falsity in the expression on his face. "I've heard a lot about the book. Thanks so much."

Our eyes hold again, but this time, I see a flicker of something I cannot quite decipher. Is it gratitude for the gift? Wistfulness over our shared moment? He looks away, distracted by Luna, and I rise to my feet, sick of all the guessing and speculation. Half an hour later, we are dining on waffles and sausages, and when he and Luna go upstairs to shower and get ready for their trip, I proceed to tidy up.

"You're all set?" I ask, meeting them as they descend the stairs about an hour later, dressed in thick coats and scarves, and with Roman holding a tote bag with their things. "I hope you're driving. I just checked and Borehamwood is only a thirty-minute drive."

"Nope. It's still forecasted to rain this afternoon and I have no intention of driving on the M1 under those conditions."

"So, you'd rather hop from train to train then?" I laugh, amazed by his apathy to driving his own car.

"It's a straight train from West Hampstead. If it's raining when we get to Borehamwood, Ihidie will come pick us from the station." West Hampstead is the stop right after ours, justifying his argument.

Before I can say anything more in argument, the doorbell rings. He bounds over to open the door, and in walks a beautiful woman. A very beautiful woman.

"Merry Christmas, my darling!" she exclaims, throwing long, slender arms around him and kissing him.

My brows raise in surprise. Her darling?

Interesting.

She detaches from him and bends to embrace Luna. "Merry Christmas, precious. I've missed you both."

As she talks, I notice the strong resemblance she has with the late Sekani and wonder if she might be her sister. But would she really be kissing her late sister's husband as passionately as she's done?

"Umm, Merry Christmas, Itunu," Roman says, the look on his face a reflection of his own surprise.

Itunu. Not Sekani's sister then.

"Were you on your way out?" she asks. "Thank God I caught you then. I got you and… and the angel gifts!"

I cross my arms and watch as she hurls in two large boxes; one bedecked in a flashy black and gold Versace wrapping paper with a red bow atop it the only indication of anything related to Christmas, and the other draped in a pink and yellow polka wrap.

"Can we open them, daddy?" Luna squeals, her eyes lit by the elaborate gifts.

"Maybe when we get back, sweetheart," Roman says to her. "We really have to get going."

Noticing me, the Itunu looks in my direction and then back at Roman with questioning eyes.

"That's Legachi, Luna's nanny," he answers. "Legachi, this is my... friend, Itunu."

I smile, more from the much-needed reminder of what exactly I am to him. His daughter's nanny. "Nice to meet you."

"It's lovely to meet you too," she offers me a stiff smile, before returning her attention to Roman. "Good call. A Nigerian minder is a much better idea than those horny Au Pairs you used to have."

Horny Au Pairs? *Ah,* so we've been many?

I watch them as they talk, taking a better look at the glamorous woman. She is dressed in a brown leather puffer coat over a black turtleneck, tight black leather pants and shiny black, patent leather, thigh-high boots, looking like someone commanding the weather, and not the other way around as is the case for us mere mortals. Her jet-black, bone straight wig hangs well past her bottom and the gloss of her milk chocolate skin is evidence of premium care. But *of course,* this is the kind of woman he will want. She looks just like his late wife, meaning he very clearly has a type. When she leans closer and kisses him again, I smile and shake my head at my foolishness. If I needed any proof that yesterday meant nothing to him, this is it in the flesh.

Fed up with the spectacle and in search of a distraction, I reach for my phone in my pocket.

Roman

As Itunu talks, I stare at her, still in a daze. If I were to have predicted who would show up at my doorstep on Christmas morning, Itunu would have been one of my very last guesses. I look from her moving mouth to the obscenely large gift boxes on the floor. What the hell is happening here?

"You didn't need to get these gifts, Itunu," I say, keeping my voice low, so as not to embarrass her.

She leans closer and kisses me briefly on the lips, prompting a horrified wide-eyed look from me. For goodness' sake, my daughter is watching.

"I've missed you," she says, imploring eyes looking back at mine. "I did everything I could to forget you, but I couldn't. You're the love of my life, Roman."

I steal a glance at Luna, who is distracted by the yellow bow on the pink gift box. My eyes also dart to Legachi, and I feel a stab of disappointment to see she is scrolling through her phone, disappointed she doesn't even seem to care that I am talking to another woman.

"You already know my position on that," I mutter, returning my attention to Itunu. "I'm sorry, but we have to leave now."

"Where are you going, sweetheart?" she directs her question at Luna.

"To see my cousins. We're going with the train."

Itunu looks at me and I shrug. "We're off to Borehamwood."

"I could drive you. You don't have to take the train. I'd love to drive you there."

I shake my head but before I can verbalise my refusal, she returns her attention to Luna.

"Would you like to ride in my car, sweetheart? It's much nicer than going in the stupid train. What do you say?"

Luna shrugs, uncharacteristically unenthusiastic. "Okay."

"It's settled then!" Itunu says, clapping her hands with glee. "Come on, darling. Your daughter has spoken."

I look at Luna, but she has run to Legachi to hug her goodbye. As they say their goodbyes, I try, with no success, to meet Legachi's gaze. For some reason, I am desperate to read her mind through her eyes, desperate to non-verbally communicate Itunu's irrelevance. But her eyes stay on Luna, and even when Luna walks back to me, they remain averted as she walks behind us to the door.

"Have a wonderful Christmas!" she calls out, her voice bright and loud, waving as if she can't wait to see the last of us.

My eyes linger on the door long after it has shut and I have to fight off the urge to pound it open and ask why the hell she doesn't care. The realisation of that annoys me more than Itunu's very unwelcome appearance.

Legachi

The smile wipes off my face the very moment the door is shut. As soul crushing as it is, I am grateful for this finger-snap back to reality. *Omo*, I'd actually started to believe Roman might have a thing for me. Making my way to the living room, I shake my head and chuckle. Talk about being a big dreamer!

Stretching on the couch, I watch TV all day, from *Top of The Pops*, to *The Jungle Book*, to the *Strictly Come Dancing* Christmas show, to *Michael McIntyre's Big Christmas Show*. I can't remember ever having this opportunity to just laze in front of the TV all day since getting to this country. I speak to my parents and sisters again and receive a call from Nonye.

"Merry Christmas, *nne*! I thought I would see you today."

"My dear, I'm so sorry. I had to move from Alero's on Saturday, so it's been really hectic."

"I hope you didn't go back to Mezie's place *o*."

For someone who has been the biggest promoter of my holding on to Mezie, this is very surprising to hear.

"I didn't go back there. We've broken up."

"Thank God! My dear, that boy is no good! You made the right decision, *biko*. Tayo's friends that go to his club say he is a community prick. Very wayward, useless boy. You're better off without him."

I chuckle at her colourful words, not even upset by yet another confirmation of everything I have suspected. "I thought you were his fan. Weren't you the one telling me I had to 'hold on to my man'?"

"That was before that first night at the club that he talked down on you," she admits. "Even Tayo complained bitterly about it all the way back to school."

I think back to all the years of verbal abuse and can't even understand how I subjected myself to that for so long.

"Anyway, we'll talk more about it when next we see," I say, changing the topic. "I got you a nice Christmas gift. I'll find time to bring it to you later this week."

"*You no dey ever disappoint!*" she squeals. "I trust you! Meanwhile, how is that your handsome, smoking hot boss?"

"Now my handsome, smoking hot *landlord*. I moved in to take care of his daughter full-time."

Her squeal is so shrill, I have to move the phone far from my ears.

"You're living with him? You're living with the fine doctor?"

"Hold your horses, madam!" I say, reining her in. "Let's not get carried away. *The guy dey im lane, I dey my own.* Let's leave it like that, I beg you."

And that is exactly how I need it to be!

Twenty-Four

Mess You Up

Legachi

I am watching *Mrs Doubtfire* on Channel 4 when I hear the door open the following evening. Sitting up, my eyes widen when I see Roman walk in... alone.

"I didn't know you were coming back today," I say, rising to my feet. "Where is Luna?"

"Paris took her along when she left Borehamwood for Chelmsford. She'll be there till after the New Year," he answers, before smiling at the TV. "*Mrs. Doubtfire.* I hope that's not an indication of how bored you've been. Sorry about that."

I manage a smile in response. "I actually like the movie. I haven't been bored at all."

And then it dawns on me that if Luna won't be here until after the New Year, he might not have any need for me to stay.

"Do I need to leave until Luna gets back?"

He shakes his head. "No, of course not. You can use the time to settle in properly," he smiles again. "I'll try not to get too much in your way."

Our eyes hold, and I am still wondering what he means by this and if it is any reference to our kiss, when Itunu walks in through the door. Aha. I was wondering why he hadn't yet shut it.

"Hello there," she throws at me, without even sparing me a glance, her eyes on Roman instead. "Sweetie, should I give these to her to heat up for us?"

My eyes go to the bag of takeaway in her hands and a bubble of rage starts to well up inside me. But I quickly catch myself. Of course, she... *they*... would expect me to run errands for them. Why else am I here?

"No, no, I'll do that," Roman says, quickly taking the bags from her, shutting the front door, and walking towards the kitchen, all without looking at me.

Itunu lingers at the doorway and turns to me, her smile completely gone. She gives me a onceover, from the crown of my hair to my socked feet, and she must decide I pose no threat as she offers a thin smile. "You alright?"

I nod, not bothering with a smile of my own. "Yes. Thank you."

The unmistakable smell of Chinese food wafts in from the kitchen, reminding me that the lovebirds are about to feast on their meal. Even though I have been procrastinating my own lunch and am already decidedly hungry, I decide it is in my better interest to retire upstairs. I neither want to be a third wheel nor do I want to witness the lovers in action. So, as Itunu heads to the living room, changing the channel from my Channel 4 movie, I turn around in the direction of the stairs.

Roman

"Where is Legachi?" I ask as I walk out of the kitchen.

Itunu shrugs, sitting cross-legged and idly flicking from channel to channel. "She must have gone upstairs. I told you that you didn't have to order a third pack of food."

I look up in the direction of the stairs, disappointed. I'd been hoping to at least dine with her. I turn back to the kitchen to prevent myself from verbalising the deep resentment I have for Itunu being the one I will be stuck with that evening.

All through the ride to Borehamwood the day before, she was extremely chatty, talking non-stop about having spent the last four months at Gucci's headquarters in Florence, flying intermittently to style more stores in Los Angeles, New York and Vegas. I'd had no choice but to endure all that yack, hoping to be able to dismiss her upon getting to our destination. But with Sean and Lara already there, Itunu had felt right at home with her friends, and stayed back to enjoy Ihidie and Tosan's annual Christmas party. I'd managed to avoid her by sticking close to Ojie and his friends the rest of the day, even leaving with them when they went to their local pub, but alas, through Tosan, Itunu found out my plans of returning to London this afternoon and showed up at the house right on the dot of 3pm to pick me up. With Luna already having left with Paris earlier in the day, I had no tangible reason to decline her ride back to London. But this time, I made sure to restate my position.

"Itunu, nothing has changed from the last time we spoke," I'd said to her in the car. "I'm not interested in anything romantic with you."

"You've said that a million times, Roman," she laughed, looking at me. "I get it. Is there anything wrong with just being friends?"

"So, is that what this is?" I asked, my tone incredulous. "The Christmas gifts, the rides to and from Borehamwood? You just being a friend?"

"Just being a friend, darling," she grinned, squeezing my cheek with her free hand.

I was not at all convinced. I'm still not.

To buttress my point, after I've taken her food to her on a tray, I return to the kitchen and sit alone to have my own meal of dumplings and sweet and sour pork. The meal of prawn fried rice and shredded beef I got for Legachi is sitting on the counter, and I can't tell what I am more upset by; that she isn't happy I've returned or that she hasn't been bothered to even sit with me for the meal. Maybe she is inconvenienced by my returning earlier than she expected. Maybe, while I'm here bemoaning not sharing a meal with her, she is upstairs talking to that good-for-nothing boyfriend of hers.

The last thought irks me.

"Why did you leave me all by myself, Roman?" comes Itunu's voice from the door. "You're not being a good host."

I will myself to smile at her and beckon her over. I might as well eat with her.

Legachi

Roman's guest doesn't leave until 11:13pm.

The next day, he leaves early for the hospital, and I don't venture to the living room the whole day, not wanting a repeat of what happened the day before. Maybe this is what he does every time Luna is away; bring his women back to the house. The last thing I want is to be a fly in his ointment, cramping his style. So, after making sure the house is tidy, I retreat to my bedroom, not even opening my door later that night when he returns from the hospital. I repeat the same pattern today, making extra sure not to get in his way or inconvenience him at all.

But what has been an inconvenience are the calls and text messages I have been receiving from Mezie since Boxing Day.

So, you really didn't call me on Christmas Day? was the first message he sent.

When I didn't reply, he'd followed this with a call, which I also ignored.

You're ignoring me now? Girl, you too dey vex! he'd texted. Again, I ignored it.

Since then, I have lost count of the calls and messages from him. Why on earth is he harassing me now? Isn't Miss 'Hairy' satisfying him enough? Or the several other women I know are in the picture? He made it crystal clear he doesn't think enough of me to accord respect, talk less of be faithful to, so why is he blowing up my phone with these calls that mean nothing? I am tempted to block him, but I realise I am deriving immense pleasure from seeing his missed calls and ignored texts.

Let him have a taste of his own medicine.

I successfully ignore him until that evening when my phone rings. It is a number I don't recognise, and I answer it. Big mistake.

"So, it has come to this, Legachi. I can only reach you through a number you don't know?"

I hiss under my breath hearing his voice, a voice that only a short time ago made me weak in the knees. But after all the mess of the last few months, it is no surprise all it does now is grate.

"You told me to do what I fucking like, didn't you?" The petty side of me feels the need to remind him. "You told me my *wahala* is too much, *abi*?"

"I see," is his scant response, followed by a mirthless laugh. "*No wahala.*"

I find myself a little disappointed, having steeled myself to hear his relentless begging. Even though I have absolutely no intention of going back to him, I was hoping to at least have him grovel. But it appears I'm not worth even that.

"Your scholarship documents are still here with me," he says. "The *Skyline* contract and information pack."

I wince, remembering that I indeed did leave the vital envelope at his place. After my registration, I haven't had any need for it, but I know I might need to refer to it over the course of the rest of my stay in England. Leaving it at his place is not an option.

"Can you mail it to me?" I ask, but even I know the folly of that wish. Besides, the last thing I want is for him to have Roman's address.

He grunts, confirming the futility of my request. "Come get it, so I'll know I'm free of you and all your belongings."

"I'll come this weekend to pick it up," I retort, eager to communicate that I too am in a hurry to rid myself of him. "If you won't be there, just leave with one of your friends."

"We're all away this weekend for Ubosi's birthday party in Bristol. I'd come now if I were you."

I glance at my wristwatch. It is almost 5pm. I decide it's early enough to make a quick dash to Hackney and back.

"No problem. I'm on my way."

Walking up to the apartment block, even though it has only been days since I was there last, I am already as emotionally detached as someone who hasn't been there in years. Making my way up the stairs, I have a vivid flashback of battling up them with my suitcases when I first arrived and battling down them with the same suitcases as I fled to Alero's place. I smile and shake my head as I think about all the lofty hopes and dreams I'd come to London with, believing Mezie would take me to a cute, small apartment and, with what was left of my living expenses allowance after he paid for his exam, we would live happily ever after. But now, only three months later, everything has spectacularly imploded.

Tragic.

"Hey, our wife!" Diran remarks when he opens the door, even though his eyes look somewhat flat. "We didn't see you this Christmas."

I just smile in response as I walk in, not bothering to tell him Mezie and I have broken up and I'm no longer their 'wife'. I wave a greeting at Nedu who is sitting on the couch, eating a plate of rice, marvelling anew over what layabouts the lot of them are. Apart from Diran who leaves for his job as a Project Manager somewhere in the city, and even Mezie who at least has a job at the club, the rest of them are content to lie on the couch, eating and playing video games all day.

Pathetic.

I push open Mezie's door without knocking, perhaps hoping to catch him in the act, to see in the flesh everything I know he's been up to, pun intended. But he is there sitting on the bed, my envelope in his hand. The sombreness of his mood sends a chill down my spine. It isn't like him to be this pensive.

"Hey," I say, hoping my voice isn't betraying my rising anxiety.

He gets up and hands me the envelope. I smile at him, my sense of unease multiplying.

"Thank you," I say, putting it in my bag, desperate to get the hell out of there now that I've gotten what I came for.

"I was at Alero's place this morning," he says, his voice still uncharacteristically mellow. "I went there so I could get your new address." His eyes meet mine. "What's this about you living with that *Mandem* doctor? You told me you got school accommodation."

I hiss. "I told you nothing of the sort. I was trying to tell you the last time I was here, but you didn't even… "

A slap across my face sends the rest of the words flying right out of my mouth. I hold my cheek as I stare at him, shocked to my marrow.

"You slapped me, Mezie?" I yell, my eyes welling with tears, stating the obvious. "Are you out of your mind?"

"Shut your fucking mouth!" he yells back, bloodshot eyes glaring at me. "You're sleeping with that doctor? You're fucking sleeping with that *Mandem*?"

At that point, I too want to draw some blood.

"That *'Mandem'* is one hundred per cent more of a man than you will ever be!" I yell back.

His eyes narrow to small slits before he grabs my neck with both hands. "I brought you to London and you're sleeping around? You're fucking sleeping around?"

Even as I am struggling with his vice grip, I still want to hit him where it hurts.

"You brought who to London? After stealing my money?" I manage to gasp. "Could you even bring yourself to London? Isn't it the loan I took that helped you complete your travel funds?"

It is the last thing I can say before he slams my head on the wall and knees me in the stomach. He catches me before I fall to the ground, securing me with one hand and punching my face repeatedly with the other. I feel myself losing consciousness but know if I do not muster the strength to scream, he will kill me right there in his room. And so I scream. I scream as I fall to the ground and as he straddles me, still punching me anywhere and everywhere his fists land; my face, my chest, my arms, everywhere.

The door is flung open, hitting him in the process.

"Wetin dey happen here?" an outraged Nedu yells, as Diran pulls him off me. "Guy, you dey crase? You dey fucking crase?"

I struggle to my feet, wheezing and choking. I grab the doorknob to steady myself, the room spinning. Wiping the wetness from my nose, I am aghast to actually see blood.

"Get off me!" an irate Mezie is yelling as he struggles to free himself from Diran's strong hold. *"Leave me make I beat her sharp mouth commot! Person I bring London, she dey straff Mandem! Leave me!"*

"Na deportation dem go knack you straight! Fool!" Diran yells, throwing him to the floor. Then turning to Nedu. *"Carry her commot from this place."*

His words are the reminder I need to leave their apartment while I still can. Without even waiting for Nedu, I bolt out of the room and out of the flat, running down the stairs like a bat out of the hell, desperate to get as far away from there as I possibly can.

It isn't until I'm on the train and I am getting curious, and even concerned, looks from the people around that I realize I probably look just as banged up as I feel. I reach for my phone, turn on my camera, and grimace at the sight that greets me. My right eye is almost swollen shut, there are several ugly purple bruises on the left side of my face, and my nose is still bleeding. I open my mouth and I am grateful that I have no missing teeth and that the laceration on my lip isn't as deep as I'd feared. I position myself and take several pictures of my injuries from every angle I can manage, knowing they will come in handy one day. That foolish boy is going to pay for what he has done.

Roman

It is past 8pm, and I have started to wonder where she is. Sitting on the train on my way home, I'd thought about how awkward things have been since Christmas and I made up my mind to sit her down so we can talk about our Christmas Eve kiss. We can't continue pretending it never happened. At least, I can't. Getting home and finding the house empty wasn't something I'd expected, and after waiting over an hour, I have started thinking the worst, worried she might have decided staying with me isn't a good idea.

When I hear the jangle of her keys at the door, I'm relieved. Until she walks in looking like someone who has been attacked by an animal.

"What happened?!" I exclaim, rushing to her.

She starts to shake her head, as if wanting to brush it off, but instead she bursts into tears. I lead her to the living room and sit her on the couch, my blood already boiling.

My eyes scan her wounds, mentally trying to ascertain their severity and if I should be calling 999. Even though there is a trail of blood from her nose, it is no longer actively bleeding and there is no broken skin beneath the bruises on her face, meaning she might be out of any clear and present danger. Sitting her in an upright position regardless, I go in search of my First Aid kit. She winces as I clean her bruises and I eyeball a small laceration on her eyebrow to determine if it needs stitching. Thankfully, it doesn't.

"What happened, Legachi?" I ask again, after I have cleaned her bruises and the blood stains on her face, doing everything I can to keep my voice calm.

"I went to Mezie's place to pick up my scholarship documents," she answers, her voice hoarse. "And he attacked me. When he heard that I live with you now, he lost it."

I can feel the anger building inside me like a fire seed, a hot burning anger that is fast morphing into a fire dragon. That louse, that scoundrel, attacked her?

"He didn't know you'd moved here?"

She shakes her head. "We broke up and I no longer saw the need for him to."

She grimaces and holds her head. That is when I notice the bruising on her hands and neck, and I grit my teeth as I realize the extent of his attack.

"Let's get you upstairs," I say, helping her to her feet.

She leans on me as we make our way upstairs. Once in her room, I help her out of her jacket and shoes. Tucking her into bed, I go to the kitchen where I make chicken soup from a packet I always have handy, taking it to her with a glass of orange juice. She is only able to manage a few spoons of the soup, but that is all I need for her to be able to take some much-needed pain relief pills.

"We have to call the police," I state, as I take the tray from her. "He can't go unpunished for what he's done."

"No, not the police. He'll end up deported and that will kill his mother," she pleads, much to my chagrin. After what he has done to her, she's still concerned about him. She raises her phone. "I'll find another way to punish him. I took pictures of my face."

I take the phone from her and seeing pictures of her freshly injured face makes me want to explode. I sit with her and when I'm sure she's asleep, I transfer the gory images from her phone to mine.

A quick glance at my watch shows me it is now past 10pm. Walking out of the room gently so as not to rouse her, I take the tray to the kitchen and then go for my jacket.

I might have agreed not to call the Police, but the bastard sure as hell has to pay for what he has done.

Tonight.

By the time I park my car on the High Street in Shoreditch, it is almost midnight. Getting out, I walk towards *Liquid Nitrogen*. A long line has already formed outside the club, and I join the queue, doing everything to maintain my composure. I look ahead and, sure enough, there he is, standing at the door. Watching him, laughing without a care in the world, talking and flirting with women only a few hours after he almost killed another, incenses me anew. I grit my teeth as I move down the line, taking in his bulky chest and thick hands, the same thick hands that almost snuffed the life out of someone whose importance to me I realize a little more every day.

I wait my turn and as I approach the door, he sees me, and the narrowing of his eyes is confirmation he knows who I am. His nostrils flare and he takes a step in my direction, but I beat him to it as I grab him by the collar and punch him hard in the face. There is a collective gasp from the bystanders, all of them stepping aside as we crash our way through the barrier and stumble into the club, Disturbing Tha Peace's *Move Bitch* blasting loudly from the speakers. I pin him to the wall and land another punch square on his face, satisfied by the crack I feel in his nose. He aims for my face, his hands reaching for my jaw, but I knee him in the groin. He still manages to grab me, and we both topple to the ground, fists flying as we exchange punches. I finally get the upper hand and pin him to the floor, punching him in the face several times. As hard as he struggles, he is unable to overpower me, and I continue to hit him until I am dragged off by his colleagues.

I put up no resistance, already satisfied with the pound of flesh I have already gotten, every pun intended.

"I'm going to mess you up!" he is now shouting, having been helped to his feet, his voice a high-pitched shriek. "I'm going to fuck you up in this town! I'm going to make you fucking lose your license. By the time the Old Bill gets here… "

"You want to call the Old Bill? Please, be my guest!" I yell back, whipping out my phone, flashing the worst picture of Legachi's injured face. "I'll bet they'll be only too glad to see this! You'll be on the first plane back to Nigeria, you dumb fuck!"

He deflates upon hearing this and is bustled further into the club by his friends.

"You better get out of here!" one of them, a dreadlocked guy with large eyes, turns to me. "Better get out of here before we call the Police."

I know nobody will be making any such calls, considering his immigration status. I also know he will most definitely not be setting foot near Legachi anytime soon. Satisfied, I walk away.

Mission accomplished.

Twenty-Five

Alien Sensations

Legachi

I drift in and out of sleep all of Saturday, unable to do more than open my eyes the few times I awake. The trauma to my body is just as potent as if I have been drugged, compelling me to obey it and not even move as much as a muscle.

I am aware the several times Roman comes into the room to check on me, and when he places trays of food on my bedside table, meals I can't even look at talk less of eat. I know when he comes in to take away each uneaten meal and replace it with another one, and even notice him hover over me for a few minutes, probably concerned about how long I have been in bed, but I can't even open my eyes in acknowledgment. It isn't until much later that night, at about 11pm, that I am finally able to wake up. Sitting up in bed, even though there is still a dull ache in my head, I feel considerably better.

I find my way to the bathroom, and I am consoled to see the swelling on my eye has gone down and the bruising on my face and neck are no longer quite as purple. I have a hot shower and feel even better after it. After my bath, I wear a cotton pyjama set and devour the sandwiches and glass of juice on my table, the last meal Roman dropped earlier in the evening. Thinking about how he has cared for me since I stumbled into the house yesterday warms my heart, and I can't help but wonder if it's still just him being nice. But just as my mind starts to wander with wild romantic notions, I hear the hum of his voice from his bedroom, talking to someone on the phone. At that time of night, almost midnight, the chances of the call being a non-romantic one are very slim. He is probably talking to Itunu, or any of the other women he might have in his life.

In resignation, I lie back in bed and bring out my phone, watching videos of Nigerian comedians performing skits on Instagram, my earphones plugged in to drown out the sound of his voice. But even though my ears can no longer hear his voice, the realisation that he will never be mine still reverberates in my heart.

And it hurts even more than the physical injuries Mezie has inflicted on me.

I wake up early the next morning and take my tray downstairs, with the intention of washing up and maybe even making breakfast. But I am surprised to meet Roman already there, frying sausages. His eyes light up when he sees me.

"You're awake," he remarks. "I'd started getting a little worried."

"My body just needed to shut down for a bit," I answer. "I guess it had a lot of healing to do."

He nods in agreement. "You look a lot better. Are you still in any kind of pain?"

Come to think of it, even the headache I felt last night is gone. I smile and shake my head. "None. I feel way better. Thanks so much for taking care of me, Roman. I really appreciate it."

He shrugs and returns his attention to the pan. But that is when I notice the bruising.

"What happened to your hand?" I ask, never having seen him with that extensive an injury.

He turns to me, and I gasp, my hands flying to my face when I see the purple shadow around his left eye.

"Don't worry, the other guy looks much worse," he chuckles, returning his attention to the pan, turning off the cooker and dishing the sausages to two plates on the counter.

I gape at him, realisation hitting me. "You went after Mezie?"

He turns to me and, even though he says nothing in response, the set look in his eyes is every confirmation I need of what he has done... what he has done for me.

"Are you out of your mind?" I shriek, walking up to him and turning his face to give me a better view of the bruise. "Why would you do something like that? Those people are ruffians! They are wild! He could have really hurt you. Roman, what if they'd called the Police? You could have lost your license."

Roman

As she holds my face, my injuries, and even my license, are the last thing on my mind. I hear nothing as she rattles on, intoxicated by her minty berry fragrance. I look at her full lips moving, glistening with their natural juices. My eyes drop to her snug cotton pyjamas, its top stopping a few inches before the bottom's waistband, revealing a bit of her midriff. By the time my eyes return to her face, as those light brown eyes stare back at me, all I can think is how much I want her.

Legachi

I see his eyes skim my body and I'm uncertain about what I see in them. But by the time they return to my face, as they hold mine, I'm one hundred per cent sure.

It is desire.

Without a further thought, I throw my arms around him and kiss him.

Roman

I need no further promoting, grabbing her by the bottom as we kiss, her plump lips even juicier than I remember, my excitement heightened not just by months of anticipation, but by the feel of her supple body, by the eagerness with which she is also kissing me, by the feel of her hands as they reach underneath my t-shirt.

This girl is killing me.

I hoist her to the counter, wanting more of her.

Wanting all of her.

Legachi

I have lost every sense of rationality, every iota of control. As our kiss deepens, I slide my hands under his t-shirt, his body feeling just as taut as I have imagined, his heart pounding a million trillion beats a minute. His rough stubble rubs against my chin in the most delicious way, and it feels like my brain has shut down completely.

His arms are wrapped around my waist, cinching me to him, and I put my hands in his hair, sliding my fingers through his curly strands. He hoists me to the counter and my eyes open, just as his also do. As our eyes hold, I know one thing for sure.

I don't want him to stop.

Roman

As I look at those beautiful brown eyes, I am afraid she will ask me to stop, and two things flash through my mind; how I'm not sure I can, and how all I want to do is worship her body with every part of mine… but not in the kitchen.

I lift her off the counter and she wraps her legs around my waist as she kisses me again, harder and deeper, with a fervour that matches mine. We stagger out of the kitchen, up the stairs and to my bedroom. My arms have started to weaken from her weight by the time we get there, which is just as well as we fall in a heap to the bed.

Legachi

I gasp as he undresses me, the feel of his hands on my skin electric. He is kissing me as he does, his lips soft… scorching… tender… demanding. I feel the strength of his arms, intoxicated by his natural scent of sweat and woody cinnamon. He pulls away to take off first his t-shirt and then his track bottoms, and my eyes remain riveted to his stunning body. Our eyes hold again and there is a spark in his gaze, a darkening of his eyes, a fire and hunger, a raw yearning.

Roman

I look at her body and my breath catches at the sight of her naked perfection. She pulls me down to her and the feel of her soft, lush curves against my body makes me want to explode. Literally.

I ease into her, and it feels like I have been teleported to another dimension. We ride together in perfect rhythm, the feel of her hands on my chest and the sound of her soft moaning heightening my excitement, and when she arches her back as she reaches her climax, I let out a guttural moan as I release mine.

Legachi

And everywhere is still.

I am trying to catch my breath, feeling like I am in a hot air balloon… no, a parachute… that is floating back to earth. My body is tingling with this alien sensation of euphoria, something I have never experienced with anyone before. This is everything I thought it would be… and so much more.

As lucidity takes over, I am filled with awareness… the awareness that I have just had sex with Roman, my boss, and that I am still lying on his bed stark naked. Desperate to quickly take my rounded stomach and thick thighs out of sight, I reach for his comforter, but he pulls me closer instead. Looking up, I brace myself for what I will see in his eyes, indifference or maybe even repulsion. But I am unprepared for the tenderness I see instead. We say nothing for the longest time, as if we're trying to read the other's mind.

"You don't know how long I've wanted this," he finally says. "My body has yearned for you for so, so long, Legachi."

As our eyes still hold, I know there is no pretence or deceit in his words. And just like that, all my worries, doubts and insecurities dissipate.

Roman

Her lips part in a smile and it takes my breath away. I have convinced myself that my attraction to her is only physical, but even as we lie in the afterglow, I am overcome by a feeling so strong in intensity, it is alien and familiar at the same time. Looking at her brown eyes and freckled face, she is the most beautiful woman in the world.

"You're beautiful," I say, my voice only a few decibels louder than a whisper.

I lower my head to kiss her, and as we melt into each other's arms, as we make love again, but this time slower and more sensual, I feel a completeness I haven't felt in a very long time.

Twenty-Six

More Than Enough

Legachi

"I've never felt enough before," I say, lying in his arms the next day. Time has become one endless continuum and I don't even know if it's still morning, now afternoon or even evening. "With everyone I've ever been with, I've never felt enough. I've always felt like I'm the one being done a favour."

I look up at him, knowing this isn't what I should be saying to him, especially not now. But in the newness of this thing I'm feeling, I am unable to help myself. He looks at me and it feels like I'm levitating.

"I've never had anyone look at me the way you do," I say, not breaking our gaze. "I've never had anyone hold me the way do. It's all so new... so new and wonderful... so new and terrifying."

Roman

Her exhilaration and fright mirror mine.

"This is also new for me, and the intensity also scares the crap out of me." I tilt up her chin. "But you're more than enough, Legachi... and I can't get enough of you."

And I truly can't.

We remain in our bubble for the rest of that day and into the next, New Year's Day, pausing only to take calls from our families. By evening, we finally make our way out of bed and luxuriate in a bubble bath in my bathroom until the warm water goes stone cold. But cold as it is, we remain there, her lying with her back to my chest, loving the feel of her body, basking in the glow of this thing growing between us.

"You officially need to win the prize for the oldest braids on a human being," I chuckle, holding her close lest she buckle and bolt like she did the last time.

"These braids have served their function, please," she giggles. "Can't you see how tiny they are? When I had them made, I knew they weren't coming off anytime soon."

"Your undergrowth is probably shoulder-length by now."

She turns to glare at me, brown eyes twinkling. "Well, if you hate them so much, maybe you can do something about it."

And I do.

Later that night, seated in the living room, I help her take them out. As my hands work her hair with a tail comb she's given me, as I sift through layers of accumulated dirt and untangle tight knots that have formed, it is the most intimate thing I have ever experienced with any woman. The next morning after we shower, I put her washed hair in the same plaits I learned how to make for Luna.

"Roman, you're very wicked!" she cackles, looking at her reflection in the mirror. "What is this? I look like an *mgbeke*!"

"I hope that means gorgeous, beautiful and sexy," I say, holding her from behind and nestling my face in her neck, my body already craving hers. It has been 72 straight hours but rather than abate, my desire for her is growing in leaps and bounds.

"My greatest fear is ending up with a man who treats me the way my father does my mother," she says, as we lie in bed that night. "Cold and condescending, that's the only way I've ever seen the man treat her," she chuckles. "I guess that's why she has been on *omugwo* for four years."

"*Omugwo*, I know what is. Don't tell me," I frown, trying to remember where I heard the word. "Ah yes, that's when an older woman helps take care of a new baby, right?"

She nods and laughs. "My sister's daughter is four years old, but my mother has refused to go home."

"And why has that been your fear?"

She shrugs. "Precedence, I guess. None of my sisters are particularly happy with their partners, and when Mezie was treating me the way he did, I just accepted that was the way it was also going to be for me."

We lie in the darkness and all I want to do is tell her that won't be the way it will be for her. I want to tell her how her every touch ignites me, making me feel almost reborn. I want to tell her that in just a short space of time, I want to do nothing but protect her, cherish her, love her. But instead, I pull her closer, hoping our burgeoning intimacy will speak the words for me... the words my heart is screaming, but my mouth is cautious to say.

All too soon, it is the morning of Sunday, January 6th, the day Luna is to return home, and one week since Legachi and I have been locked in our bubble of passion. But with work set to resume for me tomorrow, and school for Legachi as well, we will soon be back to reality.

"Sweetness, can we keep this between us for now?" I ask as we sit in the kitchen where she is baking a pound cake. "The abrupt change might confuse Luna. Maybe we could ease her into it slowly?"

She nods in agreement.

"For everyone else, a lot of people might think us being together inappropriate, so maybe we should keep things quiet in general, until you're done with your program in June," I continue. "Then I can fire you and we can introduce you to everyone as my proper girlfriend."

Legachi

I see the sense in keeping things quiet, and not only because I also don't want to confuse Luna. As much as I love this beautiful thing with Roman, I don't want it to jeopardise my job either, and having a Nanny slash Lover will be very hard for him to explain to anyone.

For the first time in a week, I shower in the bathroom I share with Luna and dress up in my bedroom, to try to get back in the mind-set of staying there. Reaching for my cardigan, it smells so much like Roman, I close my eyes and inhale, a small smile playing on my lips. Keeping this is a secret is not going to be as easy as we think. I reach for another cardigan and douse it in my body spray for good measure. It's better not to take any chances.

When I return downstairs, I see he has also showered and is wearing a smart polo shirt and cargo pants, a far cry from the t-shirts and pyjama bottoms he has lived in all week. The doorbell rings before I can say anything and when he looks at me, I am afraid to look at him, scared something would have changed in his eyes, scared that our bubble has indeed burst. But I do… and he winks… and I'm no longer afraid.

He opens the door and Luna jumps into his arms, squealing in her glee. Paris and his mother walk in behind her.

"Look how much you've grown!" Roman exclaims, spinning her around. "What have you been feeding her, Mom?"

"Plantain!" Luna beams.

"Looks like she's a Plantain Ninja like her father," Mrs. Isibor chuckles, before smiling at me. "How are you, my dear? Happy New Year."

"Yeah, Happy New Year!" Paris says, her smile wider than it needs to be. "Were you here all through the holidays?"

I make a pointed effort not to look at Roman as I nod, straight faced. "Yes. I had a lot of catching up to do with schoolwork."

"I was hardly ever home myself," Roman chimes in, nodding for emphasis.

But from the way her smile keeps getting wider, it's clear his sister isn't buying any of it. "I'll bet you weren't."

"Stop harassing them, Obehi," Mrs. Isibor chides, but the glint in her eyes is just as roguish as her daughter's. "I'm sure they were able to get some much-needed rest, whether studying or… being 'hardly ever home'."

I flush and immediately turn to Luna, who is now vying for my attention. Lifting her in my arms, I make a show of listening intently to her Chelmsford tales as we head upstairs, away from the all-too-knowing eyes of his mother and sister, because one more minute in their presence, and they will be able to see through my already very shaky veneer.

After they have left and a tired Luna has fallen asleep, as I am clearing up dishes in the kitchen, I feel Roman's arms around me as he snuggles me from behind.

"I've been waiting to do this all day," he whispers in my ear, prompting a wide smile from me.

Then taking me by the hand, he leads me upstairs, back to his bedroom… and we pick up right where we left off.

Twenty-Seven

Down Low... Not

FEBRUARY 2019

Legachi

Ontrary to any fear I had about our love abating, it flows into the New Year, waxing stronger and stronger every day. We fall into a pattern of falling asleep together, sometimes in his bedroom and sometimes even in mine. We are conscious to awaken well before Luna does, returning to our respective bedrooms so she's none the wiser. As Luna has her breakfast, we enjoy cups of coffee together, drop her off at day care together, and walk hand-in-hand to either the bus stop or the train station. If he doesn't have an early day, he rides the bus with me to Hendon before turning around to go back, and if I don't have early classes, I ride the train with him all the way to Westminster. Just as much as he has become my lover, he has also become my best friend.

And I am the happiest I have ever been.

Roman

She makes me feel like an excited schoolboy and I long to spend every second of every minute of every hour of every day with her. She has invaded my thoughts so much that it is a struggle to stay focused on anything else. And it isn't just about the sex.

The conversations we have in our quiet moments are so deep and intense, she has made me comfortable enough to reveal things about myself I haven't shared with anyone. And what makes it even more special is seeing in those light brown eyes the same feelings I have in my heart. She has bewitched me in every sense of the word... and I wouldn't have it any other way.

It is soon Valentine's Day and I love the way her eyes light up when, before she returns to her bedroom, I present her with an ornate earring and necklace jewellery set, in 24-carat white gold and set with a rainbow of precious stones.

"Oh my goodness, Roman!" she gasps. "This is too much!"

I smile as she continues to gape at her gift. If only she knew I would give her the stars if I could. And if only she knows I still have a whole lot more planned today.

"It's so beautiful," she says, before looking at me with doleful eyes. "I only got you this perfume set."

"And I love it! It's my favorite perfume ever!" I laugh, pulling her in for an embrace. The truth is, it's not. It's an *Azzaro* fragrance that I have used, and not particularly liked, in the past; too much of an incense undertone for my taste. But coming from her, it might as well be gold dust.

We don't leave together that morning as she has an early class. I stay back under the pretext of getting Luna ready, happy for the chance to put finishing touches to the surprise I want her to receive in school.

I have just gotten off the phone with the flower delivery company and walk into the kitchen where Luna is having the last spoon of her cereal.

"Is Legachi your Fallytine?"

I look at her, realizing she might have heard me order the flowers. My first inclination is to deny this, but after almost two months of tiptoeing around her, I decide I might as well come clean.

"Yes, darling. She's my Valentine."

It feels so good to say it out loud. And I get another chance only a few minutes later when I get a call from someone I haven't heard from since Boxing Day; Itunu.

"Happy Valentine's Day, handsome," she coos. "I just got into town yesterday. Some friends invited me to Aspen in January, and I decided to spend a few more weeks visiting other friends in the States."

"Nice one. Welcome back."

"So… what are you doing tonight? And please don't come at me with that 'let's be friends' garbage," she giggles. "Get a sitter for your kid and let me spoil you tonight."

"Sounds amazing, but I'm afraid I'm going to have to pass," I answer. "I already have plans."

She is quiet for a few seconds. "Plans? What kind of plans? You're seeing someone?"

"Yeah," I answer, unable to stop the grin from forming on my face. "Yeah, I'm seeing someone."

"So, what was that about not being ready for a romantic relationship with anyone?"

It is at the tip of my tongue to tell her I meant *her* specifically, but I'm much too happy to be that cruel to anyone today.

"Things change," is all I offer.

"Is it serious? You and this person?"

"I hope so," I beam, eager to get off the phone to put finishing touches to the rest of my surprise for the woman who now has my heart.

"Anyone I know?"

I hesitate. As much as I want to scream her name for everyone to hear, I don't trust Itunu not to be malicious enough not to say or do anything nasty.

"Wow, is that the time?" I answer instead. "I really must go. Have a lovely Valentine's Day, Itunu."

And without waiting for her to say anything in response, I terminate the call. Just then, the doorbell rings and I smile, happy that my sister has kept her word to pick Luna up early.

"You're a star!" I say, kissing Paris on the cheek as she walks into the house.

She looks at me, her brow raised and an amused smile on her face. "So, what's this about having 'plans' for today?"

"Just a bit of this and that," is my evasive answer as we walk to the kitchen.

"On Valentine's Day, conveniently."

"Legachi is daddy's Fallytine!" Luna declares, rushing up to hug her aunty.

Paris returns Luna's embrace, throwing me a wink and a grin. "That doesn't surprise me at all, luv."

"Just leave it," I say to my sister, trying not to smile back.

She continues to grin at me, and I am grateful for Luna's presence, as my sister would have done a lot more than grin if she weren't there.

"I'll be looking forward to all the details, fam," she says, nudging me on the shoulder as she walks past, holding Luna's hand.

"See you tomorrow, daddy!"

I blow my daughter a kiss as the door closes. I'll deal with the fall out of Paris knowing about Legachi and I later. Right now, I have another surprise to plan.

Legachi

The largest bouquet of red roses I have ever seen is delivered to me in class that morning. As everyone *oohs* and *aahs* over the beautiful flowers, I am tickled pink by yet another Valentine's Day surprise from Roman, feeling for the first time ever the butterflies and exhilaration of the romantic day. I never got anything more than a bottle of perfume from Mezie, and even though I always sent him the same perfunctory gift of boxers, perfume, and a cake, that was as far as our Valentine's Day celebration ever went. After our exchange of gifts, it was always back to normal with no added frills, as he believed it was a commercial holiday manufactured by socialists. So for me to be on the receiving end of yet another incredible romantic gesture, when I haven't even recovered from the first one, completely blows my mind.

Before I can stop her, Nonye snatches the card from the bouquet.

For each petal, I send a kiss. Roman, she reads aloud, before turning to me, a large grin on her face. "A *keees*?!" she exclaims. "And Roman, as in your boss? Roman, as in the fine doctor?"

I giggle as my face flushes, no longer able to contain it.

"*Hei*! Tell me something!" she exclaims in a stage whisper, moving closer to me. "You and the doctor? Since when?"

"Girl, it's a long story," I giggle, unable to even stop, happiness bubbling over in my stomach, my hand fingering the chain on my neck.

"Did he give you that as well?" she asks, wide eyed. "I noticed it when you walked in and was going to ask."

I nod and giggle again. "I've never been this happy, Nonye."

She claps her hands in her glee. "Immediately after this class, you must give me this gist!" Her face suddenly clouds over. "*Chelu.* I hope you gave him a nice gift as well."

My smile wanes, reminded of how my gift doesn't even stack close to his. "I gave him a perfume gift set. *Azzaro.*"

"Girl, *why you fall hand like this*?" she retorts. "As soon as this class is over, we're going to the West End. You're not paying rent, so what are you doing with your money?"

And she is correct. What really am I doing with my money? I have managed to save a little over £3,000 now, but I have been unable to touch a penny of it, worried I might have cause to use it short notice. But it is no reason not to splurge on a better gift for my boyfriend.

Boyfriend.

Thinking of him that way still gives me butterflies. Never in a million years would I have imagined a man as handsome and sexy as him even looking at me twice. But not only do I not feel inadequate or self-conscious when I'm with him, the affection and desire he has for me is not just evident, but grows more and more every day.

How did I get this lucky?

After our class, I put up no resistance as Nonye and I set off for the tube station, headed to Regent Street. She carries my flowers proudly and I am happy to let her. Having not heard from her fiancé in Nigeria, I know she's feeling some type of way. We are switching over to the southbound Victoria line train at Euston station, when I hear someone call my name.

"Legachi!"

I tense, recognizing that voice, that voice I once loved so much but now despise more than anything. With grit teeth, I turn around and see Mezie walking up to us, a sneer on his face.

"What does this fool want?" Nonye mutters, glaring at him.

"Legachi Onyema of London!" he cackles. "*You don become full London babe now, abi?*"

I hiss and I am about to turn around when he grabs my hand.

"If you don't leave her alone, *I go tear you one slap now*!" an irate Nonye yells.

He laughs and lets go of my hand. "That's how you sent that *Mandem* to me at the club. If it wasn't for our history, I would have reported him to the Police and made sure he lost his medical license."

I scoff. "You can't even try it. He told me he showed you one of the pictures of what you did to my face, and I have several more of those. Try any nonsense and let's see who'll be on the first flight back to Lagos."

He shakes his head and chuckles. "*'He told me'*," he mimics. "Of all the things I thought of you, I never thought you were a fool, Legachi. I hear you both have been acting like lovebirds all over town. A lot of my friends have seen you with him on the train, holding hands and acting like life is a movie."

"*E dey pain you*?" Nonye taunts. "He gave her these flowers I'm holding, for your information. Flowers that are your one month's wages, *ode*!"

"I'm sorry for you, Legachi," he continues, ignoring her. "You think he's taking you seriously? A hardcore London boy like him? And a doctor for that matter? You think you're the only one he's seeing? A minted guy like that?"

"Oh, he's minted now? He's no longer a *Mandem*?" I retort.

"*Girl, you funny sha!*" he cackles in response. "So, with this your wide nose and big forehead, you think that kind of man will ever think of you any more than a quick shag? *When na manage me sef dey manage you.* That guy will use your heart to sweep the streets of London. If you think I was bad, he will show you the real meaning of the word!" he shakes his head, his shoulders vibrating with his laughter. "You're a real comedian. *So, for your mind now, you don find husband for this London.*"

"Abeg, getaway from here. Who dey manage who? You wey tiff all her money come dey squat with hundred men for Hackney? Who dey manage who?" Nonye yells, before grabbing my hand and pulling me in the direction of our platform. "Let's go jor!"

I am frowning as we enter the train, hating having seen him again but, even worse, hating that his words have struck such a sensitive chord.

"Don't just mind the fool," Nonye says, as we alight at Oxford Circus station. "Standing there, talking like an idiot! He thinks every man is as useless as he is!"

Her emphasis on the word makes it sound like *yoooseless*, and this finally prompts laughter from me. She is right. He is indeed *yoooseless*, and I am more than happy to have shut the door on our relationship. He might be a part of my history, yes, but I will not allow him to ruin my future.

She takes me to the pricey *Aspinal of London* on Regent Street, and I buy sterling silver cufflinks engraved with Roman's initials, R.I., for almost £200. It is a lot of money to spend, but rather than feel as panicked as I do when I have to spend so much, I am instead excited and eager to present him his gift as quickly as possible.

Nonye and I part at the station, with her headed to the northbound Victoria line train, and me, the northbound Bakerloo line train, switching at Baker Street to the Metropolitan line and getting off at the next stop, Finchley Road. Walking into the house, I still have a couple of hours to kill before picking Luna up from day care, but as I walk into my bedroom, a smile breaks on my face when I see a shimmering black dress and a burnt orange *Jimmy Choo* shoe box on the bed, with a note beside it.

You. Me. Date Night. 7 o'clock. P.S., Luna is in Chelmsford tonight.

I giggle as I sit on the bed, grabbing the dress and inhaling the luxurious fabric, feeling like Julia Roberts straight out of *Pretty Woman*, Mezie's ugly words forgotten. This has got to be the best day of my life.

I take a long soak in the bath before taking even longer with my makeup, wanting to make myself perfect for him. I apply the blue eyeliner he likes and the scarlet lipstick I haven't had cause to use in a while. I secure my newly done wet and wavy braids into a bun, dropping a few ringlets to frame my face, and, slipping into the long-sleeved, mermaid silhouetted dress, I feel more beautiful than I ever have in my life.

At 7pm, I hear the front door open and wear the black pumps with an exaggerated bow detail. It is a little higher than I typically like, but today that doesn't matter. It is the perfect finishing touch to the perfect outfit.

Smoothening the dress and picking up my purse, I walk out of the room and down the stairs, my heart beating fast in anticipation of the look of surprise, and hopefully admiration, I will see on this face. But instead, I'm the one who gets the surprise when I see him standing at the foot of the stairs, dapper in a black suit, snow-white shirt and black bow-tie.

My breath catches in my throat as I look at him. God really took His time with this man. He smiles at me and the butterflies in my stomach almost lift me afloat. I feel like a Princess at the end of her fairy tale, getting her happy ever after. It is so surreal, it feels like I'm dreaming. I ask myself if this is the same unremarkable holiday I used to celebrate with Mezie, and even the few guys I dated before him. I ask myself if this is the same Valentine's Day I actually dreaded in the past, a day which meant spending money on my part and receiving nondescript gifts in return. It can't be the same. It would be an insult to this day to classify them the same. Today, this glorious day, was made by God Himself for us... for Roman and I.

"Wow!" he remarks, his wide eyes mirroring my admiration. "You look absolutely stunning."

"Where did you change?" I ask when I get to him. "I didn't expect you to get here all dressed."

"I told you 7pm, didn't I? I wasn't going to keep you waiting," he grins at me. "You like?"

"I like," I smile at him. "I like very much."

"Happy Valentine's Day, sweetheart." He raises my hand to his lips. "Will you be my date for the night?"

My lips curve into a smile. "What happened to keeping things quiet, Doctor?"

Roman

I smile at the reminder of my request weeks before, when we started our love affair. As her blue-rimmed brown eyes twinkle at me, I am overwhelmed by how beautiful she is.

"All I want to do is shout from the roof tops that you're mine," I answer, lowering my head to kiss her, not minding the red imprint doing so will leave on my lips.

Minutes later, after wearing our coats, I lead her out to my car, which I have had specially cleaned for the evening.

"This must be really special for us to be going in the car!" she exclaims as I open the passenger door and help her in.

"Special treatment for a special lady," I answer with a wink, before walking over to my side of the car.

It is a nineteen-minute drive to Park Lane, and we soon pull up in front of The Dorchester hotel. Holding her hand, we walk into the fine dining restaurant run by renown chef Alain Ducasse. Our three-course meal will cost me over £500, but it will be money well spent. After six weeks of pure bliss, I want to celebrate her the way I know how.

"So, Luna told Paris that you're my Valentine," I chuckle, as the appetizer of artichokes and Kristal caviar cream is served. "I guess it's safe to assume the whole of Chelmsford has heard by now."

"Well, I guess we're officially out in the open now," she laughs, large eyes twinkling at me.

"I guess so," I beam back, pleased she appears just as glad about that as I am.

We both opt for lobster medallion, chicken quenelles, Périgord truffle and homemade semolina pasta for the entrée, and a pineapple and galanga sorbet for dessert. The food is good, and it is no wonder the restaurant has earned itself three Michelin stars.

"I got you something," she says, reaching into her purse and handing me a wrapped gift box.

"But you already got me something, Legachi," I protest, accepting the box. "I hope you didn't feel compelled to get me another gift."

She shakes her head, her smile still on her face, her eyes prompting me to open the box. I acquiesce and I am touched when I see the expensive cufflinks I know she can barely afford.

"You didn't have to do this, Legachi," I say, looking at her.

"I know. But I wanted to."

And in that statement, I know that, just like I want to make the day special for her, she also wants to do the same for me. And that in itself is the best gift of all. Reaching into the pocket of my jacket, I bring out a flat, wrapped item, with an elaborate red bow on it.

"Another one?" she exclaims, accepting it from me.

"Don't worry, it's the last one. I hope you like it."

She takes her time to delicately unwrap the gift, a far cry from how I tore off the wrapping on mine minutes before. She smiles when she holds the CD in her hand.

"I know CDs are old school, so I hope you don't mind. It's a collection of love songs," I say, suddenly feeling a little self-conscious. "Curated by me... for you."

Legachi

Tears pool in my eyes when I look at the list of songs typed in calligraphy on its sleeve. From UB40's *Kingston Town*, to Lauren Wood's *Fallen*, to Lauryn Hill's *Can't Take My Eyes Off You*, to Jamie Cullum's *Pure Imagination*, to Madonna's *Crazy for You*, I am emotional that he has chosen all these songs with me... and only me... in mind.

Later that night, as we sit by the fireplace and listen to the CD, I say a silent prayer of thanks for the beautiful blessing of the most beautiful love of all. Maybe minted doctors do fall for big-forehead girls after all.

Twenty-Eight

The Doctor... and His Lover

APRIL 2019

Legachi

L ife is beautiful. Life is perfect. My life is beautiful. My life is perfect. These are my sentiments every single day, as our love blossoms into spring.

On the 6th of April, a beautiful, sunny Saturday with clear blue skies, we celebrate Luna's 4th birthday. We have a party in our backyard, with pink and yellow streamers and balloons decorating the house and garden. It is a full house, and I am comfortable enough to co-host, comfortable enough with Roman's friends and family to present myself as his girlfriend. So at home am I that I even invite my own friends over. It is a day full of fun and laughter, and as we pose for pictures with the ecstatic birthday girl, it still blows my mind what difference a few months has made. From being homeless and stranded, to being a member of such a beautiful family unit. I feel like Cinderella.

But what has gotten harder every month is to continue receiving a salary from my boyfriend.

"You really shouldn't be paying me, Roman," I said to him after getting paid in March. "It doesn't feel right having you pay me to live with you."

"Even though your evenings are still committed to watching Luna? Even now with my own timing all crazy?" had been his response, a smile playing on his face. "That wouldn't be right, would it?"

I didn't know how to counter that argument.

The truth is I still do have to watch Luna a whole lot, especially with him now spending more time at the hospital. But I love the child so much, I would do it for free. That, and the fact I am no longer so scared of the unknown to keep piling money in my account for a rainy day. Even though we are only four months in, I am certain that, with Roman, there will be no 'rainy day'.

"We should go on holiday after your exams," he says as we lie in bed the night after Luna's party. "We should go somewhere nice, just the two of us. Maybe Bali or the Maldives. Then later in the summer, we can go on another trip with Luna. I promised to take her to Disney World in Florida."

I beam, the plans sounding like music to my ears. With my final exams only a month away, I will be done writing my dissertation by September, and the world will indeed be my oyster. Even though graduation isn't until March next year, I am confident that I will be able to get a decent job by autumn, upon the completion of my Master's degree. And Roman agrees.

"There are loads of supply chain opportunities. You'll be spoilt for choice."

"But if I'm away at work, and so are you, who's going to watch Luna?" I ask the obvious.

"She starts school in September, and she can always go to Cheryl's afterwards," he answers. "We could extend the pick-up time till 6pm, when you're back from work. The penalty doesn't start until then, and any day you have to work late or hang out with your mates, we could always get a sitter."

A few days later, we are lounging in the living room when he asks, "Do you think we should redecorate the house? It just occurred to me that you might not like the monochromatic theme. That's where my head space was when I got this place, but we could change it to something you'd like?"

I have no problem with the monochromatic theme, but I am heart warmed by yet another confirmation that he is planning for us into the future. From aligning our potential work schedules and now redecorating the house, I can see that this is not a brief fling for him and that he has every plan for us to live together long-term.

But I can't help but wonder if that's all he's planning; just living together.

The following weekend, with Paris watching Luna, Roman and I head to a bar in Leicester Square for Tayo's 30th birthday party.

"Nonye used to call it *Leychester*," I giggle as we sit in the southbound Bakerloo line train to Piccadilly Circus station.

"The same way you called Worcestershire, *Warchestersheer*?"

"I told you that?" I gasp, marveling over just how much I have revealed to him.

"Anytime I need a laugh, I only have to remember that story and it cracks me up!" he chuckles.

"You British people *sef*. Why spell something one way and pronounce it another? Why would Worcestershire be pronounced *Wu-stuh-shuh* anyway? Or Leicester pronounced *Leh-stuh*? It makes absolutely no sense."

"Take it up with the early Anglo-Saxons. I'm just the son of immigrants, luv!" By now, he is laughing so loud, we are drawing curious glances from other people in the train.

I laugh along with him, amused by the contradicting names and their pronunciations, and bursting with contentment over how comfortable and happy we are in each other's company.

Roman

I am still laughing as we arrive the venue of the party, the story of my beloved's mispronunciation of her one-time employer's company name always hilarious. My hand is on the small of her back as we walk into the brightly lit rooftop bar. Having already met her friends, there is no unease or awkwardness on my part. Quite the contrary, I am very relaxed in their company, a reflection of how comfortable, at ease and, most of all, happy I have been in the last four months. I watch her as she smiles and hugs her friends, loving how relaxed and stress-free she looks, loving how the mere sight of her still makes my body burn. Whether barefaced early in the morning or dressed up to the nines like she is now, those plump lips, those brown eyes still turn me into a ball of mush. I have never felt this way about anyone before. Not even Sekani.

"Nice to see you again, Roman," Tayo says, embracing me and squealing as I present her with her wrapped gift. "Awww, for me?"

"Hey, Romanus! *How far na*? *Chop knuckle!*" the lively Nonye greets, giving me a fist bump.

I grin in return. Yep, I'm definitely one of them.

My phone rings and I frown when I see the hospital number. Walking out of the bar, I rush downstairs far from the music to answer it. Thankfully, it's a nurse clarifying a patient's prescription and not them calling me in for an emergency. Done with the call, I am about to make my way back upstairs, when someone calls my name.

"Roman!"

I turn around and see a plump, familiar looking woman walking up to me. From the determined set of her face, I can already tell it's not for a friendly discussion. I want to turn around and walk away quickly, but I decide against it. I haven't had to run from anyone in months, and I'm not going to resume now.

"You think you can get away with what you did to Torera?" she hollers, wagging a finger with red talon-like nails as she approaches. "You think you can do what you did and get away scot-free? *Wo*, we will show you in this town, Roman. We will show you!"

I turn around and walk away, her voice louder and louder the farther I go. I am scared she will chase me into the building, but she opts to remain on the street, yelling. Regardless, I take the stairs two at a time, my heart racing a mile a minute. Will I never be able to shake off this menace? Will I have to run from them for the rest of my life?

"Are you alright?" Legachi asks when I join her where she is sitting, concerned eyes searching mine.

I force a smile. "Yeah. Something came up at work that left me a little shaken, but I'll be fine."

She squeezes my hand reassuringly and I lift hers to my lips. I hate having to lie to her, but this is one murky mess I do not want her involved in at all.

Legachi

The Tuesday after the party, I am trying to study in the library, but my Instagram feed distracts me. Tayo has uploaded pictures from her birthday party, and I smile at the images of Roman and I. We hadn't deliberately colour-coordinated our outfits, but the peach mesh mini dress I wore and his rich burgundy shirt make us look picture-perfect. In all the images, I have a large grin on my face while his eyes are doing most of his smiling, our chemistry palpable, confirmation to anyone who does see them that we are a bona fide couple.

How did I get this lucky?

Long shadows cast over my books make me look up, and I smile when I see Nonye and Tayo standing over me.

"I was just looking at the pictures from Saturday," I say, beaming. "They're awesome. Please send me the ones of Roman and me. We've started putting up our pictures around the house."

But they don't smile in return.

"Babe, let's speak outside?" Tayo asks.

My smile wanes as a sense of foreboding overcomes me. "What's up?"

Nonye looks at Tayo, who can now not look me in the eye. "Tell her," she prompts. When Tayo hesitates, she proceeds to take a seat opposite me, her cue that the discussion will happen right there and then in that library.

"Tell me what?" I ask, my heart pounding so hard, I can hear it as if I am surrounded by a group of drummers at an *owambe*.

Tayo shrugs and takes the seat next to Nonye. "Some of my friends saw the pictures from my party and recognised Roman as the guy who kidnapped their friend's daughter in Nigeria. Apparently, his kid isn't his late wife's child but one he had with their friend, Torera. Things didn't work out with the babe, and she took the kid back to Nigeria when she was on the verge of deportation here. But, according to them, Roman took advantage of her immigration status and, knowing she couldn't do anything to stop it, went to Nigeria to kidnap the child."

I raise my hand to silence her before she can repeat one more word of this garbage. "What on earth are you saying?" I demand, my voice rising higher than it should be in the library. "Can you even hear yourself? Roman kidnapped who? His own daughter? The one he had with his wife?"

"That was what I said to them," Tayo says, bringing out her phone. "Until they showed me these."

My lips part as she scrolls through pictures of Roman and a beautiful, high cheek-boned woman with a pointed chin, the older version of Luna, looking happy and in love all over London. In one of the pictures, they are walking hand-in-hand and, if the distension of her stomach is anything to go by, she is clearly pregnant. I take the phone from Tayo and scroll through myself, willing them to be nothing but Photoshopped images. But they are as real as they come.

And I am floored.

Roman

I am in the study when I hear the front door. It's only a little past noon and much earlier than I am expecting her home.

"Did you change your mind about the library, babes?" I call out.

There is no answer. I am rising from my seating position when the door to the study opens. The smile on my face fades when I see the flat look on hers.

"Who is Torera?"

I deflate upon hearing that question, my heart crashing all the way to my feet.

"Torera?" I repeat, my mind running a mile a minute trying to think of what to tell her... because I can't tell her the truth.

"When did Sekani die, Roman?" she asks, her gaze now pointed.

I am rendered speechless as I look at her; no word, not a single word, surfacing in my brain as an answer.

"Is Sekani Luna's mother?" she asks, an edge in her voice I have never heard before. "Or is it this Torera person?"

I rub my eyes so hard they almost blister.

The gig is up.

Legachi

His crestfallen face is my confirmation.

All the way home, I managed to convince myself that it's all one big mistake, that Tayo and her friends are mistaken, that the father of their Torera friend's baby is just Roman's lookalike. But seeing his shoulder slump, his eyes downcast, I can see that it is no mistake after all.

"How could you lie to me?" I ask, my voice only a little louder than a whisper.

His eyes meet mine. "I meant to tell you, Legachi."

"You meant to tell me?" I exclaim. "When? You've had months, Roman. We've been sharing a bed for four months. We've talked about everything under the sun. I've told you things I've never told a soul. At what point where you going to tell me?" My voice wobbles and I shake my head, determined not to cry. "You never planned to. You would have found the time to tell me if you wanted to."

"Legachi, it isn't that simple," he says, reaching for my hand. "I can explain everything."

But I step away from his hold, afraid his touch will unravel me.

"Legachi, please."

I realise that I am on the verge of either a total eruption or complete breakdown, so I turn around and leave the study.

Roman

I flinch as the door slams shut. As much as I want to go after her, I realise it might be best to give her some time. As it is, it is unlikely she will listen to anything I say right now.

I exhale deeply as I sit on the chair and cover my face with my hands.

The result of my mistake is now attacking me like a pack of bears

Twenty-Nine

Torera

MAY 2014 — DECEMBER 2016

Roman

It was a few days after the third anniversary of Sekani's death, but I was in no better place than I was on that black Monday of July 12, 2011, when she succumbed to the cancer that came after her less than a year into our marriage. As doctors, we'd both known her frequent vaginal bleeding wasn't good but neither of us had been prepared for so ominous a diagnosis as cervical cancer, not even when her Gynaecologist, after what was supposed to have been a routine pap smear, had insisted on performing a colposcopy and running a biopsy on the extracted cervical cells. Not even then.

I will never forget where I was when I got that phone call from her, the phone call that changed my life forever. I was on the escalator at John Lewis, on my way to buy a gift for Kennedy's birthday, when my phone buzzed.

"It's cancer."

Her voice was flat with the delivery, almost as if she were relaying the news of a stranger's predicament to yet another stranger. And then she hung up.

In a daze of confusion, I'd turned around and started walking down the ascending escalator, not even minding the less than pleased people on it. I'd rushed out of the store and onto the road, narrowly escaping a bus ploughing down the busy Oxford Street. I didn't even wait till I was on the other side of the road before I reached for my phone, getting increasingly frustrated as her number rang off each time I dialled it. I continued to dial as I walked, as I walked past the train station and the 94 bus that I could have taken home, as I walked the fifty-minute distance to our house in Holland Park.

Opening the door, sitting in the living room with the drapes drawn, was Sekani, her phone still vibrating with my incoming call. I rushed to her, my wife of only ten months, and as we held each other in that dark room, I was determined that we were going to fight it together. We were going to beat her cancer together, God help us.

But we didn't. Eleven months later, she was dead.

Three years later, sitting in that same living room where we'd mourned the news together, I was still as angry and bitter as I'd been that day. Angry with the vicious disease that chose her, angry with her genetics and any other factors that made her prone to the disease, angry with her for not fighting hard enough, angry with God for letting it happen, angry with Him for not even allowing us enjoy a full year of wedded bliss before her devastating diagnosis after so many years of planning for a life together, angry with Him for taking her away. But even in my anger, at that point, I knew I couldn't allow it fester too much longer... or it would kill me.

My phone beeped with another message from Dapo, my childhood friend from Harlow, reminding me about his birthday party that evening. Just as I'd been doing to other similar invitations, I ignored it. Socialising was the last thing I wanted to do. Yes, I'd had a few nameless, faceless hook-ups since Sekani's death, but those had been prompted by my pent-up sexual cravings and not the need for any form of human interaction. Not even my siblings, cousins and close friends had been able to draw me out of the shell I'd retreated so deeply into. All I wanted, even then, three years later, was to be left well alone.

I made my way up the stairs of our house, our beautiful house in Holland Park we'd finally been able to afford shortly before our wedding, our beautiful house she'd decorated with so much excitement in anticipation of the larger family we would one day be, our beautiful house that now felt more like a grave than a home. Getting to our bedroom and sitting on our bed, just like I usually did, I felt her presence so strongly, it was as if she was still right there. Her clothes still hung from the closet, her dressing table was still exactly as she'd left it, and even her notepad and pen were still on her bedside table. But that evening, rather than feel comforted by all these things I'd kept around to still feel close to her… I felt haunted by them.

Picking up my phone, I read Dapo's message again. Maybe a party was what I needed that night to clear my head.

Knocking on Dapo's door in Bethnal Green after driving for almost an hour, I started to wonder if coming had been the right decision after all. And seeing the crushing crowd of people when he opened the door had further heightened my anxiety. This wasn't the small house party I'd been expecting.

"Hey, bruv! I'm so glad you made it!" Dapo exclaimed, pulling me in for a crushing hug. "I didn't think you was gonna make it."

I forced a smile and handed him the bottle of wine I'd picked up on my way, sorely reminded about why he and I hadn't stayed friends over the years. Even though we'd been thick as thieves back in Harlow, our paths had taken different turns when I'd chosen medical school and he, a career in rap music.

We were both now in London, but we had less to talk about when we saw each other, which, over the years, became less and less frequent. But as different as we now were, there was still a sense of brotherliness the few times we did see. We might no longer have had much to say to each other, but I knew he would always have my back, just like I would always have his. Maybe that was why I chose his, of all the invitations I'd received, to honour. But as he led me through the throng of what looked to be at least a hundred people in his small terrace house, I had started regretting my decision to come.

"Yo, I'm so sorry about the Missus," he said, his arm still over my shoulder. "That was some tough luck."

I smiled and nodded. "Yeah, it was."

"But life's got to go on, it has," he said, before snapping at a heavily tattooed guy. "Oi! Get my mate a bottle of bevvy. Quality bevvy."

"A bottle of Ace?" the guy asked.

"That's the one!" Dapo answered, giving him a thumbs-up sign, before turning back to me. "I'm going to take good care of you, Rommy. Just sit right here, and your every wish is my command."

Seated, I watched haplessly as he walked away, feeling like a fish out of water. With the loud music, and louder talking over the loud music, I was filled with an eagerness to be back at home and under my sheets. Coming there was a mistake.

"This is my cousin, Torera," Dapo said, returning with a young woman. "She's going to take care of you. Whatever you want to eat, let her know, and you'll have it. Has Axle brought your champagne?"

"Errm, no."

He clucked his tongue in his annoyance. "The wanker! I'll go get it myself."

He walked away, leaving me and the smiling Torera.

"Wow, you really look excited to be here!" she remarked.

I stared back at her, momentarily confused, until I realised she was being sarcastic. "I haven't been out in a while."

"Nah, you don't have to explain," she said, sitting next to me. "Daps told me all about your wife. That must have been rough."

I shrugged, not wanting to get into a discussion about Sekani. I'd gone there mainly because I didn't want to think about her that night.

"So, what would you like?" Torera asks. "There's a whole lot of barbecue from earlier in the day… "

"Maybe later," I cut in, the thought of food making my stomach churn. "Barbecue later might be good."

She looked at me for a few minutes before rising to her feet, stretching her hand to me. "Come with me."

Not wanting to be rude, I accepted her hand and stood, allowing her lead me past the merry guests, into the kitchen and out to the garden which, surprisingly, was empty.

"We were all out here earlier when Dapo and Segun were barbecuing," she said, pulling out two fold-up chairs. "So, please forgive the mess. I figured you might need some peace and quiet."

I sat, grateful to be away from the noise inside. She sat opposite me and as she lit a cigarette, I was accorded a better view of her face. With clear skin and angular features, she was a whole lot more attractive than I'd earlier thought. She caught me looking at her and smiled.

"Daps says you two grew up together."

I nodded, grateful for the distraction. "Yeah, we did."

"He says you're a doctor now."

I nodded again, then decided to turn the spotlight on her instead. "And you? You're cousins?"

She let out a puff of smoke. "Well, 'cousins' is a bit generous. We're old family friends. Our mothers used to be good friends, but we only ever saw each other when they came to Lagos for Christmas. When I moved to London four years ago, I got in touch with them, but we only ever get to see when they have these parties of theirs."

I listened, intrigued. "You grew up in Lagos? I've never been there. Back when my father was alive, we'd go straight to Benin from the airport, and since his death, we haven't even been back to Nigeria at all."

She took a deep puff of her cigarette. "You're not missing anything. Lagos is a dump. Nigeria is a monstrosity. I hope I never have to see that place again."

Realising talking about our home country wasn't her favourite subject, I switched to another. "So, what are you up to here?"

"I'm a skin and beauty consultant with *L'Oréal*," she answered, her face lighting up.

We spent the next few hours with her talking about how much she was enjoying her job, and me about how I was looking forward to beginning my specialization training after putting it off following Sekani's death. She asked me questions about her, and for the first time, I was able to talk about my late wife without too much of the sadness that always followed it. Before we knew it, it was almost midnight.

"Shit!" she exclaimed, shooting to her feet. "I might not be able to find a bus back home."

"I'll take you," I immediately offered, standing.

She turned to me and grinned. "I'd really like that. Thank you."

After accepting the champagne from Dapo, who said he'd thought I'd snuck out when he didn't find me where he'd left me, I led Torera to my car.

"So, where is home?"

"Dalston. Just about ten minutes from here."

Getting into the car, her short dress rode up her thighs, revealing fleshy, brown skin, and my eyes lingered there for a little longer than they should have. Catching myself, I looked away quickly and started the ignition. If she noticed me leering at her, she didn't let on, instead she cranked on the radio, singing and rapping aloud to Chris Brown's *Loyal*. Several times, I stole glances at her as she danced and waved her arms around in the car, finding her happiness and carefree nature a breath of fresh air.

When we pulled up in front of her apartment building, she turned to me. "Do you want to come upstairs?"

I didn't need much convincing. Apart from not being ready to return to my lonely house, I wanted to spend more time with this vivacious woman. Once in her studio apartment, she made no attempt at small talk, immediately pulling me in for a kiss, and for the first time since losing Sekani, sex with another woman didn't feel as dirty or leave me guilt-wrecked afterwards. For the first time since Sekani, I didn't want to run for the hills the morning after. Instead, I was happy to lie entangled with the lovely Torera for several hours, and even days, after.

We became an item after that weekend. When I eventually made it back home, she came with me, and I found myself coming alive again. With her, I was able to emerge from the shell I'd hidden myself in for so long, much to the delight of my friends and family. The downer was that, because we were out on the town almost every night, it soon started to take its toll on me during the day, as I was often tired and sometimes even hung over at work. But when I was reprimanded by a Medical Attending, who threatened to report me to the Hospital Authorities the next time I showed up plastered, I had to scale back.

But that wasn't the only thing that made me start to pull away from Torera.

As we started to settle into the routine of a regular couple, I discovered two things about my new girlfriend. One being she was a pathological liar.

"I'm waiting for *YSL* to reassign me to a new store," she'd told me when I asked why she'd never gone to work even once in almost two months of us being a couple.

"*YSL*? I thought you said you worked with *L'Oréal*?"

She'd rolled her eyes. "I told you I left *L'Oréal*, Roman."

But I was certain she never did.

"Joke and I have been besties since our days at London Guildhall University," had been another one. I didn't even bother reminding her she'd told me she'd spent only a year at City University before dropping out.

Or when she'd complained about being too broke to even pay for a travel card, only for me to get to her apartment and see shopping bags with shoes and bags from luxury stores. Or when I found out that her claim of only seeing Dapo a few times at his parties had actually been a long-drawn off-and-on sexual relationship with him.

The second thing I discovered, which turned out to be the real deal breaker, was that she was a thief.

At first, I tried to explain away the missing notes of money from my wallet, convincing myself I'd simply misplaced my Rolex watch, and even the black opal cufflinks Sekani had gifted me for our wedding, and which hadn't been moved once from my bedside table. I tried to convince myself that all the things that were disappearing around me, a brand-new iPhone I'd wanted to gift my mother, a limited edition pair of *Gucci* trainers Reagan had sent me, even vintage bottles of wine from my cellar. But when I saw that Sekani's jewellery box had been vandalised, with almost everything, even her diamond engagement ring and platinum wedding band, gone, I knew I could no longer continue to turn a blind eye.

"You're breaking up with me?" she asked in disbelief when I told her we were done. She'd come to the house after I'd stopped taking her calls, and rather than get into any ugliness accusing her of stealing all she had, I'd chosen to go the more polite route of telling her were done.

"We both know this is for the best." It had taken everything in me to remain that civil, considering all I wanted to do was grab her by the neck and hand her over to the Police.

"You can't break up with me, Roman," she scoffed. "Not when I'm pregnant with your child."

But I'd been anything but impressed.

"Spare me with your lies, Torera."

"Then let's go get a test if you don't believe me," she declared. "That's what I've been trying to tell you all week. If you don't believe me, I'll take a test right in front of you."

And that was exactly what we'd done. I drove her to the nearest *Boots* store and picked up, not one, but two pregnancy test kits. Getting back to my house, I followed her to the toilet, standing there as she peed on the stick, and waiting with her for the result to appear. And there it was, as clear as day on both sticks; two solid lines. She was indeed pregnant.

"I haven't been with anyone else in months, and you know that," she'd muttered, upon seeing the flash of doubt on my face.

And I knew she truly hadn't. Inasmuch as she was a pathological liar and thief, I'd had no reason to suspect she was cheating on me.

"So, after all the wonderful times we've had, you want to leave me now, Roman?" she asked, her eyes filling with tears.

I held her, comforting her as she cried, overwhelmed with guilt. There was no way I could leave her, not when she was carrying my child. I'd once felt strongly enough about her to consider her an important part of my life, so surely, I could find a way to overlook her vices, vices that I hoped we could correct in due time.

And so I stayed with her, remaining at her beck and call for everything she wanted, indulging her every whim, ignoring the lies that still persisted, my growing desire for the child she was carrying helping me forget my rising distaste for its mother. Because despite how much I tried, I couldn't feel for her what I once had.

But things came to a head when I found out she'd hacked into my bank account and taken money running into several thousands of pounds. For me, that was the very last straw.

"I needed the money, Roman!" she'd conceded, after at first denying it. "I have a lot of needs, especially now that I'm pregnant, and the money you give me isn't enough."

"So you had to steal?" I'd exclaimed. "I've always known you to pinch things, but this is on a whole other level! This is criminal behaviour, Torera!"

"Maybe if you gave me enough to sustain myself, I wouldn't have to 'pinch things'!"

I'd stared at her defiant, unrepentant face and knew I could no longer go any further, not even if she was pregnant with my child. And I told her just as much.

But that was the beginning of hell. Literally.

With only weeks to go before the delivery of the child, I wanted us to work out an amicable custody arrangement. But it hit a stall when she demanded for a whopping £3,000 a month.

"You're a doctor. You can afford it," had been her justification.

What followed were several days of caustic back and forth exchange, and it finally took her friend computing that, based on the percentage of my weekly income and the fact the child would be with me half the time, she wouldn't be awarded anything more than £331 a month in court, for her to agree to my final offer of £1,000 a month, which was more than generous.

On that beautiful day in April, I was present for Luna's birth, and I fell head over heels in love with her from the moment I held her in my arms, still covered in blood and vernix. My heart melted at the sight of the crying infant, born into the world on the same day of the week the woman I loved departed it, and I knew Sekani had returned to me through her. Hours later, after she'd been cleaned and lay asleep in the crib next to her mother's bed, I still couldn't keep my eyes off her. She was the most beautiful thing I'd ever seen in my life.

"She's gorgeous," I said, more to myself than anyone. I remembered what Sekani had told me as far back as when we were in medical school, and I knew there was only one name for her. "Luna. Beauty straight from the heavens."

That had led to another argument, with Torera insisting there was no way in the world her child was going to be named after a celestial body. It had taken my mother and her visiting cousins to mediate, and in the end, the child's birth certificate read Tifeoluwa Beverly Ejemhen Isibor. It broke my heart not to be able to name her what I really wanted, but I'd had no choice but to agree to the compromise.

Despite our now very acrimonious relationship, I took time off work and moved in with Torera to help out with the baby, as none of her relatives, whether in London or Lagos, had volunteered to. My mother had offered but I'd immediately declined, not wanting her to witness how toxic a relationship I had with the mother of my child. Knowing that if she moved in with me, she'd never agree to leave, I rented a larger flat for her in Lower Clapton.

In those first few weeks, I was very hands-on with the baby, staying up every night and even most of the day. Torera used her recovery from her caesarean section as an excuse not to lift a finger, so I did everything until she finally felt strong enough to help out. But as hard and stressful as that time was, I wouldn't change a single thing about it. From learning the nature and sound of every cry and what I had to do to pacify her each time, to rocking her to sleep and feeling the rhythmic beat of her little heart on my chest, to when she would give me a priceless smile, it soon felt like my daughter and I had our own special language. That was why I remained in that flat with them, even when I had to return to work, and even when Torera got it into her head to make sexual advances at me.

"You've got to be joking, right?" I scoffed, the first time she tried to kiss me after I'd put the baby to bed. "I've told you several times already. I'm here for my child, not for you."

"Keep telling yourself that," she'd laughed. "I see the way you look at me when you think I'm not watching."

She couldn't have been more deluded if she tried, and this was evidenced by the few more attempts she made to rekindle our sexual relationship. By the time our daughter was six months old, I decided I'd had enough of fending off her mother's advances. As she was now old enough to stay with me half the week as Torera and I had agreed, I moved back home. Between my mother, Paris, Kennedy and his wife Arin, everyone chipped in to help me with my new infant on the days I had her.

Everything was going well. We'd all settled perfectly into a great pattern that worked for everyone. Or so I thought. A month to our daughter's first birthday, Torera's best friend and, it turned out, her partner-in-crime, Jojo, got arrested for stealing thousands of pounds from Jojo's employer, an elderly woman. Basically, her entire life's savings. In her confessional statement, Jojo implicated Torera, and she was arrested. But as the money was transferred directly to Jojo's account, and as Jojo claimed she only ever gave Torera cash, there was no paper trail leading to Torera, making the case against her circumstantial, so she was released. But, and as I found out only then, she had been on the Police's radar for a long time, having been indirectly linked to several well-known cyber criminals in the not-too-distant past, so it was only a matter of time before the Police would have a solid case around her to arrest and prosecute her.

For the sake of the child we shared, I paid for an expensive lawyer, hoping to find a way to help her out of the mess she'd created for herself.

"It's not looking good, Roman," Max, the lawyer, said to me. "My source tells me there's enough CCTV footage of her entering and leaving the building with Jojo to make her an accessory to the crime. That, and the fact they've discovered an account she has under an alias, one in which she received a whole lot of money from

Ade-Gold, one of the worst cyber fraudsters in the country. Not to mention she's been living here on a long expired visiting visa. If the Old Bill doesn't get her soon, the Home Office will."

Even though I knew she was crooked and slimy, hearing just how much still blew my mind.

"Roman, if you marry me, all this will go away!" she pleaded, when she came to pick up our daughter after her weekend with me. "Help me, please! I beg you!"

"That will only solve your immigration issue, but it's not going to help with the criminal investigation," I'd answered. I wanted to ask her what the hell she'd been thinking. I wanted to ask her if she really thought she could go scot-free after cheating and stealing from people for so long. "Max is a great lawyer and I'm sure he'll do everything he can to help."

In hindsight, I never should have allowed her leave with my child that night. I should have insisted on having her stay with me longer, especially with all the uncertainty swirling around. But I guess in all my naiveté, I never imagined just how far Torera could really go. Until my phone calls went unanswered the next day, and a visit to her apartment the day after confirmed my worst fear.

She had fled with my child.

Standing in the empty apartment after letting myself in with my keys, it felt like I'd been kicked in the gut, like my heart had been ripped out of my chest. That evening, I drove around London like a mad man; from Lower Clapton to Dalston, from Peckham to Whitechapel, from Colliers Wood to Wimbledon, going anywhere I knew she even had the merest of acquaintances. But the response from all of them was the same. None of them knew where she was. It wasn't until I banged on Dapo's door at 1am in the morning, my eyes bloodshot from crying and driving around the city all night, that I finally made some headway. After several calls to relatives, he got an answer.

ADESUWA O'MAN NWOKEDI

"Her half-sister says she left for Nigeria last night," he said, his eyes lowered and unable to meet mine. "She says she decided it was best to leave rather than face the possibility of going to jail."

I glared at him, the realisation of his words hitting me one by one. Torera had run away to Nigeria? With my daughter? With my child? Letting out a loud cry, I'd lunged at him, grabbing him by the collar and pinning him to the wall, needing an outlet for my rage, the person who introduced me to Torera no better candidate for it.

"She wasn't supposed to be for anything more than a shag or two, mate!" he'd cried out in his defence.

And he was correct.

I got home at 3am, feeling just as bereft as when I'd walked in from the hospital after Sekani died. In my bedroom, I opened my safe to see if Torera had found a way to steal our daughter's passport that had only just arrived a month before, but saw the red booklet still tucked safely in it. I frowned as I imagined the sort of clandestine manner in which she'd smuggled not just herself out of the country, but our innocent daughter as well. Dropping to my knees, I wept like a baby.

Despite the efforts of not just my friends and family but pretty much anyone I knew who had even the most distant of relatives in Nigeria, nobody was able to trace them. It was like they had vanished without as much as a trace.

But after a month of going crazy trying to find her, she finally called.

"Hello, Roman."

I'd been at work when I got the call from an unknown number but hearing her voice had sent adrenalin coursing through my body, making me feel equal parts like strangling her and... well, strangling her.

"Where is my daughter?"

"You better relax that your uptight body," she'd had the audacity to chuckle. "We're back in Lagos."

The cavalier confirmation filled me with so much rage, I wanted to throw my phone to the wall. "You had no right taking her away, Torera."

"When you refused to do what you had to, to keep me in the country *nko*?" she laughed again, clearly enjoying hearing the frustration in my voice. "I had to do what I had to do."

I'd swallowed, knowing I would get nowhere by shouting or calling her the names I desperately wanted to. "Please, Torera, I need to see my daughter. Please."

"Send me £1,000, and we'll make it happen. I'll send you my cousin's account number and I'll arrange for a video call for you to see her."

Without thinking twice about it, I'd done the transfer to her cousin, Yomi, and when she Facetime'd me later that day, I'd wept upon seeing my daughter, giggling and laughing at my image on her mother's phone, innocent and carefree, oblivious of what was happening or that her father had missed her first birthday a few weeks before. That was how we continued for the next few months. I didn't tell any of my friends or family about these calls, knowing they would frown at me depleting my savings just for video calls with my daughter that were sometimes only two minutes brief. But as the price tag kept getting higher for every call, I finally had to put my foot down when she demanded for £5,000.

"Are you out of your mind?" I exploded. "I don't even earn that much a month. Where do you expect me to get that from after everything you've already extorted from me?"

"Continue speaking English there!" she retorted. "You better not try me, Roman. If you try me, I swear, you will never see Tife ever again!"

As much as I wanted to explode and call her every nasty name in the book, I knew I couldn't afford to lose my cool, especially as I was yet to speak with my daughter that week.

"Well? Are you going to pay or not?"

"I'll pay," I answered, beaten. "Let me speak with her, please."

"You only have one minute with her today," she said, before reaching over for the kid from where she sat out of my view. I winced as I noticed the rough way my daughter was dragged and noticed, for the first time, how her eyes widened in fear as she looked at her mother.

"Hi, sweetheart," I cooed, waving at her, despite the rock-sized lump now forming in my throat. "You look gorgeous."

Her eyes brightened as she back waved at me, a sharp contrast to how frightened she had looked only seconds before. I sang at her and blew her kisses like I usually did, despite my rising anxiety. I had never had cause to question the way Torera was treating our daughter, but seeing not only how she'd manhandled her, but also how terrified the little girl was of her, was causing several alarm bells to go off in my head.

"That's it. Time's up," Torera's voice came, turning the phone back to herself. "£5,000, or you best believe this is the last time you will ever speak to her in your sad, sorry life!"

"Torera, please," I pleaded. "I don't have that kind of… "

"£5,000 or consider this a permanent farewell."

Her face disappeared from the screen, and just as I was about to disconnect the line, I heard the muffled sound of voices. I realised she'd forgotten to disconnect the call and had merely dropped the phone, face down. I strained to listen, but couldn't make out any words, only Torera's now incoherent voice and the unmistakable voice of a man.

And then I heard my daughter scream. Her scream was followed by what sounded like moving furniture, and, in horror, I realised she had been pushed.

"Please, take her away from here!" Torera's raised voice finally made her words coherent.

By now, tears were pouring down my face, fast and furious. It was at that point I knew, without a shadow of doubt, that I had to find a way to get my daughter. Considering how much money Torera was still asking for, I was under no illusions she was going to simply hand the kid over nicely. She was a hardened criminal, and to deal with her, I was going to have to sink all the way down to the depths of her depravity.

It was no secret that Ihidie and Ojie had been involved with a nefarious fraternity in their days at the University of Benin. Even though it was now a thing of their past, they were still able to draw on a few of their contacts in Lagos and we were soon able to trace Torera's exact location; an upscale apartment in Ikoyi. Without hesitation, and for the first time in almost twenty years, I set off for Nigeria.

Ojie's friend, Evans, picked me up from the airport, and we headed straight to her place. Getting to the luxury block of flats, after a heavy tip, the guards allowed us into the compound, and as we made our way up to her flat on the 10th floor, I could see with my own eyes the kind of lavish lifestyle I was funding, in full or in part. Ringing her doorbell, I got the satisfaction of seeing her eyes widen with shock upon seeing me, the man she'd taken for an entire rodeo ride.

"What are you doing here?" she yelled. "Who the hell let you up here?"

"Where's my daughter, Torera?"

She hissed and placed her hands on her hips. "Yomi's account hasn't been credited, to the best of my knowledge."

I was so incensed, I took a step towards her but was restrained by Evans. No, nothing good would come out of my doing the unthinkable and striking her. I wasn't going to stoop that low.

"Madam, please be reasonable," Evans said. "He has come all this way. Let him see the girl."

She shrugged, a coy smile playing on her lips. "She's not even home. I don't pick her up from the crèche until later in the evening."

"Can we come back to see her?" Evans pressed.

"*Na so!*" she'd cackled, before glaring at me, all traces of laughter suddenly gone. "You better get off this property, you good for nothing fool who couldn't even do the needful to help me when I needed it. If you ever come back here, I'll be sure to have you arrested. This is my town, not London. All it will take is a phone call and you'll rot in jail here."

"I just want to see her, Torera."

She'd flipped her finger in response. "You see this, Mr. High and Mighty Roman? Go fuck yourself! When you're ready, you know what you need to do."

And the brass door was slammed shut in our faces.

But we'd gone prepared.

We already knew that she dropped Tife at a nearby crèche every morning, sending her maid to pick her up later in the evening. Evans had already done the necessary groundwork and, by capturing an image of Torera's maid, had duplicated her pick-up card, complete with name and signature. That was our Plan B, a plan I really hadn't wanted to resort to.

But Torera had left me no choice.

From her place, we'd picked up a lady Evans hired, a lady with an uncanny resemblance with Torera's maid, and left for the school. Upon getting to the crèche, the security guards gave the access card a cursory glance before allowing us in. My heart was beating so fast as we entered the room where the children were busy watching a Disney movie. Our female accomplice presented the card to a woman, who examined it with more scrutiny than her counterparts at the main gate. She glanced from the card to our partner several times, and I was worried she'd realise it wasn't the same person.

"You came for Tife early today?" she'd finally asked.

I almost deflated with relief when I realised she hadn't.

"Yes, Ma," our accomplice answered. "Her father is around from London."

The minder smiled at me and curtsied. "Welcome, Sir." Then turning to another minder, she pointed. "Go and get Tife. She's sitting over there. Don't forget her food flask and water bottle."

My eyes followed the second minder as she made her way across the room and when they fell on my daughter, my heart skipped several beats. The last time I'd seen her, she hadn't even been walking, and now, at 20 months, she was a clapping and singing toddler. As they made their way to us, as Tife's eyes clapped with mine, any worries I had about her not recognizing me were allayed as she let out an excited squeal and ran straight into my arms. With that, there were no more questions from anyone, and we walked out of the compound as easily as we'd entered.

Once in the car, my heart sank when I noticed the red welts and bruises on her neck and arms, some of them fresh and some several days old. That was the confirmation I needed that my suspicions about Torera abusing our child weren't misplaced, and I was filled with an intense urge to ask Evans to turn the car back around, so I could make her pay for every time she had dared lay a hand on our daughter. But it wasn't worth it. I wasn't about to gamble with my child's custody for a second longer.

Armed with her legal and proper passport, we headed straight to the airport. From the way she clung to me all the way there and even after we'd boarded the British Airways plane back to London that evening, it was evident that even she never wanted to be parted from me again.

Torera's irate call came the day after we'd arrived. "If you like yourself, Roman, you better have my child on the next flight back to Lagos. You better send her back to me, or… "

"Or what?" I cut in, smug over the fact I now had the upper hand. "You'll come here to get her? Oh wait, you can't come back here, can you? Or else you'll be thrown in the nick with other criminals like yourself. You can't do a damn thing about it, you little… " I grit my teeth to keep from reeling off the insults I was desperate to. "I've seen the bruises. I know you were hurting her. You should be lucky I didn't come back to return the favour." I had to take a deep breath to ward off the consuming anger I felt every time I was reminded of how she'd treated her. "Look, my daughter is here with me for good. You'll never have access to her ever again. So, I'd lose my number if I were you. Focus on rebuilding your sorry life over there in Lagos."

"Your daughter indeed!" she laughed, jarring me. "The child that isn't even yours."

If she'd intended it as a stone thrown, it hit its mark. Apart from the day I found out about her pregnancy, I'd never had cause to suspect Torera of being unfaithful to me. But for the rest of the day, that was all I could think of. Had she been unfaithful? Had another man really gotten her pregnant? Was someone else really my baby's father?

But that night as I put my daughter to bed, I watched her as she slept, and I knew I loved her more than life itself. She was my child, and I didn't need any DNA test to confirm anything.

In the weeks that followed, using my solicitor and an enrolled deed poll, I had her name officially changed to Luna Ejemhen Isibor. I also moved us out of the house in Holland Park, with its plethora of bad memories, and bought us the new one in South Hampstead.

Having heard what happened from their friend, Torera's cronies in London made it a point to harass me anywhere I had the misfortune of running into them, turning me into a recluse for the longest time. But if a retreat from the social scene was the price to pay for a new life with my child, I was ready to bear it for as long as I had to.

And now, I will not let it spoil this beautiful love I have been fortunate to find again.

Thirty

Fantasy

APRIL 2019

Roman

Convinced she's had enough time to cool off, I tap on Legachi's door later that afternoon. Without waiting for an answer, I push it open. She is sitting on her bed, staring ahead at nothing.

"I meant to tell you," I say. "It's such a messy, complicated story. I was just waiting for the right time."

She turns to me and the blankness in her stare sends a shiver down my spine.

Legachi

"You were waiting for the right time to tell me?" I echo what he has just had the audacity to say to me. "I find that almost laughable, Roman. Almost, because, as you can see, I'm not laughing. You and I have talked about everything under the sun, or at least I thought we had. Lying on your bed, and even this one I'm sitting on, we have talked until sunrise so many times. In only four short months, I have bared myself naked to you, literally and figuratively. I've told you things I never even told anyone."

"And it's been the same for me, I swear it," he implores, taking a tentative step towards me.

"So, your wife has been dead for eight good years, Roman? Eight, and not four like you made me believe," I cut in, still stupefied by that realization. "So, what was all that about her naming Luna? What was that story about her giving her daughter the name she chose as a young girl? All lies *abi*?"

"It wasn't a lie. Sekani did want to name her daughter that."

"Except she didn't get the chance to," I cut in and shake my head. "All this time, you've lied to me. All this time, all of this has been one big lie." I turn to look at him and I am broken as I realize that, truly, it has all been a lie. "I can never trust you again."

Roman

"Legachi, please listen to me," I say, sitting on her bed. I want to reach for her hand, but I am suddenly afraid to, afraid that my very touch will do more harm than good. "I messed up by not telling you, I accept that. But please, don't give up on us."

"All this time, I've ignored all the red flags," she says, her gaze averted again. "This relationship has just been one extended booty call for you."

I flinch at her words, and this time damn the consequences and reach for her hand. "How can you even say that? You know that's not true."

She pulls her hand out of mine. "I allowed myself to be seduced by sweet words, sweet presents and sweet holiday promises. But you don't have any plans for me, Roman. You've never had." She shakes her head again. "Mezie was right after all."

"Mezie?" I repeat in disbelief, the name sounding like a curse word in my mouth.

She returns her gaze to me. "I'll give you a week to hire someone else before I leave."

Our eyes hold and I search hers for any sign to show she doesn't mean what she has just said. But they are flat and vacant... and I realise she means every word. And that is the most telling of any words that have been spoken.

"Don't bother," I answer, steeling myself. "You can leave immediately, if that's what you want."

Legachi

My brows rise in my surprise. Our eyes continue to hold, and for a moment, I am tempted to buckle. I am tempted to tell him Sekani and Torera don't matter. I want him to tell me he still wants me, not just to stay, but in his life for the long term. I want him to declare his love for me, something he has never verbally done. I want him to tell me he has several plans for me... for us. But he does and says none of these things. Instead, cold, dispassionate eyes stare back at me.

Rising to my feet, I walk over to the closet, pull out my suitcases, and start throwing my clothes into them.

Roman

I walk out of her room, the sight of her packing too much for me to take. I go to mine and once in there, I swallow back the guttural scream that wants to let loose from my stomach, and punch the wall so hard, it scabs my hand. I am furious, frustrated, and disappointed that she has decided to not only not hear me out, but also not give our relationship a chance. I sit on my bed as I hear her door open and close, praying she will realize the reckless hastiness of her actions. Surely, she won't leave without saying goodbye to Luna. But when I hear the front door open, I look out my window and see her struggling with her boxes down the road… and angry tears pool in my eyes.

We are truly over.

Legachi

The tears don't come until I'm sitting in the bus headed to Hendon, my heart broken to pieces, crushed that my beautiful fantasy has been nothing but that.

A fantasy.

Thirty-One

Moving On

APRIL 2019 — MAY 2019

Uegachi

After a few days with Nonye, I rent a studio apartment in Hendon, switching my mind to autopilot mode, doing everything I can not to fixate on the change in my routine, the disruption to my daily schedule, or the gaping hole in my heart. I don't bother looking for another job and I focus squarely on studying for my exams, going from my apartment to school, and back again.

But as detached as I try to be from the turmoil still raging in my head and heart, I subconsciously find myself praying for Roman's call. Every time my phone rings, I wish it is him reaching out to me, telling me he misses me, telling me he is miserable without me. But the call never comes. By the time the month of May comes along, I have no choice but to accept that I was right after all. I was never that important to him.

I manage to sit for my exams, giving it my every waking focus, not just to pass well enough to make a distinction, but to keep from feeling the intense pain that has come with my broken heart, which, even though I haven't seen or spoken to Roman in weeks, seems to break a little more every day.

"*Nne*, I'm so glad this is finally over," Nonye remarks after we write our final paper in Applied Corporate Finance. "Let me go back home and see my man, *biko*!"

"When do you leave? Sunday?"

"And not a day later! Nine months without *Vitamin D*? Ah, I can't take it anymore."

I ponder her words as we walk to the café to wait for Tayo, the thought of an early return to Nigeria taking seed in my heart. After two bad breakups in such a short space of time, do I really want to remain in England longer than I need to? With how small the city of London is, the chances of my running into Roman are high. Will I be able to bear seeing him again? Possibly even with another woman? The more I think about it, the more I know that, for my own self-preservation, I need to be as far away from him, from the town, as I possibly can. And when I confirm from my professor that I can write my dissertation remotely, I make the decision to go back home.

"What are you going back for?" Nonye exclaims, when I tell her I am scheduled to leave for Lagos two days after her. "Why do you want to waste money going home only to come back shortly after? Chinedu is the one paying for me to come home briefly *o*. By the time I come back in July, *na* to remain here till further notice."

"Professor Kellard said he can supervise my dissertation remotely," I answer, all the more resolute about the decision I have made. "I won't be back here till graduation next March."

"You don't have to run away, babes," Tayo says, placing a hand over mine. "People break up all the time. It'll hurt for a while, but you'll get over it. We all do."

Except I don't think I will. Even by returning to Lagos and putting over four thousand miles between us, I don't think I will ever get Roman.

Which is all the more reason why I have to leave.

Roman

Without any childcare, I have scaled back my work hours yet again. But even outside of the inconvenience that has caused, what has been even more of a bother has been erasing every memory of Legachi from the house. Despite stripping down her room from the sheets to even the drapes, despite trashing all the Tupperware containers that have stored anything she has ever cooked or baked, despite trashing all her copies of *OK!* and *Closer* magazines lying around the house, she is still present everywhere, her minty berry fragrance still clinging to furniture and clothing, Luna's and mine, like an evil spirit. Several times, I go to her bare bedroom and stand there, remembering everything from our intimate moments to that last conversation, and I am torn between wishing I could turn back the hands of time so I could have told her the truth earlier… to resenting her for how easily she was able to just walk away; from us… from everything. And that resentment deepens every time a distraught Luna asks after her.

"When is Legachi coming back, Daddy?"

She would have been too heartbroken to hear that Legachi had walked out on her without a second glance, so I'd lied to her that she'd gone out of town for a while. But if I thought, being a toddler, she would quickly forget about her, she has proven me wrong as hardly a day goes by without her asking for her.

"Not for a while, sweetheart," is what I have taken to answering, hoping she will one day read between the lines to understand that Legachi will never be coming back.

As beautiful and wonderful as it was playing happy families, it is clearly over. It's been over a month, and she hasn't called even once. She has clearly moved on, probably even gone back to her low-life ex. It's best for us, Luna and I, to do the same as well.

It's time for new beginnings.

So, I do what I should have done years ago. I take down Sekani's pictures, including the one from our wedding day. There is no point living a lie, or even confusing Luna when she comes of age to start asking probing questions. I can't continue using Sekani's memory as a crutch, as the veneer to hide the dirty details of my past. I can't spend the rest of my life hiding and dodging from Torera and her aggrieved friends.

It is time for me to tackle this beast head on.

Thirty-Two

Haunted

JUNE 2019

Legachi

I deliberately don't notify my parents of my return until the day before my trip, mainly because of their tendency to overreact. And overreact they do.

"Hope no problem?" my mother asks, her high-pitched voice higher still.

"There's no problem, Mom. I'm done with my exams."

"Now now?" she exclaims, clearly panicked. "But you said it is a two-year program."

I sigh, remembering I'd told them I'd be away for at least two years, and even that had been an understated duration. That was when building a life with Mezie had still been on the cards. "No, mom. It's a year."

"But it's not even up to a year. June only just started, *bikonu*. Why are you rushing back here? Or are you going to return after a little while?"

I shut my eyes, not knowing whether to tell her the truth, that I'm returning home because of a failed relationship, that I am running away from the inevitable pain and heartbreak I will feel when I find out my ex has met someone else, that I desperately want to avoid the humiliation that will come when Mezie finds out he's been proven right after all… or whether I should save myself the agro and just lie. I choose the latter.

"Yes, I'll come back later," I say, hoping that will end the conversation.

"I think it's a waste of money to come back home and do nothing, but no problem. Have you informed your father?"

"I've sent him a WhatsApp message. He said he'll send Ebubedike to pick me from the airport."

She sighs and I can immediately recognise that as her own anxiety over having to see her husband soon. "No problem. I will see you on Thursday morning."

Once off the phone, I spend the rest of the day packing the few pieces of corporate clothes I've managed to buy. Having given away my winter and most of my spring wardrobe, I really don't have much to pack.

"How can you be leaving when summer is just about to start?" Tayo asks yet again, still unable to understand my decision. "This is the most fun and exciting time of the year. By the time we go to one or two parties, you won't even remember that anyone called Roman exists!"

With Nonye gone for a few weeks, she is eager not to have to miss us both. But at this point, my mind is already made up. I'm not strong enough to co-exist in London with all the reminders of what I'd thought the best time of my life. Back in Lagos, and away from all the things that could make me remember him, it will be easier for me to heal.

At least, I hope so.

"I still don't understand why you had to rush back here," my father mutters for what has to be the millionth time, as we sit for breakfast the morning after my return. As promised, my mother has come from my sister's house in Ajah, and if the look on her face is anything to go by, she is pleased by neither; my premature return nor being in her estranged husband's company. "Isn't your visa until September 2020? I hope you didn't get into any trouble over there."

I look up at him, wondering if he can see just how much trouble I did get into by falling in love with an unattainable man.

"No, Sir," I answer with averted eyes. "I didn't get into any trouble. I finished my exams and decided to come home and write my dissertation here. My topic is on supply chain risk management, with Nigeria as a case study, so I figured it was better for me to write it where I can get first-hand data."

That had actually been my professor's idea and one I'd happily jumped on as better justification for my return home.

He shrugs, reluctantly seeing reason with that answer. "If that's the case, it's okay then."

"But you said you'll soon go back?" my mother asks, her eyes wide and hopeful. "Because you can't be here and your fiancé, there. That's the reason you went there, isn't it?"

Deciding it is best to bite the bullet now, once and for all, I tell them that Mezie and I are no longer together, and that I might not go back to London until my graduation next year, and even then, only briefly. They are both disappointed to hear about Mezie and I but consoled that I have at least returned with a foreign degree in view.

"I'm sure your former place of work will be more than happy to take you back," my father nods. "With your new degree, I'm sure you will even get a good promotion and pay rise."

Even though I smile and nod in agreement, deep down, I'm not quite as optimistic.

"Don't mind that useless Abiriba boy. I always knew he was no good, stringing you along all these years," my mother says as we sit in my bedroom, or what used to be my bedroom and now appears to be everything from a laundry room to an all-purpose dump. An ironing board stands between my bed and the door, with heaps of my father's and cousins' clothes piled atop it. As if that isn't bad enough, their shoes and books are strewn all over the room, and I can't help but feel pained they weren't even bothered to clean the room up for my return. "Don't worry, you will meet a much better man soon."

I look at her, having only caught the last part of her sentence. Even though ending things with Mezie was more of a blessing than a misfortune, it isn't difficult for me to look as heartbroken as she expects. One day back home, and the pain I still feel from my breakup with Roman is showing no signs of abating.

"Let me be on my way. That traffic to Ajah is something else these days," my mother says, rising.

"Are you never coming back home?" I ask. "Chinasa is almost 5 years old, Mom. This one is no longer *omugwo* but full-on separation."

Her lips purse and her nostrils flare. "Call it what you like, Legachi. All I know is I am not coming back here."

And just like that, I have the confirmation that my parents are indeed separated. I remain seated on the bed long after she leaves, not even budging when the power goes off and my cousins, Ebubedike and Obiora, holler abuse at a man called Mukaila, who is supposed to be fixing their ailing generator. As daylight fades into evening, as the old generator finally kicks into service, supplying electricity to the house, sitting in this room I vacated almost ten years ago feels like retrogression. The faded blue and white floral print sheet on the bed and the old lace curtains are the same ones I left behind, and I soon start to ask myself if returning home without as much as a plan for myself was a wise idea.

Looking at my boxes stacked in a corner of the room, I decide not to bother unpacking. With the money I have returned with, and with the prospect of getting a promotion at work, I should be able to rent a small place for myself, roommate free.

As the days become weeks, even though work is going well with my dissertation, I am unable to derive the requisite joy from that. My despondency, rather than diminish, increases in intensity, and is my waking and sleeping companion. It has been two months since our breakup, but I miss Roman so bitterly, it physically hurts. I see his face every time I close my eyes, hear his voice in my subconscious, feel his arms around me when I cuddle my pillow to sleep. It is soon clear that the distance I have put between us has done nothing to make losing him any easier.

On June 27, I turn 32, and I wonder what it would have been like if he was still a part of my life. I smile at the memory of his Valentine's Day surprises, and I know he would have pulled out all the stops for me today. But rather than be loved and celebrated by the most wonderful, the most special man on earth, I spend the day in my bedroom, receiving only a trickle of phone calls from my sisters and distant relatives. It is a sad reminder of what I have lost.

That night, for the first time since finding out from Tayo, I return to the Instagram pages that have the pictures of Roman and the mystery Torera. I stare at their pictures, fixating particularly on her, torturing myself with how much more beautiful and glamorous she is than I could ever be. Even in the picture with her pregnant, in a fitted black dress and a fur coat that would drive the folks at PETA crazy, her face is made up to perfection with contours that make her angular face Kardashian-like. And I am eaten up with jealousy. Even more curious about her, I try to find her social media pages, but I hit a brick wall. The tags from the pictures I've seen lead nowhere, and I'm unable to find out as little as her full name. I try again the next day, and the day after, but it's one big circular reference, with everything I find redirecting me back to the pictures I've already seen. The woman's online footprint is non-existent, and the mystery of it all frustrates me even more.

The following week, I finally muster the courage to call my former boss, Mr. Ude.

"Ah, Legachi! You're back in town already?"

"Yes, Sir," I answer, forcing a smile so it will convey in my voice. "I arrived a few weeks ago."

"That was a quick one. You're already through with your program?"

"Not quite. I'm currently writing my dissertation. But I'm done with my exams, and from what I gather, I'm on track to finish with a distinction."

"That's good. Well done."

I wait for him to gush about missing me and wanting me back at work immediately, but when he says nothing, I decide to just come out with it.

"I'm available to come back to work, Sir," I say. "I've finished the data gathering for my dissertation, so I can pretty much write it in my free time. I can resume next month."

"That's no problem. You know you're always welcome back. Just send me your updated CV, and I will start processing it with HR right away," he answers, his voice just as gravelly as I remember. "On the same level of course."

"The same level? Sir, that's not fair!" I protest. "I have a Master's degree from a reputable British university. Shouldn't that count for something?"

"You just said you're still writing your dissertation. You don't even have a degree in hand yet. The only justification would be if you got some relatable work experience while you were there. Did you?"

I think back to my telemarketing job, to stacking shelves at *Poundyard*, to watching *In the Night Garden* with Luna, and my heart sinks.

"No, Sir."

"Then how can you expect anything but the same level, Legachi?" he scoffs. "Send me your CV, so I can get you in before the end of July."

Even though I reluctantly agree, as I terminate the call, I decide I'd rather slit my throat than return to the bank the same way I left.

With my dreams of a higher position and fatter salary dashed, I am reluctant to splash out on an apartment with the £2,000 I have returned with. So, I have no choice but to finally unpack. As I sort through my books, I find the CD Roman gifted me on Valentine's Day, the one he specially curated for me. My eyes pool with tears as I look at it, memories of the day, and the many times after that we listened to it, assaulting me. I slide it into my old CD player, not even sure it still works, but it does.

I sit on the floor as the songs play, tears pouring down my face. With Daniel Beddingfield's *If You're Not the One* playing, I go to the archived picture album in my phone, the album where I transferred all our memories when I was unable to delete them but could no longer bear to see them when scrolling through my phone. I look at all the pictures we took, intimate ones of just the two of us, and the very many with all three of us. And I realize one thing for sure; I want him back. I desperately want him back.

Even with the lies.

Roman

My cousin, Ogbeide, picks me up from the Murtala Mohammed Airport in Lagos on Thursday night, and the next day, we drive to a restaurant to meet Evans. A wide smile breaks on my face when I see my old accomplice, the man I owe being reunited with my daughter, and we embrace.

"You look good, man!" he exclaims. "A whole lot better than the last time I saw you. How is Tife?"

"Her name is Luna now," I answer. "And she's great, thank you. She turned 4 in April."

I show him pictures of her birthday on my phone, and as he gushes over her adorable pictures, I do everything I can not to look at the brown eyed, gap-toothed woman in almost all of them, smiling that smile I could move mountains for. Could have. Could have moved mountains for. All that is in the past now. She's my past now. Hopefully, one day my heart will catch up with my head.

"So, chief, what's the deal?" Evans asks, as the three of us are served bottles of beer. "What on earth do you want to see that woman for?"

"It's time to stop running," I shrug. "For the last two years, I've been looking behind my back. I've had to endure all sorts of trolling and abuse from her friends and cronies. I don't want to be labeled a kidnapper for the rest of my life, when all I did was take my daughter home."

"I hear you, but what exactly do you want to do?"

"I want to have a proper conversation with her. I want her to legally sign over custody of Luna to me. I don't want there to be any confusion or ambiguity about it. As Luna's only legal guardian without a criminal record, it's only right for me to be the one with full custody of the child."

"My brother, *that one na for London o! This na Naija!*" Evans cuts in. "She might have a criminal record over there, but over here, she might be as clean as a whistle. She could you have arrested for abducting her child years ago."

I nod, having already considered that possibility, but prepared to damn the consequences anyway.

"I'll take my chances."

Evans shrugs and reaches for his phone. "I have her new location. She's no longer in Ikoyi, but has moved further down Lekki, close to VGC." He raises a concerned brow. "You're sure about this? You're sure you don't want to just go back home and enjoy your life with your child? Who cares about a few angry chicks ranting now and again? They'll get tired after a while."

I shake my head. "I'm already here. Let's get this over and done with."

He nods and after we're done with our drinks, he pays, and we set off.

Pulling up in front of the modest apartment building, it is a far cry from her last flashy abode. Her fleecing game is clearly no longer as strong, is my sardonic thought as we walk up the dark stairway. I allow Evans lead the way, because he's already had the area staked, and also to compose myself. The last thing I need to do is lose my temper, something that might prove difficult, considering how well she knows how to rile me.

Evans knocks on the door and a heavily pregnant Torera opens the door. Her eyes widen, squint and widen again when she sees me, and I half expect her to lunge at me. Instead, she lets out a long hiss.

"You have some nerve showing up here after what you did, Roman," she retorts.

"Can we come in?" I ask.

She glares at me and eyes my companions. "I'm not going to have three men in my house. I'm the only one at home, so if you can't enter alone, then forget about it."

I turn to Evans, and he nods, his cue to let me know he'll be on the alert. He and Ogbeide linger back as I walk into the house with Torera. Just like the stairway, the living room is very poorly lit and, from the little I can see, very shabbily furnished.

"I see congratulations are in order," I remark as I sit.

"I don't recall asking you to sit," she retorts. "And you can shove your congratulations all the way up your stiff ass. You had the nerve to take Tife without doing what you were supposed to do."

"What exactly was I supposed to do?" I ask, truly unsure.

"Don't be smart, Roman. You know exactly what you had to do if you wanted the kid so badly."

And then it dawns on me. I realise she is more pained about losing out on the money I would have been more than willing to pay, than the child herself. I realise that all this while, it hasn't been about Luna at all... but the money.

"Is that what you're more interested in, Torera?" I voice what is in my head. "The money? You're not interested in Luna at all?"

"Luna," she shakes her head and laughs. "So, you went ahead to give her that silly name." Her eyes hold mine. "Don't act like you didn't know the right thing to do, Roman. This has nothing to do with sentiments." She shrugs. "Besides, as you can see, my hands are already full."

I am tempted to ask how that came about, this pregnancy of hers. I am tempted to ask who is responsible for it and why her quality of life has deteriorated. But I realise I really don't care.

"I need you to ask your friends to back off," I say instead. "I need you to stop this kidnap story that's killing my reputation back home. I need you to do the right thing and sign Luna over to me... legally."

She observes me for a while, before a smile curves her lips. "Only if you make it worth my while, Roman."

"Name your price."

Her smile becomes a full grin as she reaches for a pen lying on the coffee table. Flipping over a supermarket flyer, she writes something and hands it over to me. My brows raise when I see the amount; £10,000.

It is a whole lot more than I am prepared to pay, but if it will mean the end of this nightmare, then it's what I have to do.

"I'll pay this only after you sign the necessary legal documents."

She nods. "I'll sign whatever you want, as long as I get paid first."

"I'll send you 25% of the money first, and then have the legal papers drafted as soon as I get back to London. They'll be delivered to you here," I reiterate. "You'll get the balance payment after you've publicly informed everyone that I have legal custody of our daughter, and that I didn't kidnap her."

"How on earth am I going to do that? You know I'm no longer on social media."

"I don't care how you do it, Torera, just do it," I retort. "That's the condition to get the rest of the money."

She beams. "Deal."

It feels like a heavy load has been lifted off my chest. If she does sign the reassignment of custody papers and makes the public statement, I will finally be able to exhale and no longer have to look behind my back. I will finally be free.

I start to walk to the door, but then turn to her again. "What you said to me on the phone the last time we spoke, about Luna not being my daughter, did you mean it, or did you just say it to hurt me?"

She exhales deeply. "I could lie to you, Roman. I could say what you want to hear, to make sure you do as you've said and pay me what you've agreed to. But I've reached a point in my life where I've cut out all the bullshit." She shrugs. "The truth is I don't know. I don't know, Roman. You weren't the only one I was sleeping with."

I remain transfixed to the spot for a few seconds before my legs somehow move me in the direction of the door. But even as I reunite with Evans and Ogbeide and give them the thumbs-up mission accomplished sign, Torera's last words haunt me, the mere possibility of Luna not being my child a cruel spear through my heart.

Legachi

I watch Chinasa play as I sit in my sister's living room on Friday afternoon, tears in my eyes as I remember my beloved Luna, once again ashamed about how unceremoniously I exited her life, knowing I could have at least said a proper goodbye to her, regardless of what was going on between her dad and me. I sit through small talk with my mother and older sister, but all the while, my mind remains on the little girl I abandoned in London… and her father who still has my heart.

And on a whim, I decide to call. I decide to call him, so I can at least hear his voice again. Breaking away from my family, I go outside and dial Roman's number. It's 4pm and there's the possibility he might be busy at work… or maybe not. But his phone is switched off. I try several times and when it remains switched off, I find myself starting to panic. So, I call Paris.

"Hi, Legs," comes her voice, which isn't sounding quite as boisterous or lively. "It's lovely to hear your voice. You just disappeared and Roman refused to tell anyone why."

"I… I had to leave London. I'm back in Nigeria now."

"Oh, how uncanny! So is Roman!" she exclaims. "He arrived Lagos yesterday to sort a few things out."

My mouth goes dry, and my heartbeat accelerates. Roman is in town? He is here for me?

"I've been trying his number, but I can't reach him," I say redundantly.

"He refused to roam his number, so the hospital won't do his head in while he's over there," she answers. "Babes, I don't know what happened between you both, but my mom and I were shattered to hear you'd broken up. You were so good together."

We were.

"Do you have a number for him here?" I ask.

"I'll do you one better, luv. I'll tell you where to find him."

And that she does, giving me the details of the hotel he's staying at in Ikoyi. Once off the phone, I stare at the local phone number she's also given me but decide against calling. With the way my heart is racing wildly, it is unlikely I'll be able to manage a coherent conversation. I will go see him instead, at least that way, even if I can't speak, my eyes and my heart will do the talking for me.

With that information in hand, rather than book a taxi back home to Isolo, I book one to Ikoyi. I am a ball of nerves as the car navigates through traffic along the Lekki Expressway, nodding only perfunctorily when the driver explains why he would rather connect Ikoyi through Falomo instead of the Link Bridge. I start to wonder if I am indeed the reason Roman came to the country, if I am 'the thing' he is here to sort out. But the closer we get to the hotel, the less I'm convinced that I am. If he didn't come looking for me when I was still in London, would he have gotten on a plane to do that after I'd left?

Driving into the grounds of the boutique hotel, I can't help but smile as I think it is so like Roman to choose a place like this; classy but yet understated, stylish but yet low-key. It is such a vivid reminder of him, of the man that I am in love with, and a lump forms in my throat.

Getting out of the taxi, I stand in front of the hotel's doorway, feeling like a fish out of water. What was I thinking coming here to waylay him like this? What if he is here with another woman? I am still deliberating whether or not to walk in, when a car drives into the compound, pulling up where I am standing. I turn to it, and my breath catches in my throat when I see Roman and another man disembark. Our eyes make contact, but there is nothing in his to register any kind of emotion; positive or negative.

"Ogbeide and I will be at the bar. Come join us there," he says to the man driving.

The car drives off and his companion walks into the hotel. I am afraid Roman will do the same without even acknowledging me, but thankfully, he stops.

"Legachi."

That's all he does, call my name, but hearing his voice again feels like cool, refreshing water on my parched heart.

"Hi, Roman," I say, my anxiety making my voice wobble.

"What are you doing here?"

His unsmiling eyes and deadpan voice make me deflate, as I realize I am not the reason he is in Nigeria after all. But standing there looking at him after so many weeks of missing him, of longing for him, I'm ready to do whatever I need to, to get him back.

"I tried to call you but when I couldn't reach you, I called Paris. She told me where to find you," I answer. "She... she said you came here to sort out some things. I hope everything is okay?"

"I came to reach some sort of agreement with Luna's mom."

My heart crashes even further. "Torera?"

A sardonic smile plays on his lips, as if he is amused, but not surprised, that I remember her name. "Yes, Torera."

"How did it go? I hope it went well."

"It went as well as can be."

We stand silent for a while, with me not knowing what to say and him, seemingly unwilling to say anything more.

"I'm really sorry," I finally blurt out. "I shouldn't have acted the way I did. I was too hasty leaving the way I did. I should have listened to you." I pause, waiting for him to respond, and when he doesn't, I know I can't afford to hold anything back. "I miss you, Roman."

But rather than soften over my admission, he scoffs instead. "Oh, you miss me now? You don't think I'm the world's biggest liar only interested in a booty call anymore? Your fella, Mezie, isn't filling your head with any more ideas?"

I stare at him, surprised by his outburst. In all the scenarios that have replayed in my head about what speaking with him would be like, this hasn't been one of them.

"I'll bet your friends, or whomever, have told you the full story, right?" he continues. "You've heard from your pals what really happened, and suddenly Roman isn't such a tosser after all." He smiles again, the most soulless of smiles, and shakes his head. "You can believe your friends but didn't even give me as much two minutes to explain myself."

"I haven't heard anything. Nobody has told me anything since… since that first time," I protest. "All I've seen are those pictures, that's all. I don't even know her last name. I don't know anything about her or what did or didn't happen between the two of you. You have to believe that."

If my explanation has done anything to correct his misunderstanding of what has happened, his face doesn't reflect it. Instead, he looks at me with nary a single expression. At that point, a man walks up to us, the driver of the car that brought him, his brows furrowed as he looks from Roman to me.

"Everything okay?" he asks.

"Yeah, everything is fine, Evans," Roman answers. "Ogbedie is inside. I'll catch up with you guys in a bit."

In a bit. The realisation I will soon be dismissed devastates me.

"Can we at least talk about this, Roman?" I ask, trying, but failing, to keep the desperation out of my voice.

Our eyes hold, and I am certain that, like I am, he is remembering when he was the one who made the very same request of me... only to be rebuffed. All I can do is pray he won't decide to return the favour.

"There isn't anything to talk about, Legachi. You were right all along. You and I should never have gotten together. Ending things was the right thing to do... for both of us." He rubs his eyes and I see for the first time how weary and tired they look. "I've had a very rough couple of days. I really need to go inside now."

And just like that, the flicker of hope I have been fanning is extinguished. From the set of his face, I see that his mind is made up. We are truly over.

"Okay," I say, managing a smile. "For what it's worth, I'm sorry. Please give Luna a hug for me. Tell her I'm so sorry for leaving without saying goodbye."

He shrugs. "Yeah. Bye, Legachi."

"Can I at least hug you goodbye?" I ask, desperate to hold him again, even if for the last time.

I don't wait for his response and immediately reach for him. I bury my face in his chest as my arms circle his neck, savouring his smell like it is an elixir, like it is my very lifeline. And in a way, it is, because losing him feels like death. He doesn't return my embrace but instead stands rigid and unresponsive. The minute I step back, he turns around and walks away.

With tears streaming down my face, I reach for my phone in my handbag and order a taxi to take me home.

Roman

It takes everything in me not to turn around as I walk, not to look back for another glimpse of her face. Never have I had to muster as much internal willpower as I had to in the few seconds she held me, few seconds that felt like a hundred years, with me waging an internal battle not to succumb to the feelings I have spent the last two months trying to destroy. But from the moment I saw her standing there on the driveway, from when I looked into those brown eyes, it was clear that all those efforts have been wasted.

Walking across the lobby to the hotel's *Da Vinci Bar*, her minty berry smell still envelopes me and I grit my teeth to keep it from teleporting me to a time when it was the most sensual smell in the whole world, hating the fact it still is.

I turn around just in time to see her walking towards the gate and my eyes linger, watching her move in her half stomp, half strut. The further away she goes, the deeper is the despair welling inside me with the realization that is the last time I will ever see her.

But it is for the best. After everything I have been through, trust is critical… and I can't be with a woman who doesn't trust me. This is what I repeat to myself for the rest of the night, and as I sit on the plane back to London the next day. But rather than get any type of reassurance, all I feel is a deep, deep sadness. Getting over her is going to be hard.

Very hard.

Thirty-Three

Forever Love

JULY 2019

Legachi

eft with no choice, I resume at FGB in the second week of July. On my first day back, I have to smile through all the questions, well-meaning and otherwise, not to mention the subliminal taunting, about my premature return.

"*Ahn ahn*. What happened? Did they deport you?" Ukpono takes delight in asking, when she sees me at my desk, ironically the same one I vacated.

"*Abi* did your money finish?" Josephine cackles, her eyes dancing with glee over what she has perceived to be a downturn in my good fortune.

"I thought you said you were staying back with Mezie," is Chioma's comment, looking the most concerned of the three.

And I give them the same answers I have given everyone. "No, I didn't run out of money." "No, I didn't drop out. I was on a scholarship, remember?" "I finished my exams and decided to write my dissertation at home." "I didn't do too well with the cold weather." "Mezie and I broke up."

The last confirmation is received with even more derision.

"So, you just came back empty handed *sha*?" Ukpono giggles. "No man, no job with plenty pounds? So what was the use of going there?"

And that is the sentiment shared by almost anyone; if I have returned right back to the very same seat I vacated, without anything added to me whatsoever, what was the whole point? That is what prompts me to have another discussion with Mr. Ude.

"Sir, can I at least get my promotion when my certificate is ready next March?" I ask, desperate for some sort of reassurance that I haven't wasted my time.

"Promotion for what?" he sneers. "Do you know how many people are walking the corridors of this bank with M.As, M.Scs and even MBAs? If we were to promote everyone who has a Master's degree, where would that leave the organization? Bankrupt, that's where!"

Returning to my seat, I know that this is one defeat I will not accept. I might have not been able to do anything about losing the biggest love I will probably ever experience in my lifetime, but I sure as heck can do something about being overlooked at work. So, I engage an expert to properly update my C.V., determined to find myself a better job if it's the last thing I do.

But afterhours when I'm lying in bed at home, I continue to stalk Roman and Torera's old Instagram pictures. One time, I happen on pictures I haven't seen before, of Roman and Torera at what looks to have been her baby shower. She is beaming and draped with a pink *Mom-To-Be* sash, surrounded by her friends, while an unsmiling Roman hovers around. It dawns on me that that he is unsmiling in almost all their pictures, and it makes me even more curious about the nature of their relationship. In one of the pictures, she is tagged with her full name as a hashtag; Torera Akerele. Armed with the name I have been looking for, I immediately hit Google and I am stupefied by what I see. Apart from the articles I find about her complicity in several cyber-crime cases while still in England, there are numerous Facebook and Twitter call-outs from people she has apparently stolen from or duped of large amounts of money. In more recent times, there are even blog posts of a well-known Politician accusing her of blackmail and denouncing the paternity of the pregnancy she claims is his. After over three hours of reading these salacious stories, I put my phone down, my heart heavy with regret.

I should have listened to him.

Roman

I receive the signed release and transfer of custody forms from Torera after paying her the first part of the agreed amount. For the public statement, she gets her friend, Morayo, a very popular London socialite and one of my most persistent assailants, to do it for her, refuting any rumours about my kidnapping our daughter and confirming that I have the legal right to her custody. The post gets plenty of mileage, and I am assured I will not have any trouble from Torera's clan going forward.

I am arranging to make the balance payment to her when my doorbell rings that Monday afternoon. Luna is at day care, and I am using the opportunity to close things out with Torera once and for all.

"I came to check on the latest celebrity," Paris hoots, as she walks in. "Did that woman have to put up your picture on her page? I don't think there's a human being in this town that hasn't either seen or heard of the blasted post. I hear she even put it up on Twitter and Snapchat."

"Yeah, that was the whole plan," I answer, returning to my attention to my tablet, when we are seated by the kitchen island. "The more people see it, the less likely the harassment will continue."

"If you'd done like I told you and given any slapper who tried to harass you a shiner, they'd have stopped long ago."

I raise an amused brow. "You wanted me to add hitting women to my list of supposed crimes? Hmm, I wonder why I didn't think of that, instead of paying a fortune to clear my name?"

She steals a glance at my screen. "Is that what you're doing now?"

I shrug in response. "Now that she's met her side of the bargain, it's time for me to meet mine."

She curses under her breath, and I can't help but chuckle, even in the circumstance. Of all of us siblings, she has the pottiest mouth.

"What about the DNA test for Luna?" she asks.

"I already told you that's not going to happen," I retort, regretting having shared with her the disturbing piece of information from Torera. "Luna is my daughter, end of story."

"And we all love her unconditionally. But Roman, you have to know," she insists. "You have to protect yourself from whatever Torera might be plotting in the future. Who's to say what she might be already planning, especially as she's already hinted that you might not be Luna's dad? You don't want to be blindsided. Find out now, so you can be prepared and protect yourself. If, God forbid, Luna isn't your daughter, you'll lawyer up and prepare a solid case about why she should still be with you regardless."

Her verbal confirmation of my fears makes me pause. Torera's uncharacteristic candour and fluid cooperation with the custody transfer has left me suspicious about what her real plans just might be. Even though it is the last thing I want to do, a DNA test might be just what I need to protect myself.

"I've also been meaning to ask you how it went with Legachi," Paris says, giving me a cautious look. "I had no idea she'd returned to Lagos. Did you?"

I shrug and return my attention to my tablet. I didn't until seeing her there.

"I told her where to find you. Did she come see you?" When I don't answer, she leans in closer. "What happened between the two of you? Your face goes so red anytime her name is mentioned, and she sounded like she was on the verge of tears when she called me. If you're both suffering… "

"Leave it, Paris," I snap, not wanting to be dragged into that conversation. "She destroyed what we had by not trusting me."

"Not trusting you about what?"

And I tell her. I tell her everything that happened that awful Tuesday that began with me happy in love but ended with my whole world unravelling. I tell her about Legachi returning from school and accusing me of being a liar and a user… and walking out on me without giving me the chance to even explain myself.

"Well, I don't know about being a user, but you were definitely a liar," Paris says, looking me square in the eyes. "How did you expect her to react, hearing something like that from her mates instead of you?"

"I *was* going to tell her!"

"Oh, sod it, Roman!" she exclaims. "That wasn't the kind of thing for you to take your sweet time to tell her. You made her believe Sekani was Luna's mom. How did you expect her to react when she heard that was nothing but bollocks? Throw you a fucking party?"

I glare at my sister. "She could have at least listened to me."

"Nah, fam. You don't get to do that," she mutters, shaking her head, her disapproval more than evident. "You don't get to play the aggrieved party here. You cocked up, and that's fact. No woman would have stuck around after that kind of lie."

No woman would have stuck around for that kind of lie.

Those words haunt me as I lie awake in bed all night. Yes, I know I goofed by not telling Legachi about Torera earlier, but should that have been enough to make her leave so abruptly? My mind is cast back to how dejected she looked when she came to the hotel to see me, and an all-too-familiar pain grips my heart as I remember how badly I treated her. She hurt me, yes, but was that enough reason to push her away the way I did? Is it enough reason to keep forcing my heart to do what it very clearly doesn't want to; forget her?

The next morning, rather than take her to day care, and having declined the home test option, I take Luna all the way to Woodford to a DNA testing centre, wanting to do it as far away from our daily lives as I can. Even though it is a painless swap of saliva from both our mouths, it is the most distressing test I have ever had to subject myself to.

What follows are the most agonising seventy-two hours of my life. By the time the result drops in my inbox on Friday morning, I am already a nervous wreck.

My eyes skim past all the numerals and markers, and straight to the statement at the bottom.

The alleged father cannot be excluded as the biological father of the tested child. Based on the analysis of STR loci listed above, the probability of paternity is 99.99999999999%.

I drop to my knees, weak with relief. Still in that crouched position, I start to weep like a baby, relieved that Luna has been confirmed my child. Now, there is no more dark cloud hovering over us. Now, there is nothing, absolutely nothing, Torera can do to us ever again. We are finally free. My joy is complete.

But as I read through the report over and over again, I can't silence the niggling voice in my head telling me there is still something missing.

Legachi

I hiss as I read the offer letter from Pyramid International Bank, offended that, after what I thought was a great interview, they have made me an offer for a Banking Officer position, the very same one I have been stuck on at FGB for way too long. Their reason being that their salary band is way higher than FGB's, and my current salary places me at Assistant Banking Officer level in their bank. So, to them, they have actually made me a better offer. I am incensed that my current poor remuneration has been used as their benchmark, and not my pending Master's degree, or even all my years of experience. Hissing again, I rip the letter to pieces and trash it. This is just one down. Hopefully, my other applications will be more successful.

Not necessarily hungry but needing to get away for some air, I head to the company canteen downstairs. Walking in, I am tempted to immediately retreat when I see my dear frenemies on a table, as usual huddled over a phone and talking rapidly. In the three weeks since my return, I have tried to time my lunch breaks not to coincide with theirs. But alas, I have miscalculated it today. Before I can beat a silent retreat, Ukpono sights me and beckons me over, grinning as she does. As I approach them, from the way they are laughing, I know I will not like whatever it is they are calling me to see.

"*Eiya!* So, this is the girl Mezie dumped you for?" she giggles, shoving her phone in my face.

On her screen is a picture of Mezie kissing a mixed-race girl in front of what I can recognise is the front of *Liquid Nitrogen*. Ukpono scrolls to the next picture of them still standing there, but this time with him grinning at the camera, selfie-style, and her looking up at him with stars in her eyes. The post is simply captioned, **Bae**.

I can't help the snigger that escapes my lips. *No be only bae!*

Chioma mistakes my laughter for envy, and she has the good mind to pretend to be sympathetic. "*Sorry o*. These men are useless *sha*! After all the years you wasted on him."

"*Abeg, na this kind girl fit Mezie pass*," Josephine cuts in, her eyes dancing with mischief. "Fine, fresh, young girl. See how good they look together."

"See his fine suit. I'm sure he has a fantastic job and *don hammer plenty pounds. Chai, he go dey give this girl soft life!*" Ukpono chimes in.

Soft life? In that Hackney hellhole? I am tempted to tell them that the suit he is wearing is his uniform for his gig as a nightclub bouncer. I want to tell them the boy can hardly ever boast of £100 to his name at any given time. I want to tell them that he is living in squalor with too many people to count, and can only shag this his 'bae', and all the others he is stringing along, in full view of his drove of animalistic flatmates. But instead, I simply smile.

"This one that you're smiling like this," Josephine remarks. "*E be like say the thing dey pain you gaan!*"

I am only pained I didn't get out of that joke of a relationship earlier than I did.

Excusing myself, I buy my food and find a vacant table to sit and eat. One day, this will all be over.

I am walking behind them headed to the elevator, lost in thought wondering when the other banks I applied to will get back to me, when I hear Ukpono quip.

"What's with flowers being delivered smack in the middle of the day? One would think it's Valentine's Day or something."

"That doesn't look like a delivery guy," Chioma remarks. "*Omo,* that's a good-looking man, even from the back."

I look up to see a man standing by the front desk talking to the receptionist, holding a bouquet of flowers. I stop dead in my tracks when I recognize the back of that head and the way the curls of hair curl over the nape of his shirt when overgrown. I recognize those shoulders and the way that chest tapers into that waist. At that point, he turns around and it feels like my heart has stopped as our eyes connect.

And then he smiles.

Roman

Seeing her again takes my breath away and I can't help the broad smile that forms on my face.

"Never mind. There she is," I say to the receptionist, whose eyes have widened with surprise upon seeing whom I am there for.

Without waiting for any further prompt, I start to walk in her direction, nervous and excited at the same time. Even with a strange blunt bob hairstyle, she is more beautiful than I remember, and I can only hope she will not reciprocate the awful way I treated her the last time we saw. But then her lips part in a smile in response to mine, and my heart soars in recognition of the one it most desires.

"What are you doing here?" she asks, light brown eyes twinkling with unrestrained delight.

"Paris forgot to save your number," I answer. "And it wasn't until I was on the plane here that I realised I could have asked Nonye or Tayo for it." I hand her the flowers. "These are for you."

She accepts them with a smile that goes from ear to ear. "Wow! I'm speechless. I don't know what to say."

Our eyes hold, and in addition to the delight in hers, I can see the questions. After the way I treated her the last time, it isn't unexpected. It will take more than a surprise visit and a bouquet of flowers to undo and unsay the things that I did and said. I notice a group of women watching our exchange keenly and suddenly feel self-conscious.

"Can we go outside and talk?"

She nods and is about to follow me when one of the women watching us rushes to her. "Let me hold on to these for you," she says, taking the flowers from her hands.

Free of the flowers, I allow her to lead me out of the building, neither of us saying a word. Outside the building is even busier than the bank's lobby we have just exited, with long queues by the ATM machines, and customers waiting to gain entry to the banking hall through the heavy-duty security doors. Undeterred, she leads me to a spot between two cars, and I know this is as private as we will be able to manage.

"I like your hair," I tease. "Did you cut it?"

"This is a wig, Roman," she giggles. "A bad one for that matter."

"It's beautiful," I say, my own smile waning. "You're beautiful."

"I'm really sorry about jumping to conclusions the way I did," she says, imploring eyes looking at me. "I never should have left without listening to you. Since the last time I saw you, I've read so much about your ex, and she sounds like a real piece of work."

"And that would be putting it mildly," I chuckle. "The last few years have been a rollercoaster and I'm so glad to be able to put all that behind me now."

"Is that why you're back in town? To finalize with her?"

"No," I answer. "I'm here for you, Legachi."

Legachi

My heart soars, my daydream playing out before me in Technicolor. I blink to be sure this isn't just some cruel hallucination, but rather than disappear with the smoke of my imagination, he is still standing there. And then he takes my hand in his, confirming that he's indeed real, that he's indeed standing before me, that he has indeed come back to me.

"Last time, I was a total dick, and I didn't mean any of the awful things I said. When you left, it broke me, and I was hurt for a very long time. But we miss you." His eyes hold with mine. "*I* miss you. I love you, Legachi. And I want to do the forever thing with you."

Tears fill my eyes and I throw my arms around him, not minding the curious eyes of my colleagues watching us from the building or the teeming crowd of customers milling around the car park. As his lips claim mine, everything and everyone fades into oblivion. At that point, none of them matters, nothing in the whole wide world matters. Our kiss deepens and I drink in the taste of his lips, losing myself in the beautiful love I thought I'd lost, but which has found its way back to me. Basking in the fact that a big foreheaded, wide-eyed, gap-toothed girl called Legachi has gotten her happy ending.

Or better still…

Her happy beginning.

About The Author

Investment banker by day, romance writer by night, Adesuwa O'man Nwokedi began writing by accident and what started as a few scribbles for friends has led to 20 titles... and counting. A self-described hopeless romantic, when she's not creating new characters, she's a loving wife and mom of three.

Find her online: https://thefertilechick.ng/

Other Book By Adesuwa

Standalones

Accidentally Knocked Up
Faith's Pregnancy
You Used To Love Me
The Love Triangle
Golibe
Where Is The Love?
Iya Beji
You, Me...Them
A Love Of Convenience
Jaiye Jaiye
Adanna
The Sisters
The One!

The Ginika's Bridesmaids Series

Ginika's Bridesmaids 1: Ara
Ginika's Bridesmaids 2: Isioma
Ginika's Bridesmaids 3: Ife
Ginika's Bridesmaids 4: Ozioma
Ginika's Bridesmaids 5: Ginika

Malomo High Reunion Series

An Unlikely Kind Of Love
A Complicated Kind Of Love (Fall 2022)

Skyline Novels

The Skyline Novels are contemporary standalone books of students studying abroad, finding self & love. Read other Skyline Novels on your platform of choice and in any reading order!

Call Me Enitan by L. Leigh

Call Me Aarinola by Jules Rae

Call Me Naeto by Timi Waters

Call Me Jemila by Camaa Pearl

Call Me Aretta by Maggie Smart

Call Me Berwa by Mona Ombogo

Call Me Legachi by Adesuwa O'Man Nwokedi

Soundtrack

Like Legachi, I was a student in England, but all the way back in 2002 – 2003. When I got the brief for this project, I was so excited about going back to that wonderful time in my life, but I was worried I wouldn't be able to remember what that period was like, being so many years ago. So, I decided to put together a soundtrack of songs I loved in that period, and OMG, did they take me back or what? Listening to these songs took me back to that time, and it made bringing these characters to life even more of a joy. I hope you listen and get an even deeper feel of each scene, each chapter, each character. I hope you get to fall in love with Legachi and Roman the way I have. Enjoy ☺

Chapter	• Music
1	• Handbags & Gladrags – Stereophonics
2	• Never Leave You – Lumidee
3	• *Baby* – Ashanti • *Gangsta Lovin* – Eve ft. Alicia Keys
4	• *Silent Sigh* – Badly Drawn Boy
5	• *Silent Sigh* – Badly Drawn Boy
6	• *'03 Bonnie & Clyde* – Jay-Z ft. Beyoncé • *Nothin* – N.O.R.E.
7	• Writing To Reach You – Travis
8	• As You Are – Travis • White Flag – Dido • *Rock DJ* – Robbie Williams

9	• *Come Undone* – Robbie Williams • Little By Little – Oasis • Murder On the Dancefloor – Sophie Ellis-Bextor
10	• *Hey Ma* – Cam'ron
11	• Why Does It Always Rain on Me? – Travis
12	• I Need a Girl Pt. 1 – P. Diddy
13	• Don't Let Me Get Me – Pink • This Is How You Remind Me – Nickelback
14	• *Clocks* – Coldplay
15	• Complicated – Avril Lavigne • Turn – Travis
16	• In My Place – Coldplay • I Need A Girl Pt. 2 – P. Diddy
17	• Without Me – Eminem • *Dilemma* – Nelly ft. Kelly Rowland • *Somethin Stupid* – Robbie Williams ft. Nicole Kidman
18	• Ignition (remix) – R. Kelly • Crazy In Love – Beyoncé • Just A Little – Liberty X • Lights, Camera, Action – Mr. Cheeks
19	• Turn Me On – Kevin Lyttle • Lose Yourself - Eminem
20	• Be Faithful – Fatman Scoop

	• I'm With You – Avril Lavigne • From Now On – Will Young • See Me So – 2Face Idibia • Rock Your Body – Justin Timberlake • Like I Love You – Justin Timberlake • Flowers In the Window – Travis
21	• Underneath Your Clothes – Shakira • A Thousand Miles – Vanessa Carlton • Lovestruck – Will Young
22	• Sorry Seems to Be The Hardest Word – Blue ft. Elton John • Afterglow – Travis • *Addicted* – Enrique Iglesias
23	• U Got It Bad – Usher • Aserejé (The Ketchup Song) – Las Ketchup
24	• Lover, Won't You Stay – Will Young • Get Busy – Sean Paul • *Move Bitch* – Disturbing Tha Peace
25	• Don't Let Me Down – Will Young • All The Things She Said – t.A.T.u
26	• *Fallen* – Lauren Wood • Kingston Town – UB40
27	• Crazy For You – Madonna • Can't Take My Eyes Off You – Lauryn Hill
28	• Pure Imagination – Jamie Cullum • You and I – Will Young
29	• Spies – Coldplay • Bring Me Back to Life – Evanescence

30	• *Sparks* – Coldplay • Here With Me – Dido
31	• Guilty – Blue
32	• Afterglow – Travis • If You're Not The One – Daniel Beddingfield
33	• What's In Goodbye – Will Young • Overjoyed – Stevie Wonder

Glossary - Naija

1. Chapter One
   - *Abi?* – Right?
   - *Abeg* – Please
   - *Kabashing* – Prayer to subdue / bind
   - *Ke* – For emphasis

2. Chapter Two
   - *You don see am?* – Have you seen it?
   - *Which kin tension be dis na?* – What kind of tension is this?
   - *Na wa o!* – Wow!
   - *Moin-Moin* – Steamed bean pudding
   - *ABO* – Assistant Banking Officer
   - *That one still dey?* – He/she is still there?
   - *Sef* – Anyway
   - *Na* – For emphasis

3. Chapter Three
   - *ABSU* – Abia State University
   - *Nyansh* – Buttocks
   - *Abi* – Or

4. Chapter Four
   - *Efo Riro* – Vegetable Soup (Yoruba)

5. Chapter Five
   - *Sha* – For emphasis
   - *Tejuosho* – Popular market in Lagos
   - *She don come?* - Has she come?
   - *Na my Madam be dis o* – This is my girlfriend / wife
   - *Abeg, no forget your homeboy* – Please, don't forget your friend
   - *You dey enjoy* – You are enjoying / lucky

6. Chapter Seven
   - *Nne* – Mother / Term of endearment for a woman (Igbo)
   - *Wetin dey happen?* – What is happening?
   - *No mind this yeye girl! I just greet am small, na why she come dey shout* – Don't mind this silly girl! I only greeted her, and now she's shouting
   - *I just dey greet am. I no do anything* – I only greeted her. I didn't do anything
   - *Ehn* – For emphasis
   - *Conji* – Sexual desire
   - *E fear me as everybody dey say cold neva reach* – It scares me that everyone says the cold weather hasn't come
   - *Biko* – Please (Igbo)
   - *Abeg* – Please
   - *Na the money I dey find* – It's the money I'm interested in
   - *Sef* - For emphasis
   - *JJC* – Johnny Just Come (Newcomer)
   - *Osanobua!* – (My) God! (Bini/Esan)
   - *FEDIBEN* – Federal Government Girls College Benin
   - *For where?* – Hell No
   - *They no go fit commot eye* – They won't be able to look away
   - *Oba* – King in Yoruba Land

7. Chapter Eight
   - *Na so* – Yeah right
   - *I hope you don reach house and neva lost for London* – I hope you've gotten home and aren't lost in London
   - *Sha* - For emphasis
   - *E wan make sure say no be man house you wan go* – He wants to make sure it's not another man's house you want to go to
   - *No wahala* – No problem
   - *Nau* – For emphasis

- *Na so you dey vex* – Is this how you get angry?

8. Chapter Nine
    - *God don butter my bread* – God has buttered my bread / God has blessed me
    - Come add tea on top – With added tea
    - *Yigi Yaga* – Confusion
    - *Straffing* – Having sex with
    - *Na so so* – It was all about
    - *Na wa o!* – Wow!
    - *Abi?* – Right?
    - *Shining your 32* – Showing all your teeth
    - *Shishi I nor sell* – I didn't sell a single thing
    - *I for say they don jazz us o* – I would have said we've been bewitched
    - E be like say we go bounce – It's like we'll leave
    - *Tufiakwa* – God forbid (Igbo)

9. Chapter Ten
    - *You mean am?* – You mean it?
    - Abeg, go help me collect my own – Please help me get mine
    - *I go call you later* – I'll call you later
    - *You don reach there?* – Have you gotten there?
    - *I dey come na na* – I'm coming right away

10. Chapter Eleven
    - That one na small thing – That's not an issue
    - *Ehn* - For emphasis
    - *Omo (Y)Ibo* – Someone from Igbo Land (Yoruba)

10. Chapter Fourteen
    - Yeye – Silly / Stupid
    - *Abi?* – Right
    - *Shior!* – Rubbish!

11. Chapter Fifteen

- *Nne* – Mother / Term of endearment for a woman (Igbo)
- *This life na only one* – There is only one life / You only live once
- *Yeye* – Silly / Stupid

12. Chapter Sixteen
    - *How you dey?* – How are you? / How've you been?

13. Chapter Seventeen
    - *Nau* – For emphasis

14. Chapter Eighteen
    - *E dey there na!* – He's there (*na* for emphasis)
    - *But just the way he dey catch im fun, me sef go catch my own!* – But just the way he's having his own fun is the same way I'll have mine
    - *You dey take do yeye* – You're playing with / You're taking for granted
    - *She set die!* – She's hot!

15. Chapter Twenty
    - *E dey for commode* – He is in the toilet
    - *Oga* – Boss
    - *Wetin she do?* – What did she do?
    - She dey make birthday cake for her Oga – She is making a cake for her boss.
    - *She think say this na Naija where she fit buy favour with even one bottle of small stout sef* – She thinks this is Nigeria where she can buy favour with even just a small bottle of Stout
    - *This place where they go collect the cake, come sack you on top* – This place where they will accept the cake but still fire you
    - Na one yeye Mandem boy like that – It's one useless Mandem

- Na all these tall, fine girls the bobo like – It's tall, fine girls the guy likes
- *Alex don dey go Cricklewood. E say e go branch D'Den. You want any chow?* – Alex is headed to Cricklewood. He says he'll stop at D'Den. Do you want any food?

16. Chapter Twenty-One
    - *Babe, you don come?* – Babe, you're here?
    - *Gisted* – Chatted
    - *Ba?* – Right? (Hausa)
    - *This one wey you tanda like statue* – Why are you standing like a statue?
    - *Ogbono Soup* – Traditional soup from Southern Nigeria
    - *Eba* – Cooked starchy vegetable food made from dried grated cassava flour
    - *Garri* – Cassava flour

17. Chapter Twenty-Two
    - *Maybe he follow Lateef go house* – Maybe he followed Lateef home
    - *Abi im dey sleep for club. Maybe he too shayo last night* – Or he could be sleeping in the club. Maybe he had a lot to drink last night
    - Come and be going abeg – Please leave
    - *I don dey wait you* – I've been waiting for you
    - *Come parlour make we discuss that thing* – Come to the parlour/living room so we can talk about that thing
    - *Wetin happen?* – What happened?
    - *Na that their yeye school accommodation she don get wey she no wan make we hear word* – It's the useless school accommodation she's gotten that she doesn't want us to hear the last of
    - *Your wahala too much* – You have too much trouble

18. Chapter Twenty-Three

- You no dey ever disappoint – You never disappoint
- *The guy dey im lane, I dey my own* – The guy is on his lane, and I'm on mine

19. Chapter Twenty-Four
   - *Girl, you too dey vex!* – Girl, you're easily angered!
   - *No wahala* – No problem
   - *Wetin dey happen here?* – What's going on here?
   - *Guy, you dey crase?* – Guy, are you crazy?
   - *Leave me make I beat her sharp mouth commot!* – Let go of me so I can beat the sharpness out of her mouth
   - *Person I bring London, she dey straff Mandem!* – I brought her to London and she's having sex with a Mandem
   - Na deportation dem go knack you straight! – You will be deported
   - Carry her commot from this place – Get her out of this place

20. Chapter Twenty-Six
   - *Mgbeke* – A local / village girl who lacks exposure (Igbo)

21. Chapter Twenty-Seven
   - *Chelu* – Wait (Igbo)
   - *Why you fall hand like this* – Why did you disappoint like this?
   - *You don become full London babe now, abi?* – You've become a full London girl now, right?
   - *I go tear you one slap now* – I will slap you right now
   - *E dey pain you?* – Does it hurt you?
   - *Ode* – Fool
   - When na manage me sef dey manage you – When I was settling for you
   - So, for your mind now, you don find husband for this London – So, in your head, you've found a husband in London

- *Abeg, getaway from here* – Please get out of here
- *Who dey manage who? You wey tiff all her money come dey squat with hundred men for Hackney?* – Who was settling for who? You who stole all her money and are squatting with a hundred men in Hackney

22. Chapter Twenty-Eight
    - *How far na? Chop knuckle* – How is it going? Let's fist bump
    - *Owambe* – Party (Yoruba)

23. Chapter Twenty-Nine
    - *Na so* – Yeah right

24. Chapter Thirty-One
    - Vitamin D – Sex

25. Chapter Thirty-Two
    - *Abiriba* – Tribe in Eastern Nigeria
    - That one na for London o! This na Naija – That was in London. This is Nigeria

26. Chapter Thirty-Three
    - *Eiya* – Awww
    - *No be only bae!* – Not only bae!
    - *Abeg, na this kind girl fit Mezie pass* – Please, this is the kind of girl better suited for Mezie
    - *Don hammer plenty pounds* – Has made plenty of money/pounds
    - Chai, he go dey give this girl soft life – Gosh, he'll be spoiling this girl
    - E be like say the thing dey pain you gaan – It appears it's really hurting you

Glossary - Brit

1. Chapter Three
    - *Bruv* – Friendly term of address between/for males
    - *Muppet* - An incompetent or ineffectual person. Basically an idiot

2. Chapter Eight
    - *Bird* – A girl or young woman
    - *TOWIE* – British Reality Show (The Only Way Is Essex)

3. Chapter Ten
    - *Bob's Your Uncle* - And there it is / And there you have it

4. Chapter Fifteen
    - *Minging* – Ugly / Unpleasant
    - *Blimey* – Exclamation of surprise or annoyance
    - *Kip* – Nap

5. Chapter Sixteen
    - *Gits* – Fools
    - *A new bird?* – A new woman?

6. Chapter Eighteen
    - *Bollocks* – Nonsense
    - *Don't get your knickers in a twist* – Don't get upset over something unimportant
    - *Knob* – Stupid or unpleasant, usually a man
    - *Get in!* – Yay!
    - *Sloshed* – Drunk
    - *Mandem* – (In this instance) Derogatory term for low income men of African / Caribbean origin typically living in East London

* 9 7 9 8 8 4 1 1 2 0 8 1 0 *